TWENTY PIECES

a memoir by **LISA WELDON**

A walk through love,
loss and midlife reinvention.

Cover photo: Woodie Williams
New York City subway map © Metropolitan Transportation Authority

Printed in the United States of America
Published by Braughler Books LLC., Springboro, Ohio

First printing, 2021

ISBN: 978-1-955791-10-6 soft cover
ISBN: 978-1-955791-11-3 ebook

Library of Congress Control Number: 2021910722

Ordering information: Special discounts are available on quantity purchases by bookstores, corporations, associations, and others. For details, contact the publisher at:

    sales@braughlerbooks.com

    or at 937-58-BOOKS

For questions or comments about this book, please write to:

    info@braughlerbooks.com

Braughler™ Books
braughlerbooks.com

*"What lies behind us, and what lies before us
are but tiny matters compared to what lies within us."*

HENRY STANLEY HASKINS

This work is dedicated to

MY CIRCLE OF FIVE

author's note

I have changed some of the names
of those in my story in order to protect their privacy.

In writing this book I have relied on my own memory,
pulled notes from my blog and personal journal,
referred to news articles,
and trusted recollections of others.

I've done my best to present a factual truth to you, my reader.

prologue

The year I was 58, my perfectly orchestrated world collapsed. My award-winning career as an advertising art director had gone stagnant, my 25-year marriage was on the rocks, and the only home my children had ever known was featured in the foreclosure listings. Daily, I struggled to hang on to my elusive youth. I had been a tall, good-looking woman, defined by my appearance, and here I was, slowly losing that foothold of my identity. Everyone I held dear, everything that brought me security was being stripped away.

I began to hide, shielding myself from the public humiliation of failure. The guilt, I deferred by blaming my husband. But the fear of "what next?"—that paralyzed me. Only once before in my life had I ever experienced such debilitating fear. As a child I remember being in a swimming pool when my legs cramped. I couldn't kick or get myself to the edge of the pool. I yelled and no sound came from my mouth. As I realized that I was about to drown, a calm washed over me. I relinquished control. Then strong hands reached down and grabbed me. I was saved, by whom, I don't remember.

This time, however, there was no lifeguard, no one to pull me out of the mess of my life. I had to save myself.

The beginning of the end of the life I had known started on New Year's Eve 2010. Outside I could see the light fading. Dusk was moving in. I sat in my tiny office, my body teetering on the front edge of my hard-backed Windsor chair. Like a mother shaking her colicky baby, I jerked my torso back and forth, back and forth, in a nervous rhythm. Aware that my chair could fall from under me, I didn't quit. I couldn't.

"Sweetheart, you 'bout ready?" my husband Jim interrupted me with his usual optimistic glee. We were due at the Millers' house where celebrating New Year's Eve had been our family tradition for years. Dan and Joan were dear friends; our kids dovetailed perfectly in age and their parties were fun and relaxed. Fried chicken and champagne, fireworks and fellowship—all painted the Hallmark moments I needed to cloak the harsh reality our family faced.

But tonight, I was at my lowest point. Despondent. For months, financial doom had loomed over me like a noose, its grip tightening as the days and hours crept by. As hard as I tried to mute the threats of debt collectors or hide the letters from the IRS or bury the guilt of no longer being able to cover my kids' college tuition, I couldn't. The humiliation brought on by visits from sheriffs and repo men, the helplessness of watching my child fall into addiction, and the resignation that my marriage was disintegrating—they gutted me. I could smell the stench of impending death, and the only way I knew to survive was to isolate and stay numb.

When Jim stuck his head in the door, I didn't even lift my head to face him. "I have to pay some bills before year end," I muttered. "Maybe I'll come later." It was an empty promise, and he knew it.

It had been three long and painful years since the 2008 recession slammed us baby boomers. At a much-too-early age, many of us were put out to pasture, losing our jobs to young, inexpensive talent whose native, digital language was foreign to us. Even though I maintained a steady client base during the 20-plus years I raised our children, I had come to feel like a short order cook, slinging jobs swiftly and efficiently while I juggled the crises at home. I no longer had the confidence to ask for the budgets and timelines I needed to meet my standards. I hadn't taken the time to stay current, to re-educate myself in the new digital ways, so of course, my marketability was dwindling. *I was lucky to get whatever I got,* was my chant. To make matters worse, I was in advertising, whose unspoken truth claimed once you hit 40, you are "washed up." At nearly 60, I had no choice but to get back into the game. Reviving my career was daunting, but it was the only lifeline I had.

From the kitchen I could hear the energy in the boys' voices as they bagged up their arsenal of fireworks. "Witt, grab Mom's deviled eggs," Jim interjected, trying to herd them toward the car. I felt the ache of regret as Witt and Trey walked past my little office, arms fully laden. They seemed totally unaware that their mama was not going with them. The back door shut and with that, a void filled the house.

Watching Jim and the boys back out of the driveway, I slid to the back of my chair, steadying it on all four legs. I stood up and as I walked toward the door to lock it, an unexpected shockwave of freedom shot through my veins. *Four, five, six,* I counted the hours until the ball dropped in Times Square, and when my family would return. *Six hours just for me,* my heart fluttered with a bit of pleasure. For just a slight moment in time I was unleashed, magically untethered from our money worries and from my duties as a mother and a wife. Like a child dancing freely in the rain, I twirled around and around in my own imagination. I lost myself in a glow that enveloped me and warmed me. It felt good to feel happiness again, to be free, to be light.

But my high jilted me as quickly as it had swooned me. In just a snap it was gone, and my sense of duty grounded me, then rudely, slammed me back to my cruel truth. I walked back into my darkened space, sat at my desk, and relinquished myself to the myriad of problems that were reeling out of control.

Adding up the numbers, I struggled to stay focused. My heart was elsewhere, my head fogged with futility. I had tasted euphoria for just a millisecond, and I wanted more. I pushed the paperwork aside, then reached into my trashcan for a catalog from New York's Parsons School of Design, the one that held a fairy tale I'd discarded year after year. When it came each November, I'd hide it almost like candy and wait till nighttime when the house was quiet to bring it back out, to savor it all alone with no interruptions. I didn't need anyone asking questions or making me feel foolish. I didn't dare let on that I missed my career. Oh, I loved being a mother, but parenting three teenagers—one an addict—while band-aiding a marriage, and flailing financially, had drained me. I begged for the vitality my career had once brought me, to feel challenged and productive, and to be respected once again for my creativity.

Slowly and deliberately, I'd page through it just as I'd done with the Sears catalog as a child, savoring every single detail of every month-long summer course held in Manhattan and in Paris. I'd circle the classes that piqued my interest with a bright yellow marker. I felt free to choose anything my heart desired, never feeling bound by the cost or whether it would enhance my resume, because of course, spending a whole month in New York, and certainly Paris, was nothing but a hallucination.

But this time, as I turned each page, I felt a bit defiant. Taking a course would be smart, I reasoned as I turned the glossy pages. I could reinvent myself and get us out of this financial mess. *I could save my family.*

I flipped back through the pages, scanning each course I'd circled and then attempted to narrow my choices. I was most intrigued by a class titled "Integrative Design" which combined skills from all design disciplines—architecture, interior, web and graphic design, photography, urban planning—to affect social change in an impoverished neighborhood. I went online and found that Columbia University held a similar class in prior years, and the effect those students had on the then-decaying Harlem was inspiring. *Oh, to have the opportunity to peer into a New York neighborhood, into the life of real New Yorkers!*

But it would do little to further the digital skills I need to compete in today's market, my fiscal sense butted in. Choosing this course is frivolous, the back-and-forth continued. Yet, I rationalized, taking this course over one more closely related to advertising might give me more options in finding a steady corporate job, one that would pull us out of this financial mess. Age discrimination didn't seem as prevalent in fields such as architecture and interior design, even urban planning, I debated. *But if I start in another field, I'll have to start at the bottom.*

Disheartened, I closed the catalog. Spending a month in New York City was absurd! Surely there was a course in Atlanta, one more applicable and at a much lower cost. I needed to be mature, stay home for my family, and do the right, responsible thing.

I could rent a tiny little place near school, the romantic fantasy kept unspooling in my heart. I felt it race as I imagined myself zigzagging through Greenwich Village like a New Yorker, stopping for breakfast at a local cafe, and then floating through the hallways of Parsons, rubbing elbows with ponytailed professors and tattooed kids. Back in my imaginary apartment, I saw myself sitting cross-legged on an old wooden floor, with pieces of my assignment strewn out in front of me, totally in flow as James Taylor crooned in the background. *I'll work late into the wee hours of the morning if that's what it takes,* I bargained with the master inside me, already feeling the pulse of creativity and the boundless energy I remembered having in my earlier days of advertising.

I had fallen in love with New York City decades ago and had always dreamt of one day living there. This could be my chance to become intimate with it, "TO.SEE.EVERY. SINGLE.INCH.OF.IT" I sassed out loud in a staccato tone.

All hyped up, I went to Google and found that Manhattan measured a little over twenty square miles and then began doing the math. *At one square mile per day,* I inched mentally through the steps, *I could walk all twenty miles within thirty days!* Trying to restrain my excitement, I then searched "sunset time Manhattan in July" and calculated that if class ended at 4:00 p.m. I should be able to walk that mile before dark. *EASY!* I couldn't contain the uncontrollable thrill that whirled up inside me. I rose up out of my chair, and with a cha-cha swivel of my hips, I let out a squeal.

I could watch YouTube videos to teach myself how to create a blog, an online travelogue, my mind raced with ideas. After my walks, I could write about each day's experience and share those stories on Facebook and on Twitter. I imagined using myself as the client and showcasing what I'd learned and, in turn, I'd paint myself as a new media expert. Plus, I could show people that I was able to walk the entire island, which would prove to potential clients or an employer that, at nearly 60, I was still physically strong and viable. Oh, my God, it all made such perfect sense! My idea felt so real, so totally right. I was flying! I felt strong and invincible. *I can do this! I'll figure a way!*

But how could I ever present this idea to my family or to my friends? "It's so wrong!" I could hear my neighbors chatter over cocktails. Doing something so pleasurable when we were in such dire straits and when my children needed me, was wrong. "Just plain selfish," I could hear them whisper.

With a sense of defeat, I walked up the stairs and headed toward the bathroom. Slinging my shoes aside, I plopped down on the edge of the tub and began running a hot, steamy bath. In a wide swath over the rising water, as if to anoint it, I sprinkled the citrus-smelling sea salts my son had given me for Christmas, then took off my clothes. I tested the water, the searing heat blistering my skin, my foot turned a scarlet red. It was if the heat awakened my old familiar self. Fear, shame, and responsibility; all blaming me for allowing us to fall into yet another financial mess. I should have gone back to school before now. I should've never done the renovation on the house. We should've moved to a cheaper house during the recession. I should've had better boundaries and demanded Jim get a steady job. I should've. I should've. I should've. With that, I cooled the bath with cold water and stepped back in.

I pulled the shower curtain across to shut out the cold and the light of the room. I then sat down, sunk my body into the water, and pressed my back and head into the porcelain curve, my feet pressed on the other end. Feeling a bit lightheaded, I shivered, the top of my shoulders popped with goosebumps. Slowly and deliberately, I drew in a chest full of steam, my ribs burgeoning with resignation. I fought to focus on an imaginary line moving down my neck, through the muscles in my shoulders, down my arm, and to the tips of each finger.

The water cooled as I continued to lay there, deep in the numbness that had become my armor. With my eyes closed and my body limp, I began feeling a sadness invade my quiet peace. Almost instantly, tears welled up in my eyes, and my lip quivered. I so badly needed to cry but couldn't. "Get ahold of yourself, Lisa," I could hear the instructions loud and clear, the words tinged with the sound of my mother's voice.

I stepped out onto the soft mat, wrapping myself in loose-fitting pajama pants, warm socks and an old, wrinkled t-shirt, then headed back downstairs, where I dutifully returned to my office. I slumped down into the rigidity of my chair, powered up my computer, then cracked open the window beside me. A quick burst of cold jolted me.

As I pulled an old, faded sweatshirt down over my head, I caught a comforting scent of Frank, my 10-year-old dachshund who frequently snuggled in it to sleep. Tucking my feet under me, I pulled my keyboard closer. But, instead of paying bills, I began retyping the words, "size of Manhattan."

"2.3 miles at its widest point," Wikipedia claimed, and just 13.4 miles in length. How could a place so immense in my dreams, so powerful and alive, be so small? I clicked Google Maps to verify. I then reached into the cabinet under my desk and pulled an old, dog-eared map from a folder marked "Travel." I unfolded it, laid it out on the floor, then knelt down beside it and carefully smoothed its creases. Like a curious kid, I moved my finger along the tangled mess of subway lines, tracing the red ones then the green ones, all while imagining what it would feel like to jump from one train to the next, just like a native. I tried to make sense of how the avenues and streets wove alphabetically and numerically in and out of the city's center. I giggled as I saw myself escaping, skipping down Fifth Avenue and strolling through Central Park. Oh, just to wake up to the sounds from its streets!

Just as I began to believe that my crazy plan to walk all of Manhattan's neighborhoods and to breathe in every single inch of life on this magical island, all within thirty days, might possibly work, a loud BOOM! yanked me out of my fantasy. The first firecracker of the new year broke my reverie; it was a rude realization that my life was no longer what I'd dreamed. How in the hell would I finance such a foolish fling?

But an anger boiled inside me, and a will more powerful than I'd ever known shot back. I stood up, grabbed my map, then reached in my closet for a can of spray adhesive. I flipped on the outside lights, then marched out to my backyard and laid the map face down on the grass. I sprayed it back and forth, back and forth, until its back side was drenched in glue. I brought it back inside, smoothed it over a piece of the kids' poster board, then positioned it on top of a wooden drawing board. Positioning a metal ruler as my guide, and with an X-ACTO knife in hand, I sliced the island right through its heart, through its vertical core. Lining up the two halves, I moved my ruler down the map, slicing it horizontally again, and again, and again until my dream was finally broken into twenty pieces.

Determined to hang on to my will, I walked into the kitchen and poured myself a glass of wine. I returned to my office, sat down at the computer, then googled New York's Parsons School of Design. I scrolled down to find their summer courses, clicked the course titled "Integrative Design," and for a split second, I didn't give a shit what people thought. I hit ENROLL.

It was on that New Year's Eve that I trusted my heart and gave myself the one gift that would eventually save me.

Thirty days. Thirty days to walk through the pieces of my life.

All through the next week, night and day, I jostled between shame and self-reproach. "We can't afford it." "How will I explain it to people? It sounds so dramatic and far-fetched," all logical reasons why I should forgo this crazy idea.

At times I felt like a child, hiding something from my parents, something I really, really wanted and felt like I deserved but I knew I'd get in trouble if they found out. I couldn't find the words to justify my rash behavior and certainly not a convincing reason why I needed this trip. I was dying to announce it to the world, to blare it all over social media, but I kept reins on myself. I feared the repercussions.

Was this a midlife crisis? Was I falling into that trap of impulsivity that catches so many of us in our 50s and 60s? Buying convertibles, leaving spouses, or flying off to an ashram in India? I'd always rolled my eyes at those who did. Would people think I was off trying to "find myself?" Nothing nauseated me more than those two words.

"Taking a course" sounded smart, but flying off to New York all alone for an entire month and with plans of walking the streets sounded terribly immature for a 58-year-old wife and mother. *Stay home for Trey*, I reasoned as I fought the cloud of loss that moves over an empty nest. How could I abandon him, my baby, the last one to leave home for college? The constant lack of money plus the strain between Jim and me had been too much for a kid. He'd struggled his final years in high school, and I understood why. I'd watched him isolate and become secretive and hole up with others who had similar problems. I was keenly aware that these were blatant signs of a larger issue, but I had become desensitized, really. Numb and unavailable. Like a taut rubber band, I was stretched beyond my limit, constantly snapping at him, slinging harsh punishments his way, when what he needed was someone to be present with him, to hear him, and to love him. *I should stay home,* I reasoned with a heavy hand. *This is my last chance to make it up to him.*

And then my focus jumped to Emma, and with that shift came a momentary sense of comfort and relief. Away at college for the last three years, she was well into her own life, distanced from the problems at home. I found peace in knowing she had a sweet and attentive boyfriend at school who would be there for her if she needed the emotional crutch. I didn't really worry about Emma. She was the eldest and like me, strong and independent, even adventuresome. My hope was that she might understand why I needed to get away.

But, Witt … I choked as I was slammed back to reality. Emma had started dropping hints to Jim and me that Witt, our middle child, was beginning to have problems more serious than what we wanted to believe. I couldn't go there, I just couldn't. There was no more of me left, no strength to deal with a child who could possibly be falling into addiction.

My family was struggling, for God's sake, and my marriage damaged. Dangerously close to bankruptcy, we could in no way afford anything so frivolous. I wasn't even sure the check I'd written for the deposit would actually clear. I knew better than to write it, but I had written it anyway. I wanted it that badly.

Needless to say, I kept my secret to myself. I didn't dare share any of it. Why set myself up for more judgment? I was hard enough on myself as it was.

The following Saturday I was signed up to attend a daylong retreat called "Setting Your Intentions" with a group of friends. This was one of several sessions offered by Tavye Morgan, an ordained Methodist minister who'd recently left our church to pursue a master's degree in counseling. Although I hated to see her go, I admired her courage in taking the leap of faith to start a brand-new career in her late 40s. In my head I tried to paint my New York idea as a similar leap, but just couldn't justify it. Not exactly like getting a master's. And even though Tavye was the only person in the world with whom I felt safe sharing the gritty, unfiltered details of my messy life, I was too embarrassed to share my plan even with her.

It was a bitter, icy January day in Atlanta, and I dreaded leaving the house. I hated being cold. But honestly, I didn't really have the emotional strength to play along with anything that seemed as frivolous, and pointless really, as setting New Year's resolutions. I finally decided to go, knowing in my head the day could be a welcome respite from the stress at home, but I feared the potential for exposure. I felt weak and terribly vulnerable, especially in a group whose talks often fished out the raw and intimate. I'd spent a lot of energy reframing the gory details and just couldn't slip and allow them to see my real truth.

Smells of hot coffee and spiced cider swirled about the stairwell as I plodded up to the second floor of the old church near Emory University. The sight of the old checkered linoleum floor and the clanging of the steam heater immediately brought me comfort, taking me back to Spring Hill Presbyterian, my childhood church in Mobile, Alabama. In that instant, I was a child again, ten years old, race-walking down those beloved hallways. I could hear the click, click, click from the taps on my white Mary Janes, and I could feel my red leather Bible tucked under my arm as I anxiously searched for my best friend Debbie. I lost myself for a moment, and felt safe and happy and unencumbered, that is, until Tavye's voice interrupted me. "Grab a drink and a croissant and we'll get started."

I entered the classroom and exchanged greetings with the others who were already seated at a long wooden table piled high with old magazines and books, patterned paper and markers, buttons and swatches of fabric. Oh! The artist in me was instantly intrigued. As I settled into my seat, Tavye gave each of us a piece of poster board, then instructed us to go through the pages of the magazines and extract anything that tickled our fancy. We could cut out individual letters, or headlines, or photos—whatever we wanted to paste onto our boards. "Add buttons or glitter or Ric Rac," she added. "Be instinctual and don't overthink it!" Like kids at art camp, we giggled and glued for the next few hours, with the idea that our subconscious desires and goals would be made manifest so we could move forward and achieve them in the new year.

"Y'all start wrapping up," Tavye chirped toward the end of the morning, as she started sweeping the remnants toward the center of the table. "Let's break for lunch," she repeated a few minutes later, clapping her hands lightly, trying to unwind the spirited chatter. Herding us toward the lunch area, she assured us that we'd continue after we ate. "Each of you will have the opportunity to explain what's on your boards." It was then that I could feel the tension tear into the nape of my neck. I took my sandwich back to my seat, where I sat in a silent angst for the next twenty or so minutes.

After lunch, one by one each woman stood, pointing to different areas on their board, explaining their intentions, and answering questions from the group. Tavye would chime in with a little feedback, then move us along to the next person. As if in a fog, I heard hardly a word that was spoken. My mind scurried, trying to plot word for word what I would say. By the time she came to me I was wound so tight I could hardly speak.

It was now my turn. I pushed down on the seat of my chair, leaning my body forward as I scooted the chair further behind me. I stood straight and rigid, then took a slow intentional breath. I cocked my head while flashing a silly smile, as if to prep my audience. "Okay! Let's see," I started in a jovial tone, pointing at my poster, at the photo of a box wrapped in $20 bills and topped with a green bow. "I hope to increase my income…," then added, "Like we all do!" I grinned, using the recent recession as an excuse, a chance to paint my needs as no different from anyone else's.

Below that I'd pasted an Apple logo and beside it scribbled www.LisaWeldon.com. "My one-page website is soooo out of date, so amateurish," I announced, vowing to clean it up in the new year. Moving my hand to an image of a lacy black bra and a pair of red shiny penny loafers, I then added with a cheeky grin, "Lisa, take better care of yourself. Treat yourself to something new and fun once a month!" and with it I heard a rousing "Amen!" I was on stage; I knew how to entertain an audience. But in my heart, I was simply parroting the sentiments touted by self-care gurus. I would never follow through.

So, I went on: A photo of a mother hugging her teenage boy represented my longing to help my son. "Witt" I whispered then paused to catch my breath. I felt sure most everyone at the table empathized with my son's ADD and his struggles in school. ADD was socially acceptable, and thus it was ok to share. I didn't dare admit to the part about the alcohol and drug issues Emma had alluded to.

An image of an old-fashioned wooden desk in an empty classroom spoke, I told the group, to my love of learning and my hope to take classes on social media, web design, and other skills now required in my business. Next to the desk, I'd glued a picture of a tall young woman dressed in black jeans and black top standing in front of an old brick wall. That was me in that photo, me when I was young and vital, and well-respected in my field of advertising. That was me, tall and thin and pretty, with dreams that had no limitations. That was the courageous person who started a business and invested in real estate and who planned her future wisely, even traveled and saw the world. That was the me who was fearless and unencumbered with financial debt. That was the person who still wanted to live, to feel alive, and to be around people who were healthy and moving forward and whose creative fires still raged.

This was beginning to be too much, just too much to process in front of all these people. My body began to tremble, my chest burned. I wanted to run and to disappear, but I was stuck in place. I had to pull myself together. I had to. I had to go on.

"This brick wall behind her," I began slowly, then hesitating as my voice began to quiver, "represents my desire to work in a creative space, alongside young creative people." I pushed on. I could feel my friends around me become uncomfortable with my emotion. I imagined pity emanating from each of them and it sickened me that they saw me so weak. "Take your time," Tavye whispered in a soothing tone. I straightened myself and took in a long, deep breath. I laid my forefinger over my lips, as much to silence my feelings as to buy time to get ahold of myself.

I then pointed to an illustration of a woman soaring high off a diving board. I plodded through the title beside it, "How She Got Past the Fear …," then worked hard to finish, "… of Doing Something New." I then explained the only items left, the three unmatched letters pasted in the center of my board: N, Y, and C.

"You see," I stumbled forward as I pointed to the letters. "I love New York City and have always dreamed of living there," I said, trying to mask my anxiety with a forced flippancy. But right there in front of me, my subconscious had indeed made manifest my New Year's Eve experience and I couldn't deny it. The synchronicity was too much. I couldn't contain myself. Right there in front of everyone, I vomited the words with an uncontrollable force: "Last week on New Year's Eve, I did something really irrational. I put a down payment on a class in New York for this summer, for 30 days. It was stupid and selfish and irresponsible, I know," my insecurity flared. Grasping desperately for levity, I continued, "Maybe it was the wine that made me do it."

I hoped they'd laugh, but instead, my friends at the table went serious on me. "You have to go," I heard, almost in unison, "You have to go!"

I had made it public. Now I had to follow through.

All dreams and fantasies begin somewhere, and my New York dream began in the fall of 1975, the year after I graduated from college and a month into my new job as a paste-up artist in an ad agency in Birmingham, Alabama. At the blossoming age of 23, when a good Southern girl was supposed to be a newlywed, or at least picking out bridesmaid dresses, I found myself swooning over my work instead of some eligible bachelor.

I so clearly remember the afternoon I became smitten. Betty Ann, Howard, and I—the three lackeys in the creative department—were busy at our drawing boards, trying our best to concentrate on our work. Our desks were all lined up against a wall in a huge, wide-open traffic area that was every bit as distracting as Grand Central Station. "The bullpen," it was called.

On this particular day, the art director Harris and his cohort Bob, a copywriter, blasted through the door, swaggering in late from a lunch with a client. "GET IN HERE!" Harris bellowed out in a deep and authoritative tone, his laugher shining through his big ole rack of teeth. Betty Ann shot me an eye roll, both of us suspecting the lunch had been a wet one by the way he danced through the room. Bob, who didn't say a word, threw us a mischievous wink as he followed, carrying a brown paper bag. I watched in awe, like that wide-eyed little kid, the fraidy cat who followed all the rules. Yet, deep down inside I so admired those who were brave enough to bend them.

"They bought it lock, stock, and barrel," Harris announced as we crowded into his perpetually dark office, his thick wiry eyebrows flitting up and down with excitement as he told us how they sold the campaign we'd all worked on to the client. Selling work that was highly creative, and especially edgy, was quite the coup and definitely worth a celebration. I was a tad nervous when Bob handed me a pottery coffee mug, then filled it with a deep red wine from a bottle that was already uncorked. My eyes caught Betty Ann's and then darted toward the main door. I knew drinking wine at work was wrong and surely a violation of office policy, but my bosses were doing it, so maybe I wouldn't lose my job. It also felt really good to be included.

"And we've got the budget to produce it in New York," Harris added as he pumped his fist in triumph. Working in New York was the cherry on top, I learned that day. The best of the best creatives, the ones in advertising who shattered all the rules and then redefined them, worked on Madison Avenue. One day, I promised myself. One day I would be one of them. From that day on, New York and my career were intrinsically intertwined.

I often wondered why those early days of my career, smack dab in the hangover of New York's Mad Men era, were so impactful on me. Was it, in all the cigarette smoke and three-martini lunches, the adultery and rebellious creativity, that those extremes gave me permission to soften the stringent rules that choked me? Perhaps I was being honored for the first time, for my creativity instead of being ashamed of never making the honor roll. Or did I love the power I gained by earning my own money, never again having to listen to my mother's rule, "While your feet are under my table, you will obey MY rules!" It was a power I would never relinquish to anyone, ever again. Or was it that I'd landed in a profession that was radically progressive, one that made room for girls, that honored women as much as men?

Growing up, I never imagined being a career woman. Never, not even once do I remember being asked what I wanted to be when I grew up. Us girls, especially us Southern girls, were expected to go to college for at least two years, then come home and join the Junior League, maybe work a year or two, then marry and become Mrs. _____ (husband's first and last name), then of course, start a family. My destiny was very clearly defined. If the world was changing for other women, I didn't feel it in Mobile. Yes, we'd heard about Gloria Steinem, but in my circle, she was written off as some wacky, out of control, untamed woman. Never did I imagine myself conducting photo shoots or presenting in board rooms or much less running my own company. As much as I understood the destiny set out for me and as the rule-follower I'd always been, that day in Harris' office I could feel myself being lured into erring on the side of my heart.

After working two years in Birmingham, I did as many of my advertising cohorts and set my sights on Atlanta, which was often referred to as the "New York of the South." I viewed Atlanta simply as a stepping-stone to the city where I dreamed of one day becoming one of the best of the best.

To get myself to Atlanta, I got bold and designed my resume in the form of a brightly colored comic book cover, featuring Wonder Woman flying into a capital city. In the dialogue bubbles, I listed my references and the awards I'd won, all in Comic Sans font. After a couple of promising interviews, I got bolder, even risqué, and sent my prospective employers thank you notes. In the package I included blue satin shorts with white stars, just like Wonder Woman's. It was no surprise that my newfound moxie landed me a job offer in just a few weeks. I gave my two weeks' notice, then convinced my co-worker Skye to fly with me to New York to celebrate.

I so vividly remember our plane's approach into LaGuardia. It was shortly after sunset. I pulled Skye to the tiny window and whispered in utter awe as the island came into view, "Can you believe we're actually doing this?" Giddy with anticipation, I scanned the rows and rows of delicate white lights, crisscrossing each other, forming a perfect grid. I'd never in my life seen anything like it, the density of structures exploding out of a deep black backdrop, while a strong and mighty river girded its east side. I could already see and feel myself floating down sidewalks thick with smart people, all dressed fashionably in designer labels, on their way to the theatre or to their luxurious penthouses. *I will live here before I die*, I promised the little girl inside me. *I will!*

We landed, deboarded, then merged in with the river of bodies that flowed through the weathered halls of LaGuardia. At baggage claim, Skye and I grabbed our avocado green and candy red Samsonite suitcases, then searched for signs to the dreaded taxi stand. I was really nervous about this next part because, according to my mother, cab drivers in New York took first timers on wild rides through the city in order to run up the meter. "You know, people also kill cabbies in New York," she warned. "Lock your doors as soon as you get in."

"Address?" our driver barked as he jammed the gear shift into drive. Then off he bolted, wheeling us through the streets of Queens, slinging Skye and me across the plastic-covered seat. He honked and yelled out his window as he jerked in and out of the thick yellow sea of Checker cabs on the Queensboro Bridge. I couldn't help but thank God for the immense filigree arches that formed our grand entrance to the city. They'll save us from falling into the river, I prayed, searching for something reassuring about our wild and crazy ride.

Then the skyline appeared!

I swear, I've seen nothing since that has even come close to my first panoramic view of Manhattan at night! The miles and miles of twinkling city lights created a halo effect across the indigo sky, artfully framing the iconic structures I'd seen only in pictures — The Empire State Building, the Chrysler Tower, and of course, the new twin towers of the World Trade Center, the tallest buildings in the world.

As we drove onto the island, the buildings loomed, became immense, and towered over our heads. We rode on and the view transformed into one painted with neon. Flickering oranges, high-pitched blues, screaming yellows, and red-hot pinks. Oh, man, tell me I was not in love! The driver had taken us to our hotel on Lexington Avenue via Times Square. A bit of a roundabout way we later learned, but it was every bit worth of the trumped-up fare. Our first view of Manhattan was one hell of an opening scene. As we stepped out of the cab, I remember feeling so awed, so naive, very much like country-come-to-town.

I hardly slept that night. As soon as the morning sun slid through the slats of the shades, I popped out of bed, brushed my teeth, splashed some cold water on my face, and pulled on the same pants I'd worn the night before. Skye was still asleep, so I left her a note, then tiptoed out alone, my money safely pinned to my bra just as my mother had instructed. Our hotel was just a few blocks from the famous Bloomingdale's store, so I figured the neighborhood must be fairly safe.

Just as I pushed open the heavy hotel lobby door and stepped onto the wide sidewalk, a deep rumbling startled me. A guttural roar came up through the steaming grates, and it seemed to shake the entire sidewalk under my feet. After a moment of panic, I imagined that it was probably a subway train rattling along the rails deep below me, so I relaxed and began walking.

Lining each side of the street were old brick and stone buildings, all jammed up against each other, rising tall, their shadows blanketing the sidewalk. The façades, once gloried in their classic Renaissance and Art Deco styles, were all fused together by a common shade of dull, grimy grey, the color of a city teetering on bankruptcy. But to me, they were dazzling. I was just as awed by the boutiques hawking maxi dresses and leisure suits as I was the tiny slivered shops, those crammed full of dusty souvenirs and tacky jewelry. So many immigrants, I remember thinking of the street hustlers, their accents foreign to me, their aggressive tactics unsettling.

At the corner, rows of yellow taxis idled, their engines gurgling as they waited for their morning calls. It was early yet. I was enthralled by the sounds and motion of Manhattan—the graffitied delivery trucks wedging themselves into impossible places and the mass of bodies, all choreographed in perfect sync as they strode down the sidewalk. Even the smells seemed exotic. The stale exhaust and the musty scents that old things have about them, braided in perfectly with the richness of coffee brewing, with honey roasted nuts, and an occasional sweetness wafting from a bakery. It was 1977, a tough time for New York, but I certainly didn't feel it.

But I did try to stay aware of what we Southerners believed were dangerous streets. I clutched my little pocketbook tight against my body. My mother had instructed me to keep my I.D., her home and work phone numbers, plus a whistle on me at all times. Looking back, I can only imagine how nervous she must have been. New York was hit with a massive blackout just three months before my trip and the event fueled horror stories of subway riders trapped in darkness, looters and arsonists wreaking havoc on the city. The serial killer known as "Son of Sam" had also made the city famous in recent months. Although he was in custody at the time of my arrival, fear still loomed.

I returned to the hotel just as Skye was stepping out of the shower. We made our plans for the day and off we went, lollygagging up Fifth Avenue, oohing and aahing at the glitter in Tiffany's windows, and squeezing fluffy animals in FAO Schwartz. From there, we floated over to Central Park where we indulged in mustard-slathered street dogs and hot, salty pretzels. Then we walked on to the Metropolitan Museum of Art where, instead of investing our money in a little culture, we blew it on cheesy souvenir shot glasses and key rings to take back home.

In our first few days we practiced hailing cabs, swirled in the aroma of roasting chestnuts, inhaled the tunes of subway musicians, and felt electrified by every single ounce of energy this city had to offer.

It was on the last day that we walked Madison Avenue, the yellow brick road to the world's most famous advertising agencies.

Photo by Joe Benton, joebenton.net

It was on this holy ground where all my advertising heroes walked to work each day and I could feel their heartbeats. I would've given anything to grab a peek inside one of their workspaces or to rub elbows with one of them in a cafe. But I had to settle for the next best thing, a t-shirt with the iconic I (heart) NY logo that my idol, Milton Glaser, had designed.

The grand finale happened on our last night as Skye and I hopped on the overhead tram from Roosevelt Island back to the east side of Manhattan. At almost 2 a.m., the PA system crackled and the conductor announced, "Last call back to Manhattan!" It was then that I felt my heart leap. I caught another glimpse of that panoramic Manhattan skyline and cemented the promise I made to myself on our first day. *I will live here before I die.*

I took numerous trips to New York after that initial visit in 1977. Most were quick in-and-out spins for work, others were no more than extended weekends. Several times, while considering a job change or when breaking up with a boyfriend, I went so far as to spiff up my portfolio, redesign my resume, and gather addresses of the best ad agencies on Madison Avenue. But I never followed through.

Not until now, 33 years later.

It was February of 2011, a month since I made my New York plans public in that little Sunday School room. Taking off to New York for 30 days created a little flurry of excitement when I told my friends and announced it on Facebook, but the whole idea was beginning to feel like a public booby trap I'd set for myself. I had paid the deposit for my class at Parsons, but the remaining balance was due soon and I had no clue how I'd pay it, much less cover the other expenses I'd have to incur. My moods see-sawed high as a kite one minute, while slamming to the ground the next.

Break the expenses down into little pieces, I coaxed myself in a moment of clarity. I'd been over the list a million times in my head, but writing it down made me feel productive and, in some crazy way, let me concentrate on one small individual item at a time instead of getting overwhelmed by the big, scary bottom line. I started with the obvious: food. I figured that while in New York, I could squeak by on $50 per week, or a monthly total of $200. Of course, that meant no going out to eat, but that was okay. Then I added the cost of a month-long subway ticket, $125.

Next on my list was a computer. I got an estimate of $400 for a used Apple laptop, but the friend selling it warned it might not have the power needed to run the graphics software the class would require. "I'll take my chances," I told him, ignoring a problem I was afraid to face.

On down the list I went, "housing, walking shoes, incidentals" until the last item, a smartphone. My taped-up Nokia "brick," as my kids called it, was on its last leg, and although I had resigned myself that I'd have to forego one of those new fancy iPhones, I put it on the list anyway with no dollar figure beside it. I'd supplemented my income the previous year by canvassing neighborhoods for the Census Bureau, so I knew I could find extra work again by tutoring little kids, even babysitting and walking dogs. I was pumped!

With a bottom line in mind, I then searched for scholarships. The few I found for older professionals weren't applicable for this type of course, so I devised a savings plan. I printed out five individual calendar pages for the remaining months, February through June, then divided my grand total of expenses into 20 weekly amounts. On each Saturday I wrote, "Save $250." I knew as well as I knew my own name that shaving that much off my weekly expenses was unachievable, but breaking it down into smaller numbers at least gave me some semblance of hope. And, by damn, no one was going to tell me it wasn't possible.

It also occurred to me that the class I chose would require a basic knowledge of the new media space. Scanning online tutorials, I immediately felt overwhelmed by the fundamentals: a whole new language, the foreign words and acronyms—SEO, HTML, CSS... For a moment I felt leveled by the amount of ground I needed to cover. But instead of beating myself up for letting it get ahead of me, like I normally would've done, I felt invigorated, almost propelled to conquer this beast. ANYTHING to get to New York.

I knew a little about Facebook, so I decided to tackle social media first. I followed the online steps to set up a business page at www. Facebook.com/LisaWeldonNYC, then researched the best way to engage an audience, as measured by the number of "Likes." My goal was 2500 before I left for New York. Just as I did for my budget, I divided that number over 20 weeks, then sent an email to 20 or so friends, asking them to like my page. By the end of that first day I had 15. Well, that was easy!

In the next few days, I opened Twitter and YouTube accounts, then brushed up my LinkedIn page. Learning to use these new platforms was thrilling—empowering, actually—but my sense of accomplishment was slowly tempered by the sheer volume still ahead of me. So, like my budget, I faced it head on and inked in four days per week to watch tutorials.

The next calendar entries were writing practices, six of them. Just as I aimed to do in New York, I would walk a mile around Atlanta, take photos, then come home and write at least 350 words about the neighborhood I'd discovered; 350 words, because that's how many I read were needed for SEO, whatever that was! The first test around Atlanta took me an entire day to walk, research, write, edit, upload, and retouch the photos, then finally, post onto the new blog I was creating. Shortly thereafter, I began reading horror stories online about the rigor of Parsons. One Facebook post claimed, "Forget doing anything else. It takes over your life." I added "Research Neighborhoods" to my to-do list, hoping some prework would serve as a cheat sheet if I came up short on time.

The big elephant in the room was housing. NYU dorm rooms, virtually empty in the summertime, were the cheapest option. But please God, I'd rather forgo eating than share a dorm room, or more honestly, a bathroom, for an entire month. I checked Airbnb for apartments in Greenwich Village, which was close to school, but the prices were exorbitant, so I just listed that BIG item in the "bury your head in the sand" column.

As the weeks went on, I became almost obsessive about my trip preparation. I would hole up in my office at night and plow through more and more instructional videos. Learning became my drug, its high would bring me a feeling of accomplishment. I would reach out to more people on social media, make connections and delight as my "like" numbers clicked higher and higher. I'd stay up until 3:00 or 4:00 in the morning, digging into the personalities of the neighborhoods I planned to walk. Learning was cheap, and it felt like the only part of my life I could control, or perhaps the only thing I felt was inching me forward. The more cocooned I became in my little office and the more hours I worked, the easier it was to put off the confrontation and the hard decisions I knew in my gut I had to make.

Jim, likewise, spent most of his time in his basement office, shuffling through whatever problems he faced with his struggling business. He'd often fall asleep on the sofa watching Braves baseball. I'd crawl into bed hoping to have it all to myself. It was easier not to communicate.

My 12-, 13- and 14-hour days slumped over a computer were wreaking havoc, not only on eyes, but on my entire psyche. When I bragged about my ambitious goals and accomplishments with Tavye, she countered with, "Listen to your body! You've got to take better care of yourself," she urged, encouraging me to get more sleep, take breaks away from the computer, and walk. So, alongside my savings, Facebook, and learning goals, I inked in a walking routine, then invited friends to accompany me. Sadly, I didn't really hear the sleep part, but I did find that having accountability partners was critical to my physical well-being.

At this point, everything was hunky-dory. At least on paper.

Friends began reading about my upcoming trip on social media. Several stopped me in the grocery store or in Target, wanting to hear more about my plans. "I wish I had your courage," one admitted, and I've got to tell you, the affirmation was an instant high. It felt good to be validated and admired, and in a way, to be tagged the hero that would save our family.

But it was a high I was struggling to sustain. The veil was wearing thin. Deep down inside, as committed as I was to going, I couldn't see any way to pull off this trip. I wasn't meeting my weekly savings numbers. I got a few extra jobs, but my income numbers didn't stack up. They were nowhere near what they needed to be.

With only a few months to go, I began to feel a sense of resignation seeping in. How humiliating it would be to back out, and to fail, and have to do so publicly.

Late one Thursday evening, I was in the kitchen emptying the dishwasher. The back and forth between Meredith Grey and McDreamy Shepherd droned in the background, yet another episode of *Grey's Anatomy* filling the void that once held the voices of our family for 25 years. Just as I started wiping the counter, I recognized the clomp of Jim's shoe as it hit the bottom step. Clomp (pause). Clomp (pause). Clomp, his slow and heavy soles dropping sluggishly on each of the wooden treads. Like molasses, his ascent from the basement seemed prolonged and pained. His legs must be bothering him, I reasoned, referencing the damage the radiation treatment for his cancer had caused years earlier. When he reached the top, he paused, then pushed open the door. I turned toward him, looked at his face, and immediately sensed impending doom.

"Sweetheart," he started, his body frozen in a crumpled stance. His voice was toneless, his head hung low. "We need to talk," his words barely out before every muscle in my body braced for shock. I knew immediately that something terribly wrong had happened. I searched Jim's face for clues. *Please God, please, not one of the kids,* my worst fear raced through my veins like fire down a line of gasoline. Had Jim's cancer returned? "What is it?" I begged, not wanting to hear.

"The house," Jim stumbled, unable to look at me in the eyes. "The house is due to be auctioned off …" the words drifted toward me in slow motion. "… on Tuesday."

I struggled to breathe, the heat surging through my chest, flushing my face with rage. I inched through the words slowly in my head, trying hard to string together their meaning. All the neighbors must know. A foreclosure only four days away has surely been advertised. They knew before I did.

Then suddenly, I went cold. Stone cold. Every ounce of anger vanished. The fear, the panic, gone. As if in an altered state, I began stepping through my next thoughts like a robot. Very calmly and clear-headed, I began, Today is Thursday. Tomorrow, Friday. Then Monday, I calculated, subtracting out the weekend days. I've got two business days to save the house, my mind cataloguing next steps.

In the very next instant, I saw my face on a different body, on the courthouse steps. That person was haggard, crying, begging desperately for more time, but I couldn't feel a thing. Then I hallucinated, very clearly feeling myself in a cold CEO mode, standing at the head of a polished mahogany table. My three children sat on one side, straight and at attention, their eyes on me. Jim sat opposite them with his hands clasped in front of him. I felt myself delivering a difficult decision, one, I explained to my pretend board members, that was hard to execute but would ultimately benefit the company. Still, I felt nothing. It was simply business. Afterwards, I felt an odd sense of relief. All this was now out of my hands.

I came back into the present as I looked at Jim's hollow face and whispered in a voice not of my own, "You need to leave by noon tomorrow." He'd thrown the dice on yet another entrepreneurial venture and had lost. It wasn't the loss that broke me, it was the fact that I didn't know. This time I couldn't fix it, nor did I have the will to try. A higher being had taken over, a deeper power I couldn't explain. There was a peace that filled me, one like so many have written about after coming back from death. I was in a different level of consciousness, a dream state, but I was aware. Yes, all of my senses were aware, but I couldn't feel anything in my heart. It was as if I was actually relieved that I no longer had to fight.

Jim simply nodded and walked back down the basement stairs where he stayed the rest of the night. I didn't yell or scream, which had by now become my norm. I needed every single ounce of energy I could muster up to digest what I was losing.

My marriage. The only home my kids had ever known. And my heart, my little family of five.

That evening I laid in bed reflecting on our life together, Jim and me. I catalogued each of Jim's entrepreneurial ventures—some good, some bad—and ultimately blamed the demise of our family on his financial infidelity. Why couldn't he sit down with me and discuss difficult issues? Why couldn't we budget together? Would we ever be a family again? The tears welled up in my eyes, spilling onto my burning cheeks. I couldn't bear to accept the future my gut was spelling out for me.

Could I ever forgive him? Could I ever trust him again? What part had I played in our demise? I sifted through how each of us had been affected differently by tough financial times. Jim always seemed to bounce back so easily, often as if nothing had ever happened. Or that's the way it appeared. Me, not so much. I surfaced scarred, more afraid to take risks.

I first met Jim in 1971 when I was just 18. It was spring, my freshman year at Auburn University. It was a Saturday night and minutes before curfew when the doors to the dorm would be locked and woe betide any girl who had to ring the bell, no matter how good her excuse. I made it through the mad scramble at the door and saw my roommate, Martha Lee, trying to haul up Jim, her date, who had fallen, spread-eagle, on the newly waxed linoleum floor. Jim blamed his fall on the metal taps on the soles of his new shoes, but I sensed foolishness was involved.

The next time I saw Jim, it was I who acted the fool. It was 1976, five years later, in Birmingham, Alabama, where I'd moved after graduation. Jim, who was visiting from Atlanta, and his buddy Scott came to my apartment to pick up my roommate for a post-game party. We'd all just come from the Iron Bowl, the iconic game played between Auburn and Alabama, the biggest rivalry in college football.

I remember thinking how sophisticated he seemed, living and working in the big city of "Hotlanta," as it was called. He was dressed to the nines in a tan corduroy blazer with leather patches on the elbows. I could see his monogram sewn on the cuff of his starched button-down pinpoint cotton shirt. Hmmm, I remember feeling a bit interested.

I, on the other hand, was soaked from head to toe. Unfortunately, Alabama had pummeled us, so needless to say, this Auburn fan had drowned her sorrows with a few too many bourbon and Cokes. My date and I found it funny to dump coolers of ice on each other's head. Why? God only knows, but there I stood, looking like a drowned rat.

Jim came to town numerous times that following year, both for work and to play in golf tournaments. On one of his visits, my roommate encouraged me to join her, Scott, and Jim at a party a mutual Auburn friend was hosting, and I agreed. As soon as the four of us arrived at our friend's apartment, Jim gravitated toward his fraternity brothers and I headed toward my friends. After the party, somehow Jim and I ended up at the Waffle House, where the two of us yapped until 2:00 in the morning. I had set my sights on moving to Atlanta, and I wanted to know all about it.

We stayed in touch, but sporadically. Later that fall, just after I'd gotten the offer from an ad agency in Atlanta, he phoned one evening. "I'm playing in a tournament in Birmingham this week-end. Want to come to the Calcutta?" I accepted his offer to the after party, then told him about my upcoming move, to which he added, "Need any help?"

Well, what followed was a story he loved to tell for many years after. "Yes, I have just a few things," was my response to his offer. Two weeks later up and down three stories he and a friend he'd summoned went, hauling an entire apartment full of heavy furniture, with only one single beer in the refrigerator as a reward. When all was packed, he drove my clunky old Ford Fairlane, which had only one headlight, and pulled the U-Haul trailer in the pouring rain for three long hours to Atlanta. I followed behind, driving his sporty little BMW.

Once in Atlanta, Jim helped me carry everything up ANOTHER three stories. At 2:00 a.m., when we were finally finished, he asked if he could bunk down at my apartment. With only one bed and a sofa too short for even a child, I shook my head and said, "Jim, I can't let you do that." It certainly wouldn't have been proper. He drove another hour to get to his home in the suburbs, and yeah, I didn't hear from him again for months, or until we crossed paths at a mutual friend's party. It was there that I had the sense to ask his forgiveness. "Can I cook you a nice meal next Saturday night?"

From that point on, the two of us would get together on random occasions, meeting for drinks or grilling out, and comparing notes about each other's lives. I loved that he treated me as an equal, and that he used me as a sounding board for his new entrepreneurial venture. He could talk openly with me about the NBC reporter he was dating in Washington D.C. and I felt equally secure in sharing my dating woes. I came to refer to Jim as "my tuxedo date." If I needed a partner for fancy charity functions, I'd call on him and he did the same with me. I loved our casual and honest relationship so much so that I'd often brag that Jim, or "Weldon" as we all called him back then, was the only guy I ever felt comfortable enough to send to the store for Tampax.

We were that rare thing—a man and a woman who had a true friendship. Several years later when he wrote me a note telling me that I was the kind of woman he hoped he'd marry one day, I never dreamed that it was anything but an affirmation of our relationship.

All that changed one night two years later. I arrived late for dinner at a small Italian restaurant near his suburban Atlanta home, pushed past the maître d' and searched through the dimly lit restaurant to find Jim sitting at a small square table. "Oh, Weldon, you wouldn't believe the traffic," I started. As soon as we sent our waiter away with our orders, I dove straight into the woes of collecting money from a client whose invoices were four months past due. I had just struck out on my own and was horrified to learn than not everyone paid their bills on time. "I hate this part of my business," I complained. Jim, on the other hand, loved the financial part. He told me how to shake up a client by mailing a ten-day demand letter via certified mail, with a receipt signature required. "Just don't let it get into a lawyer's hands," he advised; "If you do, you might as well kiss that money goodbye."

At the end of the meal, when the waiter laid the tab next to Jim's plate, I sensed something was wrong. The conversation halted and the air between us thickened. Jim's attention had drifted elsewhere. He looked down and shifted awkwardly in his chair. He then cleared his throat and looked me straight in the eyes, and said, "I'd like to spend the rest of my life with you."

His words leveled me. I went totally blank. I could feel my heart race as I hung in the void between us, flailing through a myriad of emotions: guilt, sadness, confusion, pity, and fear that I would lose him. I even felt angry, as if he had violated the rules and ruined our friendship. I had no idea at all that he cared for me in that way. Not even a clue. In this very moment I sensed a tenderness, a vulnerability I'd never seen in him before and I liked it. Jim meant the world to me. Struggling to look at him, I finally shook my head and whispered, "Weldon, we're just friends."

That was the spring of 1983. I fled like a scalded cat. Six months went by with no contact at all from him. I missed him terribly but held back from calling him. I cared enough about him not to lead him on or give him a false impression of what our future might be. Reaching out to him felt too self-serving and I didn't dare do anything to hurt him. So, when he finally called in early October, I was thrilled to hear his voice. "I've got a business trip to New York in two weeks," he announced. "It's the weekend of your birthday, isn't it?" he asked. "I know how much you love the city, why don't you come with me?" He'd heard me reminisce about my trip to the city years earlier. I was touched that he remembered my birthday and yes, there was no other place I'd rather spend it, but I hesitated, questioning my motives. Would it be fair to him if I said yes? Am I taking advantage of his generosity? But, something deep down inside me was cracking, crumbling the walls I'd erected, giving me permission to go. Reluctant, I said okay.

Days before we left, I wrote in my diary. "It's funny but I'm beginning to feel like I'm okay, that maybe I am someone special, that I deserve someone nice. And Jim does, too. And if I give us a chance, maybe we'd be good together." My whole premise was to give him, and us together, a chance. I was tired of dating men who left me feeling unworthy.

So, that was the beginning of our love story.

Jim and I spent five glorious days together in New York. I watched in awe as he left for business meetings in the mornings, dressed so handsomely, a perfectly folded handkerchief tucked in the pocket of his double-breasted jackets. He blended seamlessly into the professional fabric of that great city—the ultimate, in my mind. Over dinner I was seduced as he recounted the difficult negotiations he and his customers engaged in, never once intimidated by the seasoned sportswear buyers at the behemoth Macy's or J. C. Penney. "I'm an old rag merchant at heart," he joked. I felt totally safe and protected as he swished me through the streets and in and out of cabs in this city that was so mysterious to me. He knew it like the back of his hand and his confidence was sexy. I loved his sophistication, that he knew what to tip the concierge or what to ask of the sommelier. I liked that he took charge. It felt good, for a change, to step aside and trust someone else to make the decisions. But most of all I loved the pride he seemed to have in me when introducing me to his colleagues. He would go on and on about my business, the awards I'd won for my work, even my skill at golf. He made me feel like I was smart and creative, like someone even more special than I thought of myself.

During our trip to New York, our seven-year friendship shifted from platonic to romantic. Less than a month later, I knew it was love and I asked if his offer of marriage was still good. Without hesitating, he said the time wasn't right. I asked again on January 1st, claiming proposal rights since it was the first day of Leap Year, but again he asked for more time. He had taken over ownership of a failing sewing plant and was working way too many hours to be distracted. Plus, his house was undergoing a major renovation due to a busted water pipe. It was pretty clear his focus had shifted, so we continued dating.

Jim called me early one Friday morning eight months later. "What do you want to do tonight?" he asked, just as he did every Friday morning. But this time I answered with, "Weldon, I have plans for tonight." I had no plans, but I was tired of waiting.

The next morning, at hardly 9:00 a.m., he called and told me to go find a house. When I pressed him for a meaning he said, "You know what I mean, just go find a house." Pause. "For the two of us." We married two months later, exactly one year after our New York trip, and the day after my 32nd birthday.

"Let's travel before we have kids," I proposed to Jim one night as we barbecued outside on a cool winter evening. When I added, "we could start with Europe," he stopped me cold. "There's plenty to see in the United States," he answered quite emphatically, then stood up and walked inside to get a plate for the chicken.

YIKES!

"Let's wait and do the States when the kids come," I countered when he walked back outside, feeling sure he'd agree with my logic. Then came the shocker: "Kids," he started. "I'm not sure I want kids." At that point I realized we'd never really hashed out the tough issues like our faith, family obligations, children, finances … or travel, which was a vital part of my DNA. But I brushed it off and, like a starry-eyed new bride, I felt certain we'd be able to work through anything that might arise, including travel and, certainly, having children.

A couple of months later I pushed forward with my travel dreams and finagled a failsafe way to lure Jim out of the country, to the European Tour Qualifying School in La Manga, Spain. For six weeks, golfers would vie for 25 spots to play all over Europe for the following season. Being the consummate golfer that he was, yes, he went for it hook, line and sinker. The following November we were off to an experience of a lifetime. In the end he wasn't one of the top 25, but he made the first alternate list, which meant he would be invited to compete in just about every tournament held in Europe in 1986. We came home after those glorious six weeks in Spain, he sold his business in order to fund the next year, turned pro, and off he went again with my blessings. I flew over once for a tournament in Sweden and again for the British Open Qualifying in Scotland. He went on to play for six weeks all over Africa, in the Safari Tour. He made friends all over the world, and to this day we both agree it was one the best investments of our lives. When that dream of a year was over, Jim came home and started an apparel company. I expanded my business, and we put an offer on a four-bedroom house. It was then that we faced our first financial roadblock.

"Jim, we need to clear up this old debt so we can get this loan written in time," I heard the mortgage banker say on the answering machine, his voice flaring with urgency. I was stunned. I'd never heard any mention of an old debt. Jim waved it off as an old business expense. He got it cleared up and the loan on the house went through. Nothing else was said, but the idea of it gnawed at me.

I quickly learned that Jim and I were polar opposites in the way we managed our finances. He kept a haphazard checkbook, never subtracting the few checks he had entered. I knew at any given time how much money I had in my account, down to the penny. I was anal about maintaining zero balances on my credit cards and funding my IRA each year. Jim was much more of a risk taker. "You make money through managed risk" was his mantra. I didn't want to hear about managed risks any more than he wanted to listen to me preach about retirement 30 years down the road. By the time we got married, we'd both handled our own finances for ten years, and had done so quite well. In that time each of us had secured mortgages, car loans, and lines of credit for our businesses. I couldn't imagine, like many of my women friends, having to ask permission from my husband to buy a new dress or a chair for the living room, or even running the idea by him. I just bought it. Jim was the same way. So, our modus operandi was to split responsibilities. We took turns paying the mortgage and splitting the utilities and food expenses. Each of us handled our own credit cards and car payments. Once in our new home, I enjoyed renovating, so I normally picked up those costs while Jim footed the bills for entertainment and travel. We never argued about who was spending more or what surprise expense belonged to whom. Ours was "the perfect 50/50 relationship," I used to brag to my friends. I was simply spinning a story that never really felt 100 percent right. It wasn't until years later, when a uniformed IRS officer knocked on our front door and surprised me by serving paperwork for a lien they'd placed on Jim's and his partner's business, that I realized our way of handling money, and our inability to discuss it, was terribly unhealthy.

I was overcome with anger and felt violated and humiliated, even dirty. I lost all dignity as the emotionless IRS agent questioned every charge on our credit card statements and emptied our bank accounts. Every attempt to fight or coax or plead with the steel wall of the IRS was futile. I had two little babies and another on the way. I had no choice but to pick up the pieces and go on, and that I did.

Jim rebounded quicker than I did. He didn't seem stymied at all by failure. I envied his ability to brush himself off, pick up the phone and hustle up new business. It wasn't long before he was walking into boardrooms and pitching new ideas. He had no qualms about approaching bankers and investors with big-ticket requests. "They stand to make a lot of money off my deal," he would say confidently. And although I admired his resiliency and moxie, deep down inside, I became guarded.

His most brilliant idea, a cable channel dedicated solely to golf, sounded like such an unattainable goal when he threw several thousand dollars at trademarking the name, "The Golf Channel." After two years of planning, he was in the final stages of negotiating with the European Golf Tour when Arnold Palmer and a cable operator heard about his plans and rushed to beat him to the punch. They'd done some legal spy work and found they could grab the name from Jim by simply using it publicly three times, which they did on February 26th of that year. The loss nearly killed Jim, and I was devastated for him.

Over the next year, Jim rebuilt his entrepreneurial reputation to the point of being courted by Arthur Andersen, one of the "Big Five" accounting firms at the time. They chose to fund a new software system he and a partner co-created. I was elated for him and so proud of his accomplishment. But within months, Arthur Andersen was indicted for their involvement with the Enron scandal and all speculative funding was withdrawn.

Later that fall, Jim was diagnosed with Stage 4 Hodgkin's Lymphoma. As hard as he tried to continue his quest for potential investment, he was flattened by rounds of chemotherapy and radiation. We scrambled to maintain a normalcy for our family, but it was hard to juggle my work, Jim's treatments, and three kids under the age of nine. I relied on friends and family to help with meals and carpooling, even a little leniency from the kids' teachers. For six months, or until he was deemed "in remission," I prayed one and only one prayer: "Please, God, give me the strength to handle whatever comes next."

Even though Jim found success in the following years, he and I never learned how to sit down and compromise on tough issues. The mere mention of us discussing money erupted in a fight, or Jim brushing me off, or in our final years, simple resignation. "Sounds like an independent relationship, not the interdependent one that you wanted, Lisa," a marriage counselor would ultimately tell me. For 27 years I had bragged about how we divided and conquered, a real 50-50 relationship. What felt like an even split, became a split indeed.

So, there I stood in 2011, hearing that we'd lose our home to foreclosure in just four days.

I walked out to our porch and crumpled in a white wicker chair. Hypnotized by the soft purr of the ceiling fan, I sat and looked out at the twinkling city lights of Atlanta. I'll miss this place, I remember thinking.

The night was hot and heavy. It set the perfect Southern stage for the symphony of cicadas that had just begun to sing. It was 2011, the

Engagement photo by Alan David.

nymphs were shedding their skin and making their final transition into their 13th year or, like me, into the last stretch of their lives. Uncanny, I thought.

The next morning I tucked my tail and asked my mother for a loan—enough to keep the house out of foreclosure. She was the last person I ever wanted to ask for help but was the only option I had.

I knew that asking her for financial help to dig out of one of Jim's messes meant I had to surrender to her ever-present negativity about my husband. I would have to break with Jim for good.

This time she said nothing. I had to make the decision on my own.

Early the next morning, I called my neighbor Patti. I told her I wanted to go shopping, but when she appeared, "I need help," was all I had to say. As she drove us through the streets of our neighborhood, I explained what had happened. "I can't be there. I can't watch him pack up," I explained.

I couldn't bear to face that this was the end.

7

Our son Trey was out with friends the night Jim delivered the news; the other two kids were away at school. There was no opportunity to sit down as a family and explain what happened. When Trey returned the next day, Jim was gone. The minute I heard my child walk through the door, I felt an immense pressure wrench my body. I recognized the urgency, the duty to sit down with him, to tell him we were losing our home, that Dad was gone, and why, and what lay ahead. But I was terribly unprepared and not at all emotionally strong enough to face my son. I was in such a state of shock myself. While I mumbled through the mess of what even I didn't understand, I fought to subdue the anger. Why was I left with this burden?

But Trey wasn't naive, nor did he act shocked; for months he'd heard the fights over money between Jim and me. As I tried to explain the situation to my son, he seemed antsy and anxious for me to quit. He asked no questions and quickly left the room, I'm sure, to call his sister and brother. Unfortunately, my child bore that responsibility and because of that, I felt great shame.

For years I'd told the kids that under no circumstances would I ever leave "Dad." I loved Jim and divorce was never an option for me, nothing I'd ever imagined having to do. They'd heard me joke over and over again: "Nope, Dad and I have a deal. If either of us leaves we have to take all three of y'all!" I could never imagine anything that would push me to break up my family. Oh, I always claimed I'd leave—in a heartbeat — if Jim ever laid a hand on me, or if he had an affair, but Jim would never do either, I was certain of that.

But that day, I'd broken my promise. I'd gone against my word, plus I wasn't even present to console my children during the most painful time of their lives. I had done them wrong.

"Mom, I got a job in the Engineering Department," Emma called to tell me the next afternoon, then interrupted me when I tried to interject. "I know all about it. Trey called," and then went straight into her next sentence. "Plus, I've applied to babysit in the nursery on Sundays at the Methodist Church." That all meant she wouldn't be coming home, not on the weekends nor between semesters. But even worse, I knew in my heart she was assuming the financial burden, and that broke me. I couldn't be there for my child, emotionally or financially, and it made me feel useless as a parent.

In the coming weeks, it became obvious that the boys, both teen-agers, blamed me for the family's demise. The few times Witt came home from college, he lashed out at me, sometimes quite violently, about that smallest things. I suspected he was high most of the time, but I hardly had the fight in me to address it. Trey, on the other hand, remained silent and distant. When I did try to engage with him my sentiments felt forced and disingenuous. I sensed he would have rather been with his dad, not me. This all happened during the last few months of his senior year of high school, a time that should have been filled with graduation festivities. I couldn't bear the fact that there was no celebration for him, no gifts, not even a family dinner. Jim and I came together for his two-hour graduation ceremony, but that's all the child got in acknowledgment of his major life event. It was all so sad, so unfair for him. *I could've prevented this*, I lashed out at myself.

A few weeks later, a "For Sale" sign would go up in the front yard, and it was time to delve into 25 years of stuff to prep the house to sell. Jim, who'd moved in temporarily with his sister south of Atlanta, rallied the kids by suggesting they all meet at the house the upcoming weekend "to help Mom." Having us all back together under one roof was exactly what my heart ached for, but I heard a voice warn me that I was weak and vulnerable, and that I might slip and let Jim back into my life. I began to crack when Emma said, "Mom, he's just trying to help." Nonetheless, I stood firm, knowing I could soldier through and work faster and more efficiently if I could distance myself from everyone and keep my emotions in check. More importantly, I needed to learn how to protect myself, to put myself first. "No, baby. I need to do this alone."

So, I went about packing up all the Little League trophies and high school yearbooks, sifting through the rubble of our life as a family. I found letters I'd written Witt when he went to sleep-away camp his very first time. I was so afraid he'd get homesick. I came across a love note tucked way into the toe of an old sneaker. "Trey, I like you because you are really nice to people," it read. The girl's frilly cursive broke my heart.

And then there were the kids' old bedroom doors, the ones we'd replaced when we renovated. I'd let each kid treat the doors as scrapbooks, encouraging them to put their handprints on them, to add stickers and photos, and suggested their friends leave messages on them. Although it made no sense to store three large wooden doors, I lugged them down two stories, and into the "Storage Unit" corner of the basement. I couldn't bear to part with these versions of my children's life stories. And, the kids' beer cans I found hidden up in ceiling tiles in the basement—I would have been angry had I found them before, but that day they only made me cry.

I did everything I could during the next few months to keep myself physically and mentally busy, anything to exhaust me. I didn't allow myself to stop, in fear I'd collapse. I shelved any thoughts of New York, because they were just too hard to imagine, to impossible to deal with. I certainly didn't have the bandwidth to negotiate refunds, nor could I face the disappointment of not going.

Then, one evening, just three weeks before my supposed departure date, my friend Cathy peered at me across her dining room table, her eyes narrowing. "We're throwing you a send-off party for your

New York journey," she said in her sweet Southern tone. And with a Scarlett O'Hara firmness, she added, "Which night's convenient?" I was at my lowest, my absolute lowest and New York was the furthest thing from my reality.

Almost in duty to my friend, I scrolled through the Airbnb listings and found the cheapest apartment I could find near the school, using the last little bit of my mother's money as a deposit. It had no kitchen, but I didn't care. I was simply checking another box. With that, my trip was now technically set. I was going, but nothing in me felt excited about the prospect. I couldn't get past the sense of irresponsibility of leaving my kids in such a shamble, nor could I overcome the fear of running out of money while there.

Then ten days before I was due to leave, the phone rang. It was Parsons, calling to tell me that my class had been cancelled due to insufficient enrollment. I was stunned. Silenced. It was if someone had snuck up behind me and kicked me in the back, slamming me to the ground. When I caught my breath, I succumbed to the realization that it was yet another thing crumbling in my life. "You can sign up for one of our other courses," the woman on the other end added, her voice as cold as a cucumber, "if there's room."

Surprisingly, her attitude got a rise out of me. She pissed me off. Does she have any clue how much money I'd lose? "I've already paid for an apartment!" I barked back at her, trying my best to imitate her New York toughness. Seemingly unfazed, she snapped back, stating that my only other option was a refund.

After hanging up I began to feel a power ignite. They should pay for my apartment! I tore through the school's website in search of their legalese. When I found their asterisked disclaimers, my fight flared. I then scrolled back to their course listing online and found two other courses of interest. Both were listed as full, and I got hotter. I checked NYU and Columbia and found they had similar summer courses, so I scoured both of their listings. Their sessions didn't coincide with the time for which I'd rented the apartment, so I looked for options at Pratt and The School of Visual Arts but again came up empty-handed.

I dialed the woman back, totally prepared to tear into her. I was steaming. I felt robbed of my home, my family, and now my money, my dream, and the only diversion I had in my life. I'd worked so hard to get to this point and I wasn't going to take "no" for an answer, by God!

Unfortunately, or maybe fortunately, I got her voicemail. As I listened to the robotic sound of her voice, I knew she'd won. Every ounce of fight sapped out of me. "Just refund my money," my voice cracked as I surrendered. I was devastated. The realization of what just happened finally hit me, and the old voices returned to console me.

This felt like divine intervention, a sign I shouldn't go. *This was stupid, Lisa, even from the beginning. All this hype you've created around this trip, what a fool you've made of yourself.*

Then it dawned on me: This is the perfect out! I could blame abandoning this New York dream on Parsons. I could do the responsible thing and collect my refund; the only money I'd lose would be my apartment deposit. I could finish packing the house and cleaning up the yard, and I could find myself a place to move. I would be the adult, put on a strong face for my children, and not flit off into fairyland, the voice reeled through my mind until I believed it.

On Facebook I typed, "Oh no! Parsons just called and said they cancelled my class!!!! Less than two weeks before I was to leave. {ok, Lisa, breathe}." Immediately I felt the pressure fall away, I felt a huge relief. I didn't fail, I assured myself. Yes, my heart was bleeding with disappointment, but staying home was the right thing to do, and a hell of lot easier.

Phew.

In less than a minute my Facebook friends began commenting and they were all of one voice. "That's just awful! … What's Plan B? … You ARE going!" One after another, these people I'd enjoined to come on this adventure with me let me know they were having none of my selflessness. Even Jim called and left a message, "Sweetheart, you have to go." But it was a comment from a Facebook friend I'd never met, my dear Constance, who lived in the middle of nowhere in Michigan, who pierced through all the voices. From day one, she'd read every word I wrote and commented on both Facebook and on my blog. She had confided in me that I was her inspiration, that my push to walk New York had helped her get through difficult days. And now she wrote, "You know, Lisa, I'm living through you. I always wanted to go to Ireland, but now that I have cancer, I doubt I'll ever get there." At that moment, I knew I had to go. I had to go for Constance. I had to also go for me.

Then it hit me: I would get my class deposit back, which would allow me to put a down payment on an iPhone. I could pay the balance on my apartment AND I could possibly afford to eat while I was there! I didn't need the class as a reason to go. I would walk New York, EVERY SINGLE NEIGHBORHOOD, no matter what.

It was early Friday evening, the 24th of June, the night before I was to leave for New York. A violent storm howled through Atlanta, its wind wailing and whistling like a band of angry souls. The tall, gangly pines thrashed violently against each other. Like bowling pins colliding, their deep, hollow cracks vibrated through the walls of my office. Hunched over my keyboard, I worked feverishly to grind out the last-minute work for my clients. I was anxious, my shoulders knotted. I pleaded silently with my internet connection as it sputtered in and out. I'd not done laundry, nor had I finished packing.

As I scooted my chair closer to the screen, I heard a slow, high-pitched cr-e-e-a-ck of a splitting sound, followed by a deep, thunderous BOOM! It shook the entire house. The lights flickered, then went out. Trey hollered from the second story, and Frank scurried down the wooden steps, his tiny little paws belying his bellowing bark.

I was first to reach the garage door, where I found a huge pine from the neighbor's yard had fallen diagonally across our driveway. Pine needles and pieces of bark were strewn everywhere; an odorous cloud of turpentine billowed in the air. Luckily, it missed the cars and the house, but it blocked our only way out. My mind immediately counted: "Seven. Eight." Only two hours to total darkness. Two hours to get the tree moved so I could get out the next morning.

In a weird sort of way, this act of nature, or fate, infused me with a new resolve. I threw everything in my being toward getting this tree, this last impediment in my life, out of my way. I felt oddly combative, even defiant, as if someone was testing me, or the world was telling me not to go. But I would show them. With no hesitation at all, I summoned the help of neighbors, and they showed up with chainsaws and rakes and wheelbarrows and helped us remove enough of the tree to clear a path out of the driveway. The electricity never came back on that night, my work didn't get finished, and my clothes got packed dirty—but, come hell or high water, I was getting out of that driveway the next morning.

As I laid in bed that night, picking at the last little bit of sap on my fingers, I gave myself one last pep talk. "Eleven more hours, Lisa. Eleven more hours and you'll be sitting on that plane!" It was all I could do to contain the eddy of joy, of wonder, of anticipation, and of fear that swirled in my heart.

The next morning, I arrived at the airport way before my flight, a real first for last-minute me. I had all my clothes, my books, even a box of Bran Flakes, and my trusty Ikea step stool packed in my one medium-sized suitcase. I was wearing my special shoes, a pair of black-and-white zebra-patterned flats. Not the most comfortable, not a pair I'd use for any kind of major walking, but I wore them because they bore a special significance. Months earlier my copywriter friend Cleve deemed my walk of New York "a dance of re-invention," and suggested I name my blog "reSoulin' My Dancing Shoes." Even though I sucked at dancing, it put a nice uplifting spin on the reality I danced around. The name stuck and these flashy shoes became my blog's iconic symbol.

I boarded the plane and ambled down the center aisle toward the back and to my place by the window. After tucking my computer bag under the seat in front of me, I pulled the seatbelt across my lap and pushed my back and head into the hard, leathery cushion. I closed my eyes and took in a long and deep breath, my chest rising as the air filled my lungs. I held it for a few seconds, just long enough to mouth the words, "Thank you, God," then exhaled slowly, and surrendered. Every muscle in my neck and every knot in my shoulders and every sting of stress finally released, the responsibilities and uncertainties left behind. There was nothing more I could do. And nothing that could stop me now. A young fellow slid into the seat beside me, but I barely gave him a nod. I fell asleep even before the engines began to roar. I was mentally and physically and emotionally spent.

Two hours later I was awakened by a jolt, a man's voice delivering orders for our initial descent. "Please make sure your seat back and tray tables are in their …" As I came to, I glanced out my window and watched the southern tip of the island come into view. I had purposefully chosen a window seat on the left side of the plane. I wanted the initial glimpse of my dream to be—DRUM ROLL—a view from above, just as it had been 33 years before. Because air traffic was heavy, we circled the area twice which gave me two hard looks at the expanse I dared myself to walk. All I could think as I looked down at the massive island of skyscrapers was, *Holy shit, what have I gotten myself into?*

After deboarding, I joined my fellow travelers in the scrum at LaGuardia's baggage claim, where I searched for directions to ground transportation. I had carefully planned my entrance into New York, choosing to forgo the most direct and expensive route—a taxi from the airport directly to my rented apartment—and instead opted for a $12 ride in a nice, slow, air-conditioned bus to Grand Central Station, on the East Side. Not only would this allow me to take in all the sights along the way into Manhattan, but the iconic Grand Central Station with its Grand Hall was most emblematic of my New York dreams. From there I could take a leisurely stroll to my apartment in the West Village. A great plan, well… in theory.

I managed to find the departure point for my bus into the city, then climbed aboard hauling the one bag that contained everything I determined I'd need for these 30 days. At last, I could relax, lean back, and enjoy the sights from Queens into Manhattan.

Perhaps I enjoyed them too much or became a bit too relaxed, because it eventually clicked that we were no longer on the east side of Manhattan. Instead, the bus was heading west on 42nd Street and, to my absolute horror, I realized that I'd missed my stop. When the bus came to the next one, I exited, stepping into the bowels of the Port Authority Bus Station, a dark and musty-smelling terminal that had the reputation of being overrun by hustlers and criminals. It was hardly the ceremonious start I intended. Even worse, the directions I'd printed off to my new apartment in Greenwich Village had Grand Central Station as a starting point.

Somehow, I found my way through the cavernous bus station to a grimy little cafe, where I slumped down with a cup of overcooked coffee and the battered banana I'd stuck in my purse before leaving Atlanta. I unfolded my crisp, new MTA subway map, laid it on top of the little round table beside me, and set to work trying to make sense of the tangled web of subways and streets on this magical island.

But instead of roadways and landmarks, I caught a glimpse of a grand panorama of what I'd accomplished. Instead of one-way streets and avenues, I saw opportunities I'd created for myself, ones I would be loping through in the coming days. I witnessed before me the barriers I'd weathered, all the heartache I left at home, just to get myself here. My eyes brimmed with tears as I finally embraced all the mystery and hope that lay ahead.

Here, in a grimy ole bus terminal, I lowered my head and let the tears drip down into my lap. The older gentleman behind the counter glanced nervously at me. Bless his heart. He had no idea how happy I was.

I took one last sip of coffee, wiped my face, and gathered my Styrofoam cup and banana peels then dropped them into the garbage can as I exited the cafe. I wove my way out of the terminal and set off to find my new home in the Village. With a false bravado, my map and suitcase in tow, I pumped up my chest and started down 8th Avenue.

As I walked block after block, I noticed the street numbers climbing, "45th, 46th, 47th …" I remembered reading that street numbers go down in the lower part of the island. *DOWN-town!* it clicked.

I secured my roller bag between my shins, unfolded my map, then verified that my walking had, indeed, taken me north, or UP-town. I made what I hoped was a graceful pirouette, tucked in my pride in case anyone had noticed, then reversed directions. The noon sun bore down hard on me, but I soldiered on and sweated for 11 more blocks before I gave up and hailed a cab.

As I hoisted my suitcase into the back of the fruity-smelling cab, I could hear a dispatcher's voice crackling in and out from the radio dangling from the dusty dashboard. "Address?" the young driver asked without even turning around. "Perry Street," I answered. "In the Village?" his Caribbean accent asking me to confirm. Still terribly unsure of the decisions I'd made and certainly of the map I was about to tackle, I mumbled "Yes," and off we flew. He took a left, then another, and down 9th Avenue he wove, in and out of traffic, jerking me through the reality that was about to unfold.

As we barreled down the wide avenue, I felt weightless, limp, like I'd put my all in the hands of the driver. I held no control over my destiny as we sailed through mid-rise office buildings that then morphed into residential areas with narrow streets of brownstones and thick foliage. Those were soon replaced with whitewashed warehouses and restaurants shaded by awnings, famous names on fancy boutiques. The grid of streets and avenues began to fall out of conformity much like my life; so did the personality of this neighborhood, and adventure, I would soon call mine.

After great anticipation, I could finally see the Village unfold before me. It was every bit as picturesque as I'd imagined. Tree-lined streets with old-world European charm: cobblestone lanes and sidewalk cafes with young people meandering fashionably in and out of low-rise buildings. It felt cozy, a tad shabby chic. Other than the occasional taxi, few cars littered the streets, mostly bicycles and Vespas parked here and there. There was a quiet bustle about the Village that Saturday afternoon, almost defiant of the frenetic pace north of 14th.

A few blocks later, my driver veered onto Hudson and I caught sight of a street sign that read "PERRY ST." "Just let me out here," I blurted out, figuring I was close enough. Like a protective son, he turned his head and asked if I was sure, "I'll just turn here and get you closer," he pressed, assessing my advanced age, I feel sure. I was nervous about the up-ticking meter, but I also was dying to be outside, walking the glittery streets, breathing in every detail. I wanted to stroll slowly to my new home, making a grand entrance to my dream finally coming true.

As I stepped out onto the street, I was struck at how weathered some of the brownstones, or townhomes, looked. Granted, these three- and four-story homes were quite a bit older than most in Atlanta, but I guess I expected them to be pristine and perfectly coiffed, especially since I'd heard that many were owned by movie stars. The sidewalks seemed haphazardly swept, a bit of paint was peeling here and there, plus I was shocked to see garbage cans visible on the street and burglar bars and air conditioning units teetering from the windows. Yet the gorgeous black wrought iron reminded me of the French influence in my hometown of Mobile and the flower boxes were beautifully lush, with bright, colorful blooms spilling over their sides. All were row houses, each delightful in their own personality. Mostly brick, some red, others gray, and one, an awful shade of mustard. Catching a glimpse inside two or three of them, I wondered why their interiors seem so much more luxurious than their exteriors.

Finally, I arrived at 141 Perry Street. I stopped for just a second, as if in honor. I needed to take in the whole of the place that would hold me safe, whose walls would protect me and provide strength in my solitude and grief. I needed to feel and trust that its sanctity would inspire my learning, my creativity, even shepherd my life forward. A bit breathless, I stood there, studying the four-story structure before me, its red brick a bit overgrown with plants. Its Federalist grandeur stood awkwardly sandwiched between an antique car showroom and a tiny sliver of a bar. I stepped forward and pushed open the black wrought iron gate that protected it and proceeded up the six or seven steps, as if to say, "I'm ready. I can do this." The doormat, a hemp-colored rug printed with a black-outlined dachshund, an uncanny reminder of my own sweet Frank, brought a smile to my face. It was a comforting sign that I took as a welcome to my new home.

"I was getting worried about you," a young woman announced as she flung open the door, standing on her tiptoes to kiss me on both cheeks, as Europeans do. Her warmth was delightful. "I'm Seema," she chirped, finally introducing herself. With her olive skin, her deep brown eyes, and chocolate hair, I wondered if she was of Italian descent. Her features were delicate and feminine, her voice was soft, almost a song. I was struck by her youthfulness. Her partner, my landlady Barbara, she explained, was out of town so she was tasked with getting me settled.

I followed her up a narrow staircase that looked original to the 130-year-old building. The worn treads creaked as we ascended the steep, narrow steps. I was hot, worn out, and struggling under the weight of my heavy suitcase as I tried to navigate the tight stairwell. "This is the hard part," Seema winced as she glanced back at me, and then promised, "but the apartment is grand."

Oh, man, and was it! She flung open the door to a huge open room, framed with stark white-washed walls to the left and paint-peeled brick to the right. Huge, floor-to-ceiling windows flanked the wall facing the street below, pulling in beams of light that swept across the entire length of the room. Its original wide oak planks graced the floors in a dark honey brown. I was stunned by its aura.

An electric-blue glass light fixture hung from the 12-foot ceiling, haloing what I pictured would become my new workspace, a small round white laminate table and two plastic chairs. On the opposite side of the room was a tiny kitchenette of sorts, a counter with a sink and a few drawers next to a dorm-sized refrigerator. No stove nor oven, but that didn't faze me. With a food budget of only $200 for the month, I figured I could only afford raw vegetables and fruits every day, no meat that required a stove. I was looking forward to the challenge, really. I was determined to make this month as healthy mentally and physically as I could.

What wasn't grand was the thick, sticky heat that engulfed us. I couldn't remember whether the Airbnb listing mentioned air conditioning one way or another, so I held my tongue. When we finally entered the bedroom, I caught sight of a window unit and breathed a sigh of relief. At least I'll be able to sleep, I thought.

Seema gave me the rundown on which keys to use on which doors, where the dishes and towels were kept, how to connect with Wi-Fi, and asked that I turn off the A/C whenever I went out. "I've left you a pitcher of cold water in the refrigerator," she said as she turned to leave.

Except for the heat, my new home in New York was so much more than I'd imagined. The décor was eclectic, a perfect mix of Swiss and industrial, modern and antique, with a dash of Ikea thrown in. The fabrics were stark in design and color—the boxy Bauhaus sofa was a white fabric adorned with big black words, all in a multitude of languages. The coffee table was an old oaken chest, probably an antique. In one corner was a large black board propped up against a wall, with a white "3" painted on it; perhaps a sign from a train station?

I remember feeling a bit overwhelmed, lost as to where to begin this grand adventure. So, I started with unpacking. I hung up the clothes from my suitcase and placed my three pairs of shoes neatly in a row at the bottom of the closet. I felt like a little girl playing house as I ceremoniously put my books and maps in the tiny room, a closet really, off the living room, dubbing it my "Map Room." I set up my computer on the round table where I imagined working late into the nights. The lime-green plastic Ikea chair didn't feel very comfortable, but it would do just fine. It sure looked cool!

I then taped my two calendar pages to the back of the table, each with blocks for each day I would be in the city. On June 25th, I had inked in "ARRIVE!" and on July 24th, "LV: 3:59p" and "AR: 6:22p," the flight times that marked the end of my trip. In the weekend blocks I'd entered scheduled visits from my sister Michele, my daughter Emma, and my friends Debbie, Annie, and Tavye. On June 27th, I listed a lunch with my childhood friend Pam, plus on July 12th, a dinner with my Atlanta friends Julie and Randy who would be in town. Also penciled in were free museum days, a taping of *The View*, and other events and classes I'd made note to attend. And finally, the dates my clients' checks would arrive.

I lined up my few toiletries, my foundation, lotion, deodorant, and a small bottle of Woolite on the one small shelf in the sliver of a bathroom. I checked the cabinets in the kitchenette, finding a plug-in coffee pot, a hot plate, and a half-full can of that expensive illy brand of coffee. I then squatted down onto the mattress on the floor, laid my tired body across the bed, and breathed a deep sigh of disbelief.

One hour later, I awoke to the realization that I had fallen asleep. I jumped up, splashed some cold water on my face, and then slipped on my tennis shoes. With a city map and my new house keys tucked in my vest pocket, I scurried down the squeaky steps. It was almost 6:00 p.m. and I didn't want to waste another minute of daylight. I walked a block up to the first corner, then turned right onto Greenwich Street, and from there, I let myself get lost in my new neighborhood.

With every step I took, I'd stop and take a photo, my mind hyper-focused on every detail. On Seventh Avenue, I stepped inside the Gourmet Garage, a tiny market with tight walking spaces woven between aisles packed high with mustards and honeys and crackers, all with exquisitely designed labels and ridiculous price tags. The vegetables and fruits were arranged in perfect lines, each piece screaming red or green or yellow. I'd never seen anything in a grocery store quite so perfect!

I watched a customer come in and dip a sample of freshly baked rosemary bread in olive oil while he waited for the order he'd called in. He chatted with the server as if they were close friends. All this newness to me seemed so ordinary to them. I so badly wanted to know it as my normal too.

The prices were steep, so I tried to limit myself to only the items I needed for dinner and breakfast. I could find a cheaper store tomorrow. I picked up a few bananas and a package of blueberries, then a carton of yogurt and some half-and-half, a must for my morning coffee. As I neared the cash register, I let my financial guard down and treated myself to some fresh flowers, Genoa salami, and a slice of peppered Brie. And yes, some of those overpriced crackers, or "rice wafers," as they were called.

The sun was just beginning to dip as I returned down Perry Street. A golden glow shone down on the buildings and bounced off the cobblestone streets. I felt like I was floating through a romance movie.

But as I neared my block, I could see a man further down the sidewalk, acting a little strange. I couldn't really tell what he was doing, so I stopped and ducked into a doorway so he wouldn't see me. His clothes hung on him loosely, and he seemed a bit disoriented as he struggled with a large piece of cardboard. I watched him unfold it and then shape it into a tent-like structure. He then sat down beside it and pulled a blanket over his shoulders. He was a homeless person, I assumed. The thought of him being so near to my place shook me. I didn't feel in any danger, really, but just in case, I crossed the street and scurried on up to my apartment. Once inside, I put away my groceries, arranged the flowers in a drinking glass, then stood in the heart of my new home. I closed my eyes and inhaled a slow, deep breath and concentrated on it as it passed down into my lungs.

I'm here. I am finally here. Brimming with so much new news, I reached for my phone to call Jim, to tell him every single detail. Then I stopped.

Things were different now.

The next morning, I opened my eyes a few minutes before five, groggy and disoriented. The walls were whitewashed with a foreign starkness; the ceiling towered overhead. There was a steady sloshing of water from the window unit, its sound almost soothing to me.

Sensitive to Seema's request, I reached over and turned off the air conditioner. As it powered down, its clickety clack, clickety clack, clack gave rise to an early morning medley of birds. The unfamiliar apartment, the sounds of the city outside, my new reality—all were a bit overwhelming. I tried to keep myself in bed to rest a little longer, to process it all, but there was no way. My heart could hardly lay still. *I need to be quiet and respectful this early in the morning*, my training kicked in. I was a guest in another's home.

I climbed out of bed, crept quietly around the apartment, forcing myself to wait to start the shower or flush the toilet. It was much too early, and I was afraid of waking my landladies downstairs. I dug around the cabinet until I found a coffee pot. I didn't see any filters, so I folded a paper towel into a cone shape, filled it with grounds, and had my coffee brewing within minutes.

OH.MY.GOD! Every single sense in my body was ratcheting up to HIGH. I felt like a racehorse at the starting gate, my heart beating wild and my body trembling with anticipation. I could hardly wait to be let loose on my first full day in New York City. At 5:20, just before daybreak, I tiptoed down the creaky stairs, as quietly as I could, then pushed open the outside door and stepped into a crisp, pink, morning light that filled me with hope and exhilaration. It was such a rush!

I stilled my body and mind, closed my eyes and allowed myself to bask in the moment's joy and splendor. *Breathe, Lisa. Breathe.* As I filled my lungs, a tiny voice urged me to take a right, to walk toward the Hudson River just a block or two away. Having grown up along the Gulf Coast, I had a deep connection to water. A spiritual pull, even. Show your gratitude, Lisa. Take a moment to thank God for providing these 30 days, a voice instructed me. But instead, I muffled my sense of duty, whispered my prayer quietly under my breath, and bolted east toward the heart of the Village.

The Village was dead asleep. As alive as it had been the evening before, it was eerily quiet this Sunday morning. Except for a cop on patrol and a few delivery guys, I was the only soul out walking.

Rounding the corner, I noticed several tow trucks removing cars from the streets. I couldn't help but grin, remembering the old days in my twenties when I'd been out partying a bit too late on Saturday nights, imbibing beyond my limit, leaving my car and getting home some other way. Was that the case here? As I walked, I saw more tow trucks, at least 20, all toting cars away. Was this a common event in New York, like a rude way to raise revenue? The mere thought of it riled me. I pitied the kids. As I approached a cop, I felt an unexpected authority to confront him, to stop this nonsense. "We're not towing 'em away," he said in a thick Jersey accent, "just moving 'em," then pointed somewhere off in the distance. "We're closing the streets for the parade and these caaahs agotta go." I let out a lukewarm "ahh," at the same time thinking how ticked off I'd be if I woke up and learned my car had been towed for a damn parade. "They'll calm down once they realize their vehicle was just relocated," he said, shining a big toothy grin. I shot him an insincere smile and moved along, doubting a single soul would find it amusing.

As I walked along, the streets slowly came alive. Trucks stopped here and there, the drivers hanging their deliveries on storefront door handles, with nary a fear that their packages might be stolen. I nodded at a groggy homeowner as he hosed dog pee off his sidewalk.

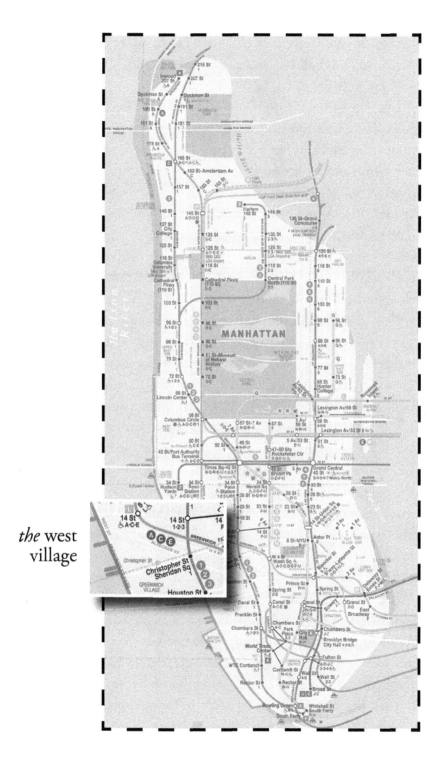

the west
village

Restauranteurs swept away last night's cigarette butts and empty beer cans. It was all so new, so captivating, and *SO Neeeewwww York!*, my heart sang!

I watched trucks dripping in graffiti deliver suits and starched shirts. The oxymoron tickled me. I passed a store dedicated solely to Tiramisu, and another to vibrators. *Yes, vibrators*, I had to repeat in my prim and proper mind. There was a little church that openly advertised an AIDS ministry. A 9/11 logo showed the two towers—its tagline, "Rise Above," spoke to forgiveness, a sentiment I seldom heard spoken in regard to the tragedy. All this new stuff, all surprises within the confines of my little neighborhood, and none of it was like anything we had back home. My world at this very moment felt boundless, and like a mantra, the words "I have thirty days, an entire month!" rattling through my head over and over again. Thirty days to absorb this richness of life and this energy I so badly wanted to experience in the place I've always wanted to know.

As I walked on, the theme of the upcoming parade became clear. Rainbow flags hung from windows, lampposts, and fire escapes. Red, orange, yellow, green, blue, and purple striped ties, T-shirts and caps graced the store windows on Bleecker Street. At Magnolia Bakery, rows and rows of cupcakes, each iced in the primary colors, reflected the diversity of the LGBTQ community. Two giant wedding cakes, one topped with two bride figurines and the other with two grooms, sat proudly in Michael Kors' shop. On Google I learned that Governor Cuomo had signed the same-sex marriage law the evening before.

A major step toward social equality for those labeled "gay," "lesbian," or "homo," as I called them as a child, would be in effect in just 30 days. It was obviously a momentous event in this neighborhood, Greenwich Village, which I later learned had seen the start of the gay rights movement in 1969, my senior year of high school.

I first heard of such sexual differences back in 1962, in fifth grade at Mary B. Austin School in Mobile. As the two new girls that year,

Debbie and I quickly became inseparable. One day, when the bell rang for recess, the two of us scurried in line together, holding hands. As we passed, our teacher Mrs. Merritt grabbed my arm and pulled us aside. "Little girls don't hold hands!" she scolded us. "It's bad!" I didn't really understand what she was telling me, but I knew I had done something terribly wrong. I remember feeling so ashamed, yet totally unaware of why.

A few weeks later, I heard the word "homo" for the first time. Choir practice had just ended; Debbie and I were running across the lawn of our church, heading home. We'd been razzing each other about who'd get the attention of the cute, popular boy we both liked. She turned to me and yelled, "Homo!" She didn't have a clue what the term meant and neither did I, but she did know it was a word she wasn't supposed to use. I did too, and that made it tantalizing. When I got home, I called my younger sister a "homo," and unfortunately, my mother heard me. She grabbed my skinny little arm and swung me around so hard my neck whiplashed. "Don't you EVER use that word in this house. If I ever hear it again, I'll wash your mouth out with soap!" And she meant it.

I asked around the next few days trying to get a definition of exactly what the word meant. I learned that when a boy liked another boy instead of a girl, or even worse, girls who liked each other and not boys—they were homos, and it was dirty, unnatural, and immoral. Just not the way God intended it to be. Suddenly I realized why Mrs. Merritt had scolded Debbie and me for holding hands. I was humiliated that she thought I was a homo. And I certainly never touched another girl's hand again.

After a short nap and a quick lunch back at the apartment, I headed out for one of the most colorful, eye-opening experiences I had ever witnessed, the Gay Pride Parade. Never in my life had I seen such free flaunting of sexuality as I witnessed in the Village that day. Drag queens perched on convertibles, waving their white gloves like homecoming queens; I couldn't help but chuckle at their flamboyance. I did a double take when a man trotted by me wearing nothing but a jeweled jock strap. I turned and followed him when I recognized the photo op. Women with mohawks and men in wedding gowns, it was quite a show.

I was initially quite amused by all the theatrics, but when I caught sight of a fairly indistinct woman, dressed much like me, tussle lovingly with her girlfriend's hair and kiss her, I instinctively winced. My reaction jolted me; it puzzled me. My 58-year-old traditional upbringing seeped back into my consciousness and I was left wondering why my natural reflexes were so different from what I now wholeheartedly believed. Memories of my fifth-grade event flooded back, and the realization of how deeply rooted my bias was, stunned me. It had resided in me for almost fifty years.

Just then a roar in the crowd interrupted my reverie. I turned to see a young woman march into my sight, her voluptuous breasts bared to the cheering crowd. At first, I was appalled, my eyes glued to her hanging bosoms. I felt anxious and embarrassed for her, my attention diverting to others, searching for their reactions. Then I read the sign she raised up over her head, "FREE AT LAST! FREE AT LAST," the bold letters rejoicing her freedom. I reached for my phone and snapped a photo. This will make the perfect blog post!

As I pulled my phone down from my face, my eyes caught those of an old cop's. He rolled his eyes, and without hesitation, I affirmed his disgust with a quick smile. But the moment I did, I sensed I'd cheated her. I felt shame and was disappointed in myself. A coward. I'd sold myself out for approval from a cop, someone I didn't even know, for God's sake.

As the parade marched on, my mind switched to production mode. I took more photos and scribbled notes in my little notebook in order to remember every single detail for the nightly blog post I intended to write. As I began to formulate my story in my head, I honestly got a bit giggly over all the content I was gathering. The drag queens! The colorful balloons and costumes! The cupcakes in the bakery window! I couldn't wait to get back to the apartment so I could post the all the pictures and details. I was sure my audience would find them as intriguing as I did.

Just as I began to mentally craft my words, I was interrupted by a loud, sonorous sound. Like a final military salute, its long, foreboding "G-O-N--G---G----G!" vibrated through the crowd and began to transfix it. *A clock,* I wondered? And then glanced down at my phone to see that it was exactly 1:00 p.m.

A crackling of a loudspeaker followed, and I strained to hear the voice of a woman asking for silence. She asked again and again until the roar of the crowd had skidded to a deafening quiet. "Let's take a moment to remember those who we've lost to AIDS, to hate crimes ...." The speaker's words were a chilling plea. This was the first time I had personally experienced, and been smack in the middle of, a gay event of this magnitude. Or of any, really. I'd certainly heard of Gay Rights parades and seen them featured on the nightly news. I'd read about the insurance challenges and the employment and religious barriers this community faced. Hell, my own Methodist denomination didn't allow them to marry or preach inside my church. But never had I paid much attention, because those things didn't affect me, or anyone in my family. I'd heard that an old co-worker of mine had lost his life to AIDS, and there was an acquaintance who'd moved to San Francisco to feel accepted. Another had been spat on, but I never really grasped how it must feel to another human being. Here I was today, in their space, with all their energy and frustration and pain surrounding me. It was if I could "physically feel" the problems lobbed at them because of who they loved, or because of their sexual orientation, an orientation I believed with all my heart was natural, or God-given from birth. As the woman's voice trailed off, and the crowd began to dissipate, I could only wonder how I could have been so oblivious.

The sun was beating down and steam beginning to rise from the burning pavement. Pungent body odor mixed with wafts of weed and cigars made me nauseous. Chatter and laughter wove in and out as the thickness of people began dispersing, but a sense of claustrophobia started muddying the child-like curiosity I'd initially felt. I began to tense up and worry, my mind firing incoherent thoughts: Would a bomber see this crowd as the perfect audience for his homophobic statements? Would some religious zealot take this opportunity to discipline the thousands on the streets according to his beliefs? *Get out of here, Lisa. Get out.*

I brought myself back to the realities of my "job" here in the city and pulled out my little notebook to find the address of the Apple Store where I'd enrolled in an iPhone Basics class that afternoon. It took me almost an hour of pushing and shoving to reach the nearest subway station, where I stepped aside and watched throngs of hot, sweaty people descend into its entrance. Feeling a bit agoraphobic and not sure if I should take a train, or which one, and thinking it would be safer to walk, I decided not to brave the subways quite yet. Even if I had to forgo my class, it was free, I reasoned, and gave myself a pass. This would give me a few more hours just to meander before I was to meet Caroline, my daughter's close friend who was in town for a summer internship. I made my way up Fifth Avenue, then walked west along 13th Street, inadvertently finding myself in a neighborhood called The Meatpacking District.

The streets were lined with warehouse-type structures, chic boutiques and restaurants, art galleries and lofts that painted a story of restrained urban renewal. Zigzagging through the streets, I came up on some interesting graffiti at the corner of 13th and Washington. The wall facing 13th Street served as a huge canvas of incongruent icons ranging from quirky peace symbols to whimsical Mickey Mouse ears, all painted in black and white brushstrokes. I took several photos.

I moved to the opposite wall and took shots of an umpire body with a slot machine head, and others that bore radios and cameras in lieu of faces. I broke a smile at the only ounce of color, a perfectly placed bright red "NO SMOKING/NO FUMAR" sign. I then strung together the words, "ART" and "LIFE" and "DREAMERS," eager to understand its hidden message and the mysterious artists who slither in at night to paint. People whooshed by, seemingly more amused by the odd old lady taking photos than by the art itself.

Walking on, I thought back to 1977 and my first trip to New York when I first remember seeing graffiti. Row after row of tall, red-brick tenement walls shouted with angry symbolism and racist rhetoric. Burned-out shells of cars, with slashed tires and shards for windows, were masterpieces of hatred and despair. The world equated graffiti with gangs, crime, poverty, and certainly danger. But I remember that something in it intrigued me.

I headed back home for a nap and later that evening met Caroline for dinner. I drilled her about every morsel of her time in the city: her internship, her dating life, the dorm where she lived, and I delighted in each of her answers. I saw so much of a young me in her. I was her age when I started in the ad business and dreamed of working on Madison Avenue. How different my life would have been!

"Let's stay in touch," I said as we hugged goodbye, the words hardly leaving my mouth before I sensed my salutation was simply an empty formality. I loved this young lady like one of my own but in my heart, I looked forward to a schedule free of commitments. The last time I'd had any sort of break was ten years earlier when Jim was battling cancer. I used his illness as a reason to cancel social functions, to say no to volunteer obligations, and to allow others to help me with our family chores. To this day, I remember how sacred that time and space felt, and how incredibly healthy. I needed another dose of that solitude, especially now, after all I'd been through.

After dinner, Caroline headed out to meet friends for the evening, and I followed the hordes of folks walking toward the Hudson River, where a fireworks show was planned in celebration of the new law. I could only get within a block and a half of the waterfront; people were as thick as fleas. "Folks were already here when we came to close down the streets," a cop told me as I commented on the size of the

As the sky exploded with thunder and glittered with streams of color, I was quite surprised at how comfortable I felt trapped inside this dense mass of strangers. I'd never seen such an array.

I found myself totally intrigued as my creative eye jumped from soul to soul, imagining each as a different piece of art. One guy wore a sleeve of floral tattoos, another a head full of shiny black braids. An aging flower child sporting matted dreadlocks stood next to a teen wearing skimpy Soffes. Crisp button downs and worn-out Birkenstocks. Wafts of body odor and perfume, each person so wonderfully different, yet all so beautifully, and peacefully, braided together.

I reflected back on how I'd happened to find myself in the center of so many historical events throughout my lifetime. I was on a college visit in Memphis the day Dr. Martin Luther King, Jr. was shot, and in France in '74, when their president Georges Pompidou died. In January of '87 my friend Susan and I were on the front lines of the largest civil rights demonstration since Selma. Twenty thousand activists, the Ku Klux Klan, and National Guard faced off in the tiny town of Cumming, Georgia. Then of course, I'll never forget being in Mexico on September 11th of 2001, shut out of my own country after the terrorist attacks. And here I stood tonight, smack dab in the middle of the victory celebration after what many in our country felt, was a full-fledged war between the Bible and the Constitution. New Yorkers had won by redefining the word "marriage." Deep down inside I suspected it had, instead, been a marriage of the two.

At nearly ten in the evening, the fireworks display came to an end with a glorious finale. Folks folded up chairs and gathered their kids and, as if in slow motion, we all shuffled off in various directions. What an awesome first day!

At Ninth Avenue I turned right and proceeded into unchartered territory. I knew my apartment was south, maybe six or eight blocks away, but I wasn't exactly sure how to get there. I felt really uneasy because, except for a young couple way ahead of me, I was the only soul on this dark, empty boulevard. I decided I might be marked a target if I stopped and unfolded my map, so I threaded my keys into my fingers, lifted up my chin and started hoofing it … like some badass local, a little voice coached my fear. With new resolve, I walked a few more blocks until I hit Perry Street. From there I knew to turn right and walk the two or three blocks to my apartment. Nearing my destination, I caught sight of the homeless man who'd set up his cardboard tent once again, right outside my apartment. This time I wasn't frightened by him.

Trudging up the steps to my apartment, I could feel the draining effects of dehydration. I'd pushed myself way too hard for one day, yet I was totally energized by what I'd witnessed. I really wanted to put my excitement into words, quickly and before I'd forget.

Men in brassieres, women with shaved heads, the blinged-out jock straps. The fireworks show. There was plenty to write about, and more than enough photos to include. *Where do I start*, I whispered as I deposited my bone-weary body in my lime-green plastic chair, and in front of my screen. I gave myself just a moment to rest, to breathe deeply, and to embrace the time and space I was in. The flashbacks, the awareness, a new understanding. It had all been so exhausting, yet exhilarating, to finally have the unencumbered time and space to explore.

I began to type:

"…I got up early this morning. Tried to stay put, but by 5:30 I could no longer force myself to stay inside…"

My fingers couldn't keep up with my racing thoughts. I went on to describe the cars being towed, the Pride colors in the store windows, the two brides on the wedding cake, and the two grooms. It was if I was a child describing my first view of Disney World. I felt the words flow out of me so freely, with such a sense of awe. In this moment I felt strong and confident, even empowered to speak my mind openly and boldly.

"All this was in preparation for what would be a celebration like I'd never seen before.

After a late morning nap, I ventured out for the parade which began with a moment of silence for those lost to AIDS or victims of a hate crime.

One thing I love about New Yorkers is that they are open to differences, they embrace change, and they celebrate personal freedom. In the crowd were preppy straight folk, bejeweled transvestites, gay and straight politicians, parents with their children—people from all walks of life, all out supporting their gay friends and the new law."

I added the photos of the man wearing only a jockstrap, men dressed as jesters, and another in a black and white jail costume. *Jailed*, I halted in a jolt of realization.

I then pulled the image of the woman with her breasts bared into Photoshop. As the pixels loaded on the screen, I searched the woman's face, begging for a story in her dark apathetic eyes. They were defined by a harsh black arch, her lids painted with shades of ash and blue. Her opulent lips, slathered in deep cherry red, gave me no hint at all of her state of mind. I wondered if all that hard, stoic paint on her face was actually her armor, her way of hiding the pain.

"The day ended with about an hour of fireworks. It was quite a celebration in the West Village of NY. I'm so glad I was able to be part of it."

With that, I began reflecting back on the battles people had fought, and the biases they faced, just in the span of my lifetime. I shuddered at the misconceptions I learned, very early in life, that one religion or one culture or one skin color was superior to another, or one right and the other wrong.

I was a child of the 60's in Mobile, Alabama, when the words "colored" and "negrah" were common terms, even quite acceptable. The two water fountains, side by side, in my doctor's office ... two different doors. Yes, I lived in that world every day. I had read all the books about how wrong it was. I had taught my children to see all people as the same. I had helped my kids write papers for MLK Day, and I had honored and respected my few Black friends and clients as I would anyone else. But never, never had it sunk in like it did today. Never had it seeped into my marrow. This was all too much, too overwhelming. Too hard to even comprehend why I had become so emotional. Why the need to speak out?

My mind spiraled on ...

... and Barbara, my childhood friend. The biases against Jews. I remembered writing in my little red leather Bible, "Why can't Barbara go to Heaven?" I was instantly back in my fourth-grade Sunday School classroom, on the second floor of Central Presbyterian Church, frantic that my friend would be sentenced to Hell. Jews don't believe in Jesus, the lesson read. "And what about the people in Africa, those who don't have Bibles?" I remember asking my teacher, trying at a very early age to debunk something that didn't jive with "Jesus loves the little children / All the children of the world."

The Japanese. Because my great aunt lived through the horrors of Pearl Harbor, she taught me never to trust anyone with slanted eyes. And how many times did I hear disparaging remarks about other "foreigners."

I dug deeper. My unconscious biases spanned gender, too. I thought back to the first time I heard a woman preach from the pulpit and how jolted I was by it. Or when I met my first stay-at-home dad, my gut deemed him a "deadbeat." My God, I know better than that!

"God made us different for a reason," my mother taught me when I first started dating at age 15. "If you ever bring a Catholic, a Jew, or a Black man to this door, I will shoot him and you both." Marrying someone outside my Protestant faith was considered sacrilegious. Marrying someone of another race or from another country "would be too hard on a marriage," I remember her reasoning, often referencing my cousin's marriage to a Persian man, a Muslim. Her mother and father disowned her for doing so.

But tonight, I felt so free to speak my mind, freer than I'd ever felt. So, I typed on:

> Today reminded me of the late 60s. I clearly remember people of color were not allowed the same rights as my family. Women were not allowed to preach from a pulpit and 'stay-at-home Dads' were frowned upon. Maybe one day we'll understand that God made us all in his image, no matter if we're white or black, gay or straight, Methodist or Buddhist. Hopefully we'll see that our differences are what make this world so great.

After typing my last word, I started proofreading from the top. I could feel my fatigue eat away at my courage. *Do I dare publish my views? Do I risk being judged by my neighbors and friends, or even my own family?* I hated controversy and I certainly didn't want to be in the middle of any.

Maybe I should soften it a bit, not be so "out there." With that thought, in that very moment, I stopped, stunned. I disgusted myself. It was if I'd been slapped in the face with a revelation: I have spent 58 years crafting the correct image for myself, saying what people wanted to hear. How wrong!

At nearly 2:00 a.m., I closed my laptop without hitting the Publish button. I reached over the bed and turned the air conditioner on low, then let my head fall into the pillow. *Read over it in the morning when you're not so jazzed up.*

I was lulled to sleep by the muffled sounds of laughter coming from the young revelers at the pub next door. I faintly remember leaving the front window open, but I was too tired to get out of bed and close it.

In just a day and a half, I had dug deep into some places that were uncomfortable for me. I had stirred something deep. For a moment, I heard a voice that warned me not to go to these places, but it was too late. I was already there.

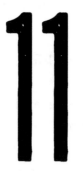

Pinch me!!! was my first thought as I came to. I pushed the comforter out of my way and reached for my phone to see that it was a few minutes before seven. "I'm in NEW YORK CITEEEE!!!!," I squealed out loud. And with that realization, a bolt of pure jubilance shot through my veins. It had been so long since I felt such unadulterated joy. Just flat-out happy!

I reached across the bed, turned the air conditioner to "Fan," and headed to the living room to start my coffee. As it brewed, I sifted through emails, scanned Facebook and Twitter, then sent an invoice to a client. I scrolled over to last night's blog post, scanned it quickly, and hit the "Publish" button before I could talk myself out of it. I'd acquired a bit of boldness since arriving in the city, and I loved the way it felt.

I filled my mug with coffee and started coaxing myself, trying to focus my mind on the two jobs still hanging over me, the ones I intended to finish before leaving Atlanta. But, at 7:25 a.m., the morning light taunted me as it streaked through my front windows. I could feel its warm invitation; my spirit was ready to fly free as a bird. I railed against my own self, my overbearing sense of responsibility. The pull to escape was strong, but I couldn't give in. It took every ounce of my being to drop my body into that damn lime-green plastic chair.

The software I'd used every day of my last 20 years began giving me fits. I could hear my friend's warning. Just as he predicted, the cheap, second-hand laptop I'd purchased wasn't powerful enough. And to make matters worse, all the files I thought I'd loaded onto a backup drive the night before I left weren't there. The power outage, I assumed, was the culprit.

I could feel myself getting agitated, frustrated, even angry. I was facing problems I didn't know how to fix. I was pissed that I had to do work, feeling even a bit violated by the control my clients had over me. All I wanted to do was break free, run out the door and escape into another adventure like I'd had the day before. But through the angst, my voice of reason won out. This time in New York was never meant to be a vacation, I reminded myself. My work was financing this dream. Working around my mechanical difficulties, I trudged through the rest of my projects, emailed them to the client, showered, and dressed myself for the day ahead. I then emailed my friend Jane and asked if her husband Craig, an IT whiz, could go to my house and set up a screen share. Not the easiest way to work, but apparently, my only option.

Next on my list was a rescheduled class at the Apple Store, and off I went. With plenty of time before it started, I meandered through the nine or ten blocks to my destination, savoring and photographing every detail of my neighboring 'hood, the Meatpacking District. In my research I'd learned that in the early 1900s, this area was filled with large red-brick warehouses, housing up to 250 slaughterhouses and meatpacking plants, plus a bustling open-air market. By the 80s, Mafia-controlled night clubs began popping up, fueling drug dealing, prostitution, and sex rings. Ten years later, as AIDS prevention slowed such activity, designers Alexander McQueen, Stella McCartney and Diane von Fürstenberg replaced the smut with haute couture. I was totally awed by the juxtapositions of fashions costing thousands hanging up against crumbly brick walls, and of the trendiest of clientele tapping their Guccis and Pradas on concrete floors that showed decades of industrial wear. The old and the new. As I strolled the cobblestone streets, my creative side was swept into the genius of the artists and architects, the fashionistas and restaurateurs, and the technical brains who were the lifeblood

the upper
west side

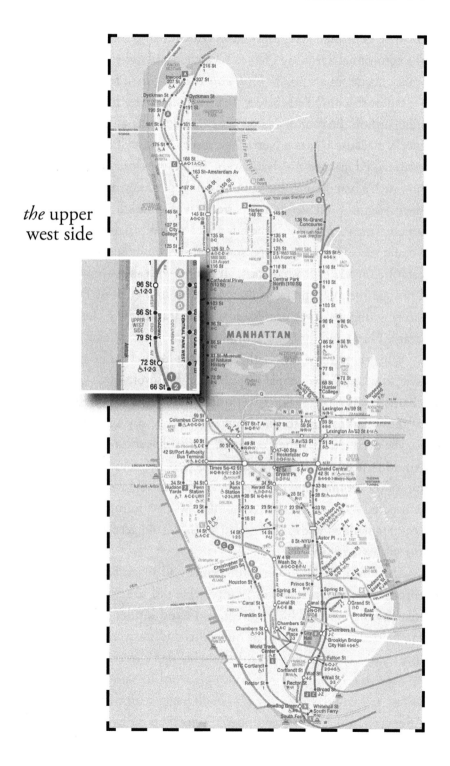

of these gentrified slaughterhouses. At the same time, I smiled at the communal harmony I felt as I watched a blood-stained butcher walk outside for a smoke. *Ah! If only I could have a studio here.*

Upon reaching 14th Street, I caught sight of a huge V-shaped billboard on the roof of a large red-brick building at the end of the block. Because it was advertising Apple's newest iPhone, the 4, I assumed I'd reached my destination. As I came closer, I marveled at how such a brand-conscious company as Apple, known for their clean, sleek designs could blend in so perfectly with a backdrop of dusty old warehouses. Peering inside the huge bank of industrial-style windows, I could see an immense spiral staircase, seemingly suspended in air, each step made of frosted glass, all bound with shiny brass railings. I pushed through the front door and was immediately faced by a lanky young man, his professional smile framed by a close-shaven beard. I hesitated for a just a moment. Am I dressed okay?

When I told my greeter that I'd come for a class, he motioned over to where I saw people beginning to fill several rows of folding chairs. I was a bit puzzled, yet quite comforted to see that most of the others looked to be within ten years of my age, one or two maybe even older. It then occurred to me that most young people wouldn't need these Apple classes because, of course, they come out of the womb knowing this stuff. "This the old folks' section?" I whispered to the white-haired gentleman next to me as I took my seat. He nodded with a half grin. I guess the old geezer didn't think my joke was funny.

The young, svelte instructor clad in all black began clicking through the ins and outs of iPhones. He did so in a very elementary manner, almost like a sweet, old-maid kindergarten teacher. He fielded the most basic of questions and answered them with great patience. *If nothing else,* I thought, *Apple teaches these kids to be respectful.* I hung on to every single word he said and scribbled as fast as I could, filling my notebook pages with new knowledge. After class, feeling totally pumped, I signed up for two more classes.

I couldn't wait to get back home and try some of the new apps, but first, I was due to meet my childhood friend Pam and her husband Ray for lunch.

Pam and I gravitated toward each other our first year in high school, I seem to remember, when we were the two in our inner circle not invited to join one of the high school sororities. I guess it was the rejection that bonded us. We remained dear friends all the way through our senior year. After graduation Pam went on to a small Baptist college in Birmingham while I headed to Auburn, a large state university just two hours away. She married shortly thereafter, while I focused on career and my move to Atlanta. Although we drifted apart over the next 30-something years, we stayed in touch through Christmas cards and news from each of our mothers. She invited me to lunch shortly after reading on Facebook that I'd be in New York at the same time she and her husband Ray had planned a visit. I was thrilled. I'm not sure I'd seen either of them in over fifteen years, maybe even twenty.

Pam had given me clear instructions, via the subway, on how to find Isabella's, a café at the corner of 77th and Columbus Avenue, on the Upper West Side. This was my first attempt to navigate the trains by myself, so just outside the Apple store I unfolded my MTA subway map and re-checked exactly where I was headed. It was a different experience being all alone. I had only myself to rely on to get the directions straight. But that was okay. I loved the challenge.

According to the map, my subway station was a straight shot, just one block east on 14th Street. East? God! You step out onto the streets and how are you supposed to know what is east or west? Guessing, I turned left. I was lucky this time.

As I arrived at the corner of 14th and Eighth Avenue, I eyed four subway entrances, one on each corner. I had no clue which one to enter. I chose the closest and was pleased to find a uniformed subway officer standing at the bottom of the steps. He kindly explained which platform and train I needed. "Remember 'A' and 'Uptown'," he repeated as I walked away, I'm sure, betting I'd screw it up. But I didn't and I got there just fine, thank you.

When Pam, a beautiful redhead with the world's most infectious smile, saw me approaching, she jumped out of her chair and ran to embrace me as if I was the most important person in the world. I admired that she always sensed the best in people, never one to gossip about anyone. She was always this joyful, even as a teenager when the rest of us were moody as sin.

Pam was your consummate Southern lady. She moved with a grace, like a ballerina, elegant and classical. Soft-spoken yet determined, she was known for her bright brown eyes, wide open and full of delight. A model champion of the archetype of self-care, she was always coiffed with a string of pearls or a bright linen scarf around her neck. She never left the house without lipstick. And man, did she love pretty clothes. Her mother was an excellent seamstress, always filling Pam's closet with handmade Ladybug and Villager-style dresses, the "in" labels back then. You couldn't tell them apart from the store-bought ones.

I adored her parents, too. Her mother was a gentle and patient soul who epitomized the sweet and patient elementary teacher that she was. Even though Pam's mom worked full-time, just like my own mother, she always seemed to have the time for us that my mother didn't. Her dad, a soft-spoken man, was a government worker. He spent many of his off-work hours tending to his acres of camellias, deadheading them, grafting varieties together, and snipping bouquets to bring into the house. "Jennie," I can still hear him say with his sideways grin. They spoke adoringly to each other. You could see in their mannerisms how much they honored each other, and how dearly they adored their only child.

Pam's home life was gentle. It seemed so different from mine.

After the waiter took our orders, the two of us jumped right in, right where we'd left off decades earlier, ping ponging memories back and forth, each followed by giggles and "wows" and great admiration that exists between true friends. Ray could hardly get a word in edgewise as we reminisced about growing up in Mobile and how the boundaries of our dreams extended only to Birmingham or maybe the Florida line. "How odd that you both felt the same pull to New York City," Ray finally added. After marriage, Pam taught ballet and brought a number of her students to Manhattan for summer programs and competitions. As we dined, it became obvious that she knew the city like the back of her hand and I was totally awed—oh, and maybe a tad envious, if I was to be honest. I never dreamed Pam would have been the one to rebel and blow past the boundaries set for the two of us.

"Oh, yeah!" I continued, my eyes cut to Ray. "Pam and I chose names for our future babies!" Merely teenagers, we also relied on our Ouija boards to tell us how many we'd bear. I went on about the many nights we spent perched atop of our beds, putting together scrapbooks of wedding gowns and bridesmaid dresses. "Oh, we even designed our future monograms," I added, shaking my head in disbelief. As a young girl I was especially excited about taking on a husband's name because I had no middle name, which bordered on being sacrilegious in the South. "You drop your middle name when you get married," my mother had reasoned, "so why waste a perfectly good name." I chuckled as I explained that she was efficient that way, and Pam nodded in agreement.

Pam then asked about my kids and I highlighted each of their accomplishments, and she followed with the same. "Ohhhhh ... but wait!" she interjected, her smile broadened, her eyes gleamed impishly as she reached down into her purse. "The grandkids," Ray whispered, leaning across the table to explain her sudden change. "Lisa, you're gonna love having grandchildren," he added. Pam placed a small photo book onto the table. Her entire face relaxed into a softness, her eyes brimming with a calm of contentment, like a sense of completion, as if she'd finally reached the pinnacle of life. There was a joy and a peace as she turned the pages, and as much as

I wanted to embrace and absorb and have this happiness myself, I could do nothing but simply nod in acknowledgement. A sudden wave of sadness had washed over me as I tried to decipher my reality.

At 58, I was supposed to be happily married and financially secure and looking forward to traveling with my husband. I should have been planning weddings for my children, gardening, and hand-smocking baby dresses for new babies in our family. Instead, I was struggling to keep my house and to restart my career. I was piling on debt to get my kids educated while imagining myself alone after almost 30 years. Where had my life had gone so wrong?

It was all I could do to finish my meal.

Pam, Ray and I hugged and said our goodbyes and, as I headed south along Columbus Avenue, I searched for reasons why our lives had taken such different paths. I assumed that my friend's seemingly idyllic childhood had affected her life's trajectory, and I credited her parents for setting quite the example for how to create a harmonious home and marriage.

Looking back, they never seemed bothered by what kind of car they drove, how big their house was, or that they didn't belong to a country club, or maybe that's just what I imagined. From the outside looking in, they seemed totally content with their lives and with what they had materially, as well as with what their Baptist beliefs might describe as, "the life God had chosen for them." Often, in my journaling as an adult, I prayed for that same appreciation of the life I had, for that contentment Pam's parents seemed to feel, and now their daughter, too. I so badly wanted that same peace.

I walked on, my legs propelling me on their own, my mind decades away, back in Pam's childhood home. I could see the light in the room; it was low, casting shadows from Pam's tall four-poster bed. I listened intently to her mother who sat on the floor between us, teaching us how to crochet. I could hear the softness in her voice as she looped the yarn around her finger, formed it into a slip knot, then pulled it through with her hook. I could smell the Mod Podge varnish that we painted on to the wooden purses we decoupaged. And the Christmas cookies we decorated together, sprinkles and icing spilled everywhere, but the messes never upset her like they did my mother.

One after the other after the other, the memories flowed through me, so incredibly vivid.

B-E-E-E-E-P! BEEP!

The sharp sounds startled me. I jumped to the curb, a car narrowly missing me. Totally unaware, I'd stepped out into the intersection after the light had changed, and the driver wasn't about to stop. A bit shook up, and a lot embarrassed, I edged closer to the building where I could catch my breath. I reached into my breast pocket for my map, unfolded it, then focused on my next steps. Once I got my bearings, I pointed myself toward Broadway where I would ultimately find my destination, Julliard, the famous performing arts school that was part of Lincoln Center.

As I arrived, I was instantly struck by the school's dramatic architecture. The front corner of the building jutted out three stories above the sidewalk, over what appeared to be a small amphitheater that tiered down a story below street level. At the bottom, on a small stage, stood not a mighty grand piano as one would have expected of such a renown conservatory, but an old, scratched and dented, well-worn black baby grand, whimsically adorned with lilac, blue, and green paint swatches.

Curious, I walked closer for a better view. One of its legs was broken and someone had steadied it on a large white box. *And these damn New Yorkers think they are classier than we are*, I thought, comparing this sight to a Southern redneck's car on cement blocks! I took a photo and chuckled while mentally composing my next Facebook wisecrack. I later learned online that this piano was one of many placed around the city, part of an initiative called "Sing for Hope."

I watched as a little girl, maybe six or seven years old, climbed onto the piano bench and began moving her fingers across the keys, her proficiency silencing the onlookers. I took a seat on the steps; a young man in light blue scrubs joined me. One by one, the concrete benches began to fill, gawkers leaning in, raising their cell phones, taking videos of this child prodigy.

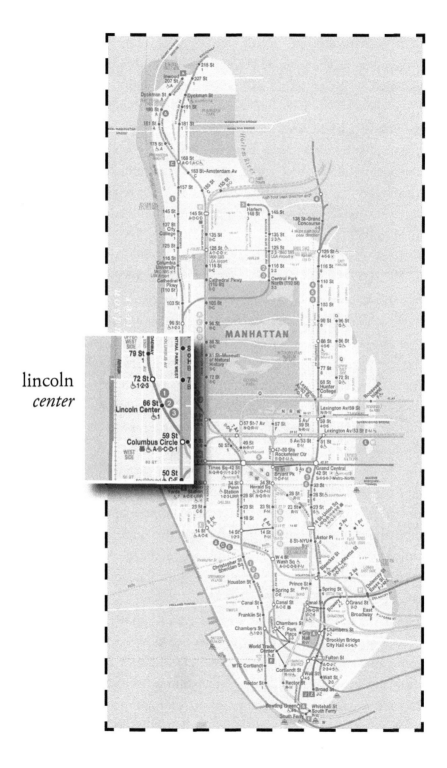

lincoln
center

A woman stood just to the side of the child playing the piano. Still and erect, she scanned the child's surroundings. The nanny, I assumed. With my mind still tangled up in Pam's mother versus mine, the scene took me back to fond memories of my nanny Rosa, the young Salvadorian woman who raised me from the time I was five until I was eleven. She first came into my life when my father, a major in the Air Force at the time, was transferred to El Salvador for a three-year tour of duty. Rosa was assigned to take care of my younger sister Michele and me. Just the mere thought of her brought me a smile.

Rosa was the one who drew my baths for me, knelt beside my bed at night, rosary in hand, and taught me how to say my prayers. She was the one who took me to market on Saturdays and walked me to school and fixed my lunches. I remember her singing with me and reading me stories. When I was sick, it was Rosa who lowered my fever, gently swabbing my forehead with a cool rag. When I was really ill, she'd lay on the hard stone floor beside my bed and stay with me all night long. In many ways, Rosa was much like Pam's mother. She was patient and had plenty of time for me, and although she disciplined me, it was never with anger. She had the tenderness, the unconditional love I longed for from my own mother.

My parents petitioned to bring Rosa back to the U.S. at the end of Daddy's duty in Central America. She'd become an integral part of our family. Once in Mobile, my parents built a house and designed a suite at the opposite end of the house where she lived. Even though Rosa was referred to as "the maid," she was like a mother to me. I couldn't imagine life without her.

The last time I laid eyes on Rosa or even heard her voice was late one evening in 1963, when my mother drove away with her, saying something about her visiting her sister in California. But Rosa never came back and five decades later, I'm still not sure what happened. In later years, I pieced together events that led me to believe she left about the time my mother got a job and started night school.

My father had retired from the Air Force and started a small business, but then lost it. I can only guess that money was tight, and they could no longer afford Rosa's salary, but I didn't dare ask my mother if that was the case.

As I sat there listening to the young child play, I became agitated. My mood turned sour. It was the only feeling I had left toward my mother. I had harbored resentment toward her for years and I was tired. I was worn out trying to earn her approval. My mother demanded perfection and judged me harshly, so my only option was to hide myself from her, to withdraw and protect myself, even lie to her about anything that might cause conflict. I was always afraid of her, and of the wrath I'd receive if I spoke my mind. The times I dared to sass her or talk back, she would come after me with the belt or the wire flyswatter. She had a fiery temper and often unleashed it on me.

Oh, I knew my mother was proud of me. All of her friends would tell me so. But I wanted to be loved. I needed to feel valued by her, like Pam's mother made me feel. I just wanted to feel like I was worth her time and her attention, but instead I felt cheated, cheated that I never got a mother like Pam's and Debbie's and others of my friends. Did she not enjoy being a mother? Was I just an impediment in her life? Why had she relegated her duties to Rosa? I had so many unanswered questions.

I left Juilliard a tangled mess. It was hot and humid, and I was wearing thin. I opted to forgo the subway for a walk instead. My apartment was about three-and-a-half miles away, but I knew I needed the exercise and more importantly, the time to process it all.

Had I been the same type of mother? Was I too busy for my children, were my career and making money too central in my life? Had I exhausted myself, martyred myself like my mother had, in order to "better" my kids' lives with the best schools and vacations to faraway places, ... and a home they'd be proud to bring their friends to? Tough questions, like leaks, sprung up everywhere.

Insecurities and self-doubt cooked my face, as did the sweltering summer sun.

My thoughts returned to Pam and how our mothers prepared us so differently. Although it was widely understood that most of us girls, me included, were sent to college for an "MRS" degree, I got a different version of that message, one that was very conflicting. Like any Southern mother, mine wanted me to marry a doctor or lawyer or one who came from money, one who could financially take good care of me and our kids. But, in the very next breath, she made it very clear that I should be financially independent of him. "You need to make your OWN money," she would preach, and I knew what she meant: "Have a way out."

My mother was a daughter of the Deep South, brought up at a time when women or proper ladies never pumped their own gas and never paid the bills. That was men's work. Women looked pretty, they cooked, herded the children, and managed the help.

Except—my mother hadn't led that charmed Southern life. She was only four when her father died unexpectedly of a stroke, leaving her mother scrambling to keep her young family afloat in the dregs of the Depression. Jobs were still tight and children were tasked with helping out, even the very young. "Shirley was the pretty one," my mother explained why her curly red-headed sister was spared of the dirty work, as was her brother William who, she explained, was artistic. "I was the tough one," she said, wearing her words like a badge of honor. "I wore the pants in the family." She went on tell how their landlord had given her mother the job of collecting rent from neighbors. "But Mama was too sweet," she started with an air of empathy. "They didn't have anymore 'n we did." So, the task became hers.

She bragged about how her mother went on to earn a certificate in typing at the University of Alabama, but added with a tad of bitterness, "We lived on the porch of a professor's home while Mama went to class." It was if she wanted me to understand why she had become so hardened and so resilient. When her mother landed a job at the Air Force base in Mobile, Alabama, she moved her family into a boarding house. "We all slept in one bed, all four of us," my mother emphasized. They slept in it at night, and another family used it during the day. "Sometimes it smelled like tee-tee."

She was definitely proud of her mother's grit, and of her drive, but she also wanted to make damn sure I was protected from the horrors of such a life. A good, respectable, high-earning husband would see to it that his family was protected.

In some ways, my mother's real life—or at least the way it was supposed to be—began when she met my father. Daddy was an officer in the Air Force; a pilot who, at age 36, was publicly deemed "the most eligible bachelor on the base." My mother, just 21 at the time, worked on the same base as a typist. Her boss set them up, and within a month of their first official date, my father proposed. In the early years of their marriage, he took her places she'd never been, showed her off, and exposed her to a grander world than she'd ever imagined. For her part, she was the perfect, beautiful, entertaining wife my father wanted. Often the youngest in the crowd, my mother was high-spirited, the life of the party, and everyone seemed to love her. As my dad got transferred from city to city, even overseas, she adapted and made friends easily. He was a man of few words, so I'm sure her social skills boosted his career.

After three years stationed in El Salvador living the charmed life of a diplomat, my father, at age 45, had a heart attack and their world changed. He moved our family back to Mobile, retired from the military, and returned to the world of the South where the rules and expectations were quite different. The loss of place in a society based on "Who's your father?" was difficult to accept for both my parents. His experience couldn't be parlayed into commercial flying because of his heart attack, so he turned to entrepreneurship. And when my father lost the car parts business in which he had invested their savings, my mother's Cinderella story ended abruptly. She was forced to go back to school, to find work, and she was slammed back into the same world she'd known as a child.

Laying it out like that, I started to see why my mother's message to my sister Michele and me often seemed conflicted. She wanted to be a proper Southern lady, but she wasn't truly: she lived a hard-scrabble life as a child and it was that experience that formed her views on raising girls.

"Be independent!" was her constant message to Michele and me. "Be your own woman. Don't ever depend on a man," she would rage, especially when embroiled with my father. Yet, in the very next breath, she'd look me straight in the eyes and say, "It's just as easy to fall in love with a rich man as it is with a poor one." It was only now, as my marriage was falling apart, that I started to untangle how my mother's conflicting teachings had twisted my own relationships.

I also saw how my past, that of my mother and of my grand-mother, are hauntingly similar. Had I unconsciously carried their generational baggage? Was it predestined? Had I inherited their emotional DNA? Did I have the power to rewrite it for my own daughter? I trembled in disbelief.

I'd never stopped long enough to see that I had, indeed, mimicked their stories.

13

… and on I walked down Columbus Avenue, which then became Ninth. It wasn't at all a pretty stroll like I'd had in the morning, not at all uplifting. My curiosity felt dulled. Office buildings, beige ones and others a drab gray, mirrored my confusion. Faded awnings and mismatched signage, nothing seemed visually in sync. Block after block of brick apartments with little or no style. Floor after floor after floor, the metal fire escapes zigzagged from top to bottom. A tree here and there, smothering in dust. Like me, gasping for air.

The months and weeks leading up to this trip had been more than any one human should ever have to bear. Bored into my psyche were wounds so raw I doubted would ever heal. As my visual field clouded into oblivion, my mind zeroed in on one of the most jarring moments I'd faced, just a month or so before I was to leave for New York. It was late one afternoon. I was juning around my living room in Atlanta, picking up coasters and vases and photos of the kids. The sun was streaming in ribbons across the nubby seagrass carpet. I could feel its summer heat warming the emptiness in the room. One by one I stacked items beside my neighbor Patti, who sat straddling an ottoman. She carefully wrapped each item in newsprint then nestled it in the box marked "LR — STORAGE." The mood was light as we bantered back and forth like two old Gladys Kravitzes, nosing way too far into our daughters' secrets. It was just a month or so after Jim told me we were losing the house, but in this little snippet of time, I felt productive and cheerful. I felt good for a change.

"Why in the hell am I keeping this," I grunted as I handed Patti the old mahogany metronome from my days as a young piano student. I'd hated the five laborious years of lessons my mother insisted I take. "… and HOURS of practicing, EVERY AFTERNOON! They cut into my friend time," I shot my friend an eye roll.

The deep, slow, repetitive tock — tock — tock — tock still hung in me as I caught sight of a burgundy-colored SUV come to a stop on the street in front of our house. The trunk popped open. Curious as who it might be, I moved closer to the window to see a dark-haired woman walking toward the back of her car. The instant I recognized her as Gala, our friend and real estate agent, every muscle in my body tightened. I clenched, bolstered myself for impact. I knew what was next. I watched her lift a For Sale sign from the trunk, pound, pound, pound it into the ground, then return to her car and slam her trunk shut. Every single movement seemed to proceed in slow motion. No one had prepared me for this. I had never visualized this finality. This stake in the ground was there for the entire neighborhood to see. There was no way I could get us out of this; I had no more answers.

My heart went immediately to my babies scampering down the steps on Christmas morning, then to the five of us sitting around the breakfast table, blowing out birthday candles and making wishes. I choked up as I visualized my little girl coming downstairs in her very first prom dress, and my boys in their Dodgers Little League jerseys. I could see Frank basking in the early-morning sunshine and Jim and I on the back porch, drinking a beer around the Big Green Egg. Friday nights were our time, our time for just each other. In that millisecond of time, 25 years of our life as a family flashed by, scene by scene, all spliced together like an old home movie. Faded and flickering and crackling with wear, the last frame read, "The End." It was a death, a hard, cruel death and I felt gutted. As Gala drove away, I knew that this chapter of my life was now over. It was the end and there was nothing I could do about it.

A swell of tears rose up through my neck, clenching my throat, and welling up in my eyes. I fought hard to repress them, but I couldn't. I remember feeling so desperate, so out of control. I didn't dare let Patti see me so fragile, so vulnerable, so I turned my back to her, but it was too late.

"It's okay," I remember her whispering, as she pulled me in for a hug, trying to console me. "You'll make it through this." She'd seen me weather our financial ups and downs over the years and soldier through Jim's cancer, all while juggling the boys' problems and the needs of my aging mother. I'd always been a steady person, the strong one, the one who could suck it up and plow through like a Mack truck. But losing this house, saying goodbye to this part of my life and to my family, was breaking me.

I wiped my tears and began sputtering through the story of our first night in the house, in 1986. "It was just a few hours after the closing," I explained to my friend. "The house was totally empty. I remember telling Jim that the first thing I wanted to do was rip up the harvest gold linoleum floor in the kitchen. It was awful …," I tried to make a joke of it all to try and hide my emotions. "I was so excited," my voice trailing off as I remembered sitting on the brick hearth, just a few months pregnant. At 35, I was finally getting the chance to fix up a baby's room. Having a baby was the one thing missing in my life, the one dream that had eluded me.

I remember so clearly asking the little baby in my belly, whom I'd jokingly named after Jim, whose middle name is Earl, "Jimmietta Earlene, you like your new home?" But she never got to see the house we were buying for her. Our little girl was born 12 weeks early, weighing a little over two pounds. "She lived for less than a day," I babbled on, my disjointed story pieces making little sense, I'm sure.

I was at an employee's wedding in Detroit. "You remember Jeff?" I asked my friend. I went on to explain feeling the first sharp pain in my abdomen. It came on so quickly and was so strong that I had a hard time concentrating on the ceremony. I was a little over six months pregnant and I sensed the pain I was feeling might actually be concerning. After the newly married couple exited down the aisle, I retreated to the bathroom where another guest found me doubled over with cramps. I asked if she could find someone to drive me back to the motel, then trying to minimize her alarm, I added "I just need to take a quick nap. It's been a long day."

Once in my hotel room, I took off my dress, my bra and panty-hose. Why I felt the need to explain all this to my friend, I don't know. It was if I was finally vomiting the details that had, over the years, festered in my gut. "I didn't have any more pain," I paused, then in vivid details, recalled how I crawled into bed and pulled the clean crisp sheets and downy comforter all the way up to my chin. As I began to doze off, I debated whether or not to set an alarm. "I couldn't miss the reception," I interjected. Then, not a second later, I felt a gush of liquid course down my legs and I knew something terribly wrong was happening. I had read about water breaking.

"I remember a strange calm washed over me," I added, question-ing my own sentiments. "I pulled the Detroit phone book from the nightstand beside the bed and flipped through the Yellow Pages to find the nearest hospital. It never dawned on me to call 9-1-1," I added with a shallow chuckle.

And with that I quit talking. In my silence I went on, recalling how I rang the clerk at the front desk and asked him to get me a cab. When I told him my situation, he assured me that my belongings would be okay if I didn't return right away. After leaving a voice mail for Jim, I then called my mother-in-law for some assurance and, I suppose, a little emotional strength. She took down the name of my OB-GYN in Atlanta and the hospital where I planned to go.

The taxi driver rushed me to the hospital in total silence. I remem-bered sitting in the back, in total abandon, disoriented, as if outside my body, watching this happen to someone else. As he pulled into the emergency area, he moved quickly around the front of the car while barking orders to a security guard. "Wheelchair. Quick!" He instructed me to stay seated until an orderly appeared with a chair.

I was whisked away through the halls and tucked into a dimly lit room, all while fretting that I'd forgotten to pay the driver.

It was in that little cell that I endured a long and terrifying night of the most intense pain I'd ever experienced. Even though I phased in and out of consciousness, I have a clear memory of a young nursing student who sat beside me through the entire ordeal. As my body wrenched with cramps, she seemed as terrified as I was. The odor of infection enveloped me, the scurrying of people in and out of my room frightened me. The constant drip, drip, drip of saline sustained me. She never left me. I remember that as clear as day.

At some point shortly after midnight, I gave birth to a tiny baby girl. At least, that's what the chart said. I don't remember the actual birth, but I have a slight memory of a large-frame, older nurse cradling my tiny child in the palms of her sturdy hands. She stood straight; her demeanor was focused and efficient. "Would you like to hold your baby," she asked in a cold and toneless voice. As she moved closer, I could see a weak up-and-down, up-and-down heartbeat through my child's paper-thin skin. She was missing a foot and one of her arms dangled helplessly beside her; it was horribly mangled.

"No," I remember saying to the nurse, "if I hold her, I will want to keep her," knowing instinctively that I had to let my baby go, that she could never be mine. "Don't try to save her," the words flowed calmly from my heart. And with that, they whisked her away. I don't remember anything else until Jim arrived six or seven hours later on the earliest morning flight in from Atlanta.

A nurse brought our little dead baby to my room. She had a tiny pink cap on her head, her eyes were closed. She looked absolutely beautiful to me. Her sweet and peaceful face, her perfect lips. Her tiny, tiny body was swaddled tight in a blanket. "You need to get some sleep," Jim said just a second later, signaling the nurse to take our baby away. The next day we had to decide whether or not to name her and how to handle her remains. Jim snapped at one of the counselors, which was so totally out of character for him, but I knew he was simply trying to shield me from as much as he could. A day later he wheeled me through the Detroit airport, headed home to Atlanta. I carefully tucked the horror of the last few days into the back of my heart. I had to keep going.

A few nights after we returned to Atlanta, Jim suggested we go to a good friend's party. "It might be good for you, sweetheart, to get out," he urged. In preparation for the party, I took a hot shower which, unfortunately, stimulated my breasts. Midway through the party two large wet spots appeared on my gold-colored silk tank top. My milk had come in. No one had warned me. The real horror of it all seared through me like lightning. For the first time, I realized I had lost the baby I so badly wanted.

The next Monday morning when I returned to the office, I started our week with a staff meeting like nothing had happened. Deadlines had to be met; bottom lines had to be right, and life went on. There was an understanding that I didn't want to talk about what had happened, and my staff complied.

But as steely as I was, guilt eroded my core. Had the stress of work harmed my baby? Had I put too much importance on my career? Was I even worthy of being a mother? I knew how to do advertising but knew nothing about having children. It was the one dream I had held my entire life, my real purpose in life, and I feared I was not worthy of it.

Two years later, when I learned I was pregnant again, I had a choice to make. I could continue at my breakneck pace and keep growing my company, or I could put my career on the back burner, close my office, find my employees other jobs, and work from home while my attention turned to motherhood. As much as I wanted both my career and motherhood, I was not willing to gamble losing this child.

The next week I closed the door to my office and relinquished the one thing that had come to define me—my career.

14

Emma was born that September, a healthy eight-plus-pound baby. A month shy of 38, I was finally a mother and I couldn't remember ever feeling more fulfilled. It was a dream come true, my purpose in life finally unfolding. I'd wished for this baby for as long as I could remember. Oh, yes, life quickly turned chaotic, but we loved it and managed quite well … well, with the help of a nanny!

Just six weeks after Emma entered our lives, so did Classie, bless her soul. She'd raised 30-plus babies, her resume claimed, and whether that number was correct or not, she certainly knew what she was doing. Within days, she normalized our lives.

In another six weeks, I enrolled my new little baby in Mother's Morning Out at the church a few blocks away. Two mornings a week I would have total quiet in my house. For six whole hours I could linger in the bathtub or catch up on laundry. I could shop for groceries or sneak in a dental appointment. But most importantly, I could focus on my hobbling career. I thought I'd hit the jackpot!

It wasn't soon after enrolling Emma that I found myself lingering in the hallways after dropping her off, meeting other new mothers here and there. Then the parents' "Meet & Greets" started, and the preschool's committees formed. "Someone mentioned you might be able to help us with our newsletter," was the call that hooked me. And so began my new life surrounded by moms instead of by the friends I'd made through my work.

It was a curious time for us baby boomer women. We were the first generation to have choice. Unlike our mothers and grandmothers, whose only career options were secretarial, nursing, or teaching, we could choose fields traditionally held by men. We could be lawyers or accountants, architects, or even astronauts. We could opt to stay home and raise our children, or we could choose a full-time career outside the home, if we liked. And although it was rare, some couples were beginning to choose not to have children at all. But that took a lot of explaining.

Becoming more and more ensconced in the preschool, I began to experience a friction, an underlying angst that affected many of us mothers of this age. I remember it vividly to this day, the morning that a mother arrived at the classroom door perfectly coiffed in heels and a fashionable gray suit. Her make-up was perfect, her demeanor smart. I felt a resentment toward her, an envy, and a sadness that I'd lost control of my professional life.

This undercurrent of resentment against those who had chosen full-time careers was very real. Their financial independence from their husbands was envied. For me, I desperately missed my creative cohorts, the structure, and the reputation I'd built for myself. I'd lost my identity, and certainly a chunk of my self-confidence.

We struggled to correct the labels we used and how we framed each other. Moms who no longer had careers were most often called upon to supplement the school and church activities. "Ask her to bring the cupcakes. She doesn't work," would absolutely rub them raw and that kind of thinking had to change. "Stay-at-home" demeaned those whose jobs were just as intense and stressful and important as those who spent their days in offices. A push to redefine them as "full-time moms" finally equated them with those who carried business cards, or those who were re-labeled as mothers who "work outside the home."

But behind their suit and high-heel façade, many of the "office" moms were jealous of those who were home full-time, raising their children. "Kept woman," I once heard an attorney friend lash out at her neighbor. Like many, I'm sure she was deflecting guilt for forsaking her maternal instincts for personal enrichment, or private schools, or a three-car garage. Others worried that their professional accomplishments and their paychecks were emasculating their husbands. One or two were just plain gut-honest, admitting that they'd lose their sanity if they were with little kids all day!

"I got the best of both worlds," I often touted as I maintained a semblance of a career, plus got to be at home with my babies. It was a good narrative, but deep down inside I struggled knowing that I was doing both jobs only halfway. Yes, all of us baby boomer mothers were finally given a choice, but if we chose to work outside the home, we were expected to do both at 100%. It had not yet kicked in that fathers were supposed to do 50% of the child-rearing or housework or meal-planning, nor was it cool if they did.

So, on we swam in this new world of ours, blissful in our little family of three. Finally getting our sea legs on, Jim and I managed quite well as we welcomed our new baby Witt into our lives, just two years later. Then Classie got married and left us. Annie replaced her, and all was good until two things would happen that changed everything: I found myself pregnant yet again, and shortly thereafter, the IRS officer knocked on our front door.

After that day, my life became all about mere survival. Sheriffs appeared regularly at our home, serving lawsuits. Our family van was repossessed in the middle of the night, and the creditors' phone calls started at 8:00 sharp every morning, continuing until 9:00 at night. I was terrified, humiliated, and teetered dangerously close to an emotional breakdown.

There I stood, a new mother with two little babies and another on the way. I had never in my life felt such despair. For the next seven months, I suffered from panic attacks. I didn't sleep. I told no one outside my family that I was having another baby. Fear replaced the joy and excitement I'd experienced during my previous pregnancies and, of course, I was too embarrassed to ask anyone for help through our financial nightmare, one of a magnitude I'd never faced.

My sweet little Trey was born in mid-May. Making the best of his gestational upheaval, this determined little boy entered this world at 9 1/2 pounds. He was perfect in every sense. When the doctor placed him in my arms for the first time, I felt a peace and a love, and an emotional attachment that for nine months I'd shut out of my heart. But that peace slowly seeped out of me, replaced by fear of how I was going to make it to the next day.

I didn't rock Trey or sing or read to him as I'd done with my other babies. I dismissed it as "the third-child syndrome," but it was much worse than that. I was juggling a three-year-old, an 18-month-old, and now a newborn. And on top of that, a household. I scrambled to get more work to keep us from being evicted or going bankrupt. I was tired, spent, scared, and unfortunately, in fits of rage, I began taking it out on my innocent children. I found myself shutting them out, just as my own mother had done to me and my sister. I became like a hard, cold robot, emotionally unplugged from my children's needs and even my own. I cut off all social interaction with friends; it was easier that way. I was forever changed, as was my trust in Jim.

My number one focus became making my own money, to protect myself and my children, and to fund a way out if I needed it … just as my mother had taught me. At 41, I finally understood.

15

It was Tuesday, June 28th, my fourth evening in Manhattan when I sat at my table with one leg crossed over the other. I steadied my hand on my knee and carefully pushed the sharp point of a safety pin deep into a nasty blister on my left heel. Once the liquid drained, I covered the area with a bandage, then turned my attention to writing a blog post for that day:

> "Stupid Is as Stupid Does. Just like Forrest Gump, I started walking toward my subway station and kept walking till I hit the East River. Then I turned around and walked till I hit the other side. In other words, I walked the entire width of Manhattan, twice. Stupid. I'm sure I'll be laid up in some hospital, in traction, by tomorrow."

I was good at frosting my emotions with humor. My Forrest Gump crack was to ensure that my readers couldn't see that I had walked over 60 blocks because I needed to process, step by step, my harsh reality. My family was bracing for the hardest series of events it had ever faced and I wasn't there for them. For the last three days, I was able to swim in the New York world of excitement, to push away any wave of fear for what awaited back home. But euphoria was fading fast.

I had left my apartment this morning and raced through the streets, walking aimlessly, with no idea which way I was headed. I picked up a new piece of map but stuck it in my pocket without even registering which neighborhood it covered. My mind paced through the steps of my family's demise, my gait mimicking my frantic emotions. With my head low, I sprinted north and east, through 20 or so blocks until I

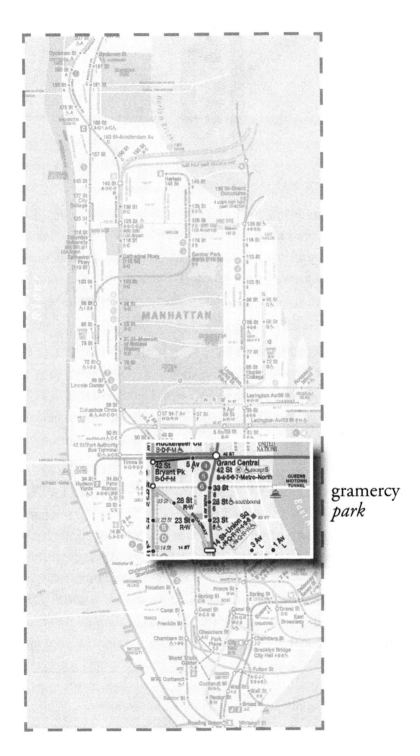

gramercy
park

came to an idyllic little haven called Gramercy Park. It was different from any neighborhood I'd seen in Manhattan. Genteel and serene, it felt totally residential, almost like a planned community. I stopped to have lunch at Pete's Tavern, an old, dank pub-style restaurant whose awning read, "THE TAVERN O. HENRY MADE FAMOUS." I asked the waiter who greeted me if I could eat outside and he waved his arm as to say, "It's all yours." No one else was on the patio and it took me only seconds to understand why. It was in the 90s and humid as hell, but I needed the sunlight.

I had read that this neighborhood haunt had fed the muse of the literary elite since the mid-1800s, including writers such as John Steinbeck, Herman Melville, and Stephen Crane. According to lore, it was here that O. Henry penned "The Gift of the Magi." I suspected this little haunt might have contributed to his untimely death at age 47, due to cirrhosis of the liver.

After placing my order for a tuna fish sandwich, the cheapest thing on the menu, I pondered how alcohol played a role in the life of so many creative greats. Does it take alcohol to hush or heighten voices in your head, to clear the way to your soul? Does it take an altered state to awaken the creative muse? It had certainly worked for me oftentimes.

I glanced inside the open door at the bar area of the tavern, my mind flashed to Witt and to the small dark counselor's office where Jim and I sat just months earlier, listening in horror as our son told us that he drank his first beer in seventh grade. One beer led to a six-pack, enough to put him to sleep. When that wasn't enough, he moved on to hard liquor, then to pills. Then it was cocaine, he'd finally admit.

"I've stolen some money," he muttered that afternoon. "Witt …" his rehab counselor interrupted, pushing him to come clean. "Several thousands," my son offered up after a long, hard pause. He'd pawned everything he could get his hands on and sold stuff out from under us so he could get the next gram. He needed those chemicals to get through the night terrors and the panic attacks that kept him from sleeping night after night. He did it to survive, he claimed, and I desperately wanted to believe him, but my empathy was bloodied with deep resentment. Deep down in my gut I sensed he was playing us with self-pity. He knew how to work me.

"You must cut him off," the counselor advised, "to the point where he may not make it out alive," he emphasized and with that, a bitterness toward Jim flared up. He was always there to get Witt out of his messes, and when he could, he'd hide the truth from me. "I hate to upset you, sweetheart," was his lack of transparency that was probably due to my fiery reaction. But how could I label Jim the enabler when both of us were incompetent? Dealing with an addicted child was new to us, we had no experience, and these instructions flew in the face of my maternal instincts. My heart and gut and being told me to hug my child tight and to protect him and never let him out of my sight. To help him financially through this horrendous disease. He'd already attempted suicide once. I couldn't bear the thought of losing my child. No mother could. And all tangled up in that confusion, anger, fear, and desperation was guilt, of course. Guilt for leaving him behind, for shutting it all out for these 30 days in New York, and for selfishly taking time away for me.

I finished my sandwich, settled the tab, refocused on my directions, then headed east on 23rd to First Avenue through the medical complexes of Bellevue and NYU, where my trance was interrupted by huge, 30-or-so-foot-tall photos of black and white faces looming over me, all extreme close-ups, their eyes glaring through me. Beside each photo was an explanation of their scientific contributions in their respective fields. Some were young, high school-aged kids, whose research papers included titles like "cellulosic biofuels" and "ethyl levulinate." I approached the uniformed guard monitoring the entrance of what appeared to be a newly built campus of sorts and asked about it. "This is the Alexandria Center," he boasted, "a life science complex." He went on about the state-of-the-art amenities it would offer, the views of the East River and the famous pharmaceutical giants who would occupy it. For a guard, he's quite good as a salesman, I thought. "And what beautiful buildings these are," I remarked as I pointed back to two old red-bricked buildings, about seven or eight stories each, that flanked The Alexandria's entrance. When I asked the guard what they were, imagining that they were cool lofts, or something of the sort, his carefully crafted answer, muffled under his breath in a totally different tone, shocked me. "It's a place where people live who have no home," he pointed to the one on the right. I understood. I wondered if he'd been coached by the marketing team, by someone like me, and told to hide the fact that a homeless shelter and the children's foster home sat right next door to a shiny new office, space they were hawking for millions of dollars. I got it. Image was what I was trained to create.

The thought didn't sit well with me. It felt uncomfortable and I questioned why, my mind racing back to how and why the concept of image had become such a part of me. I thought back to how my mother disciplined me with the phrase, "What will people think?" I clearly remember being a young teen when I heard her refer to one of my good friends as "trash" because she made out with a boy at one of our boy-girl parties. "All the mothers are talking about it," she said and warned me, in no uncertain terms, that I should NEVER embarrass our family by doing such a thing. It would "ruin my reputation," a phrase I heard over and over in my formative years. That and "no need to air our dirty laundry" were words I lived by fearfully, all through high school and college and, honestly, still to this day.

I reflected on our Sunday mornings, when my mother fussed about our less-than-perfectly polished shoes, the mismatched bows in our hair, and our wrinkling of the dresses she'd starched and ironed. "You HAVE to look nice for church!" she would bark. It was our way of honoring God, she'd explain. "The mere concept of looking pretty for church is WRONG," I argued with her years later, my first Sunday back home from college. "Everybody goes to church to show off their new clothes!" She was quite upset when I walked out of my bedroom wearing a maxi-length gauze skirt, looking quite Bohemian, very "cool" for the '70s. This was not as she'd raised me. "Just come on," my father said as my mother shook her head in disgust. "It's too late to change."

As I neared the United Nations complex, it came to me that I had perpetuated the cycle. I, too, had worn myself out on Sunday mornings, polishing my kids' shoes and starching and ironing the boys' Sunday khakis, finding the right bows for Emma's hair, worrying about their image, and subsequently, mine as a mother. *Why?* I lashed out at myself, *why, when I knew it was wrong, had I not done any better?*

I turned west on 43rd, then wove my way through the congestion at Grand Central. I kept pressing on, step by step, block after block, deep in reflection and self-examination and meditation until I found myself at the end, the opposite side of the island, at the Hudson River.

Through these 60-plus blocks, I came to understand that this time away and this time alone was not a fling nor a selfish act. It was a lifeline.

16

The next morning, I hardly had the energy to think about walking another neighborhood. The physical and emotional calisthenics from the day before had been brutal. I relaxed, pulled the covers over my aching body, then began a gratitude exercise I'd learned years before, a simple recitation of things I was thankful for in that moment. "Thank you, God, for getting me here," I began, slowly, speaking in a whisper. "…and for making this dream come true. Thank you for giving me the courage to follow through, to come here against all odds. Please keep me safe and healthy. But most of all, God, please be with Emma, and with Witt and Trey, and …" I stopped, my words choking me. I couldn't finish. I saw the faces of each of my kids, each of them in a different place, all alone. I could see them suffering through the worst trauma of their lives. I felt it in my bones and in my soul. I wasn't there for them and the guilt was eating me alive.

Why am I here?

I laid there for a moment, my tears staining the dark pillow. I wiped my face, then pulled my will out of bed and headed toward the shower.

The hot water beat down on my face, then my shoulders, as if to awaken me. The steam embraced me with the tenderness of a loving mother. "You'll be okay. You are here for a reason," I heard her say. I stood still as a stone with my eyes closed. I took in a deep breath, the steam traveling deep into my chest, my muscles surrendering. I could feel a sense of relief seep back into my vessels.

As I ran my fingers through my soapy, wet hair, I turned again to my gratitude practice, "Thank you…," but stopped. This dream. This dream wasn't really a dream. It was a call, a pull, a shift, something bigger than me, something much more profound than I could explain. I felt it like I had a duty to be here, to use my days wisely, and to take care of myself.

I refocused myself and reached for the bottle of conditioner. As I squeezed a couple of drops into the palm of my hand, I scanned the few basic things on the shelf: toothbrush, toothpaste, deodorant, hairbrush, and some basic make-up items. *How little I need, how little I need,* I thought, as I considered all the things we were about to lose.

All the stuff that litters my tabletops, I countered. All the china I'd packed up, the crystal and the silver and the linens, all pieces I'd used only a handful of times. *All artifacts a Southern bride believes she'll need,* I chuckled. What purpose do they serve?

As the shower turned from warm to cool, my mind and emotional high flipped like a switch, back to Atlanta. Oh, God, the silver! Will Jim remember to lock up the silver and jewelry before the realtor shows the house?

With that I stepped out, dried off, and wrapped the towel around my naked body. As I entered the bedroom, I caught a glimpse of a woman across the way, opening her shutters. I was struck by her bright red hair. She closed her eyes and I watched her taking deep breaths of fresh air, each time her chest rising as the air filled her. It's her ritual, I fantasized, wondering if she started each day by preparing her mind and spirit in this beautiful way.

I folded a clean towel into a small square and placed it on the pillow. I crawled back in bed, laid my wet head on the towel, then closed my eyes and did what I had imagined the neighbor doing. I relaxed and let my mind gape open. Why had I let others shape my life? Had I let my mother, Jim, my neighbors drive me? How would I have done it differently?

I put aside my plan to walk a piece of the map that day. Instead, I left the apartment and ambled over to 14th Street. Descending down into the subway station, I could hear intermittent sounds, deep and lively, staccato tones as if from a bow being dragged across the strings of a violin. As I walked further, I could see a young Asian man in brightly plaid shorts playing for the commuters, most of whom never even lifted their eyes to acknowledge him, and that saddened me.

With no destination in mind, I climbed aboard the first train to pull into the station, the northbound, or "uptown," #3 train and sank into a seat next to a young Hispanic woman. I leaned my head back onto the metal railing and closed my eyes. I wanted to focus on the sounds and smells around me, and within a few seconds, the faint conversation in Spanish behind me transported me back to my childhood days in El Salvador. Their soft laughter fueled an urge to smile, and I allowed myself to do so. The back-and-forth rocking of the train lulled me into sweet memories of me as a child, laying on the St. Augustine grass back home, making objects out of the clouds as they drifted by. It had been decades since my mind had been so empty, so clear to just think and listen and imagine. And to be at peace.

I got off the train at 103rd Street, at random, and when I exited the station, I caught a glimpse of a sign pointing to Central Park. I bought myself a street dog, a bag of Cheetos, and a bottle of water from a street vendor, then strolled into the park where I found a bench to sit. It wasn't exactly the romantic picnic I'd always dreamed of having in Central Park, but at least I could claim on Facebook that I'd picnicked here!

The bench was hidden away in a thick canopy of green. It was as if I'd stepped into another place, an idyllic retreat far, far away from the muffled murmur I'd come to know on the streets of Manhattan. The beeping horns and sirens were gone, drowned out by the sound of water gurgling over a large waterfall of rocks.

I finished my makeshift picnic and walked until I saw a small group of runners approaching. I stepped out of their way, closer into the inner ring of their path. From there I could see a huge open

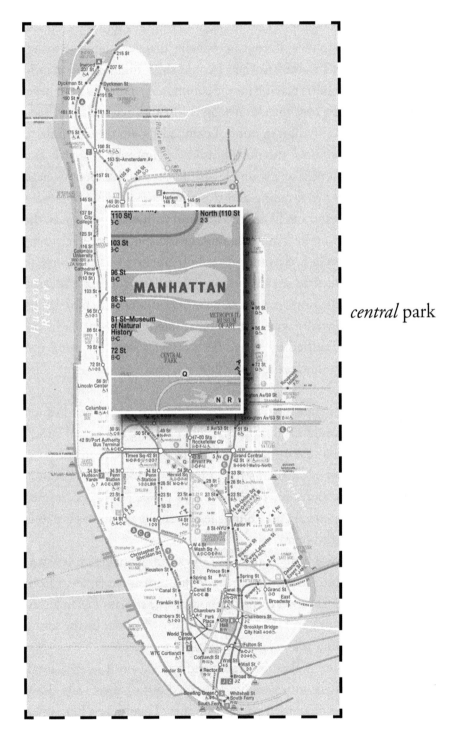

central park

meadow, drenched by the glaring sun. Sunbathers patchworked the grounds—loners with books, pairs sound asleep in each other's arms. I passed a trio of bongo drummers and a group of Latino men playing what appeared to be a pick-up game of soccer. I stopped to watch a woman who was arguing with a tree, yelling something about a war. A young man begged her to go home. At first, I felt sorry for her, imagining that she might be homeless, maybe psychotic. *Hell, I'm in New York,* I reminded myself, cracking a big ole fat smile. For all I knew, I might have just witnessed performance art, or a scene from an actor rehearsing an off-Broadway play. God, I loved this place!

In the distance of this grassy expanse, I could see the outline of a baseball diamond, its orange dust kicking up in the wind. How many times had I washed that damn red clay out of the kids' uniforms? I reflected back on the many days and nights our family spent at the kids' Little League or softball fields. Tears started down my warm, sunburned cheeks. There were so many things I wanted Jim and the kids to see, so much of my newness I wanted to share.

I walked past a bank of empty tennis courts and stepped onto a beautiful old Gothic-style bridge. "Bridge No. 28," the sign beside it read. Just as I crested the bridge, I caught sight of a calm sheet of blue, the famed 106-acre reservoir named after Jacqueline Kennedy Onassis. I peered over the old iron fence and could see a rippling reflection of the skyline on the East Side, the clouds billowing through the water, just as they did overhead. The view was breathtaking. I stood still for a long moment, almost in a trance.

I continued on the quiet path along the water's edge, the only sounds coming from birds in the trees beside me and the crunching of pebbles beneath my feet. I tossed one of the stones into the water, making a wish as I watched the rings of water ripple out, wider and wider. It was the same wish I'd made on each of the kids' birthdays, year after year. "May they come to know their God sooner than I did."

Nearing the 90th Street exit, I stopped and turned my body back and faced into the park. I caught a faint sound of a violinist playing nearby. I was warmed by the sound of children's laughter in the distance and intrigued by a man hawking rides in his horse-drawn carriage. I wasn't ready quite yet to leave this reverence, so I parked my tired body on one of the wooden benches lining the sidewalk. I wanted to linger and bask in this moment of peace.

Just as I relaxed, I noticed several small brass plaques posted on the backs of other benches, the ones in front of me. Curious, I turned to find one on my bench as well, one that read: "In honor of Brook Byers who allowed Shawn her Manhattan Fantasy." Her Manhattan Fantasy? Intrigued with what that could mean, I got up and went from bench to bench, reading all the other plaques. Some were memorials to parents. One or two were marriage proposals. One was even a remembrance to a family's beloved dog. I then took photos of eight or ten of them to highlight on my blog post that evening.

Back home that night I worked through my photos and words and wrapped up my blog post with:

> "Today was a very retrospective day. It finally hit me that this dream has actually come true. If for some reason I had to leave tomorrow, this experience will have already exceeded my expectations."

And with that I closed my day a different person.

17

As my morning coffee brewed, I opened my laptop to check my email and proofread last night's blog post. A million thoughts had run through my mind yesterday, and I wanted to make sure my head wasn't too in the clouds, that my writing didn't reflect the endorphin high I often found myself on after a day's walk. I frequently sensed my writing was a bit too enthusiastic, too Pollyanna-ish or naive. I checked social media for any feedback, either from my real friends or the virtual ones who'd begun to follow me. Had my number of Facebook "Likes" risen? Were there new comments? Were they supportive? I was still somewhat insecure about what people thought of this harebrained trip I was on. I needed the validation.

I stopped on a comment from my friend Edie:

" … we bought one for my aunt who believed that the only place in the world worth knowing was NYC, specifically Manhattan. She was a Central Park Ranger after retiring from a publishing career. Her bench is on the East Side, 78th Street near the kiosk she manned weekly. Her plaque reads:

'Marie Roth Reno. New York was her first love. Central Park her passion.'

Friends of hers call from time to time, telling me they are sitting on her bench on a glorious day. Her ashes were strewn in a lovely area of the park, Naturalists Walk, near the Natural History Museum. It is designed to look like the Park would have looked during earlier times (split-log benches, soft-surface paths), very fitting, since she wrote a couple of novels about Manhattan during the Civil War, her favorite era.

The nice thing about the bench plaques is that they are guaranteed to be in the park as long as there is a park, if defaced or damaged they will be replaced, and a bench will always be there for future park lovers."

I scrolled down to find another comment, from my friend Jane:

"My niece was given a tree in Central Park for a christening present. I've never found it. But her grandfather and I swore we'd build a treehouse in it one day!"

My curiosity was piqued. I poured myself a cup of coffee and went back through the photos of plaques I'd posted online. They read:

"The Girls: Dakota, Madison and Annabel. Forever will I hold the memories of our life together close to my heart. Because of you, I am. Juliet 2009"

"Angie, have I asked you to marry me yet today? Love, Mike"

"Jim Harpel and Katie, his smart and funny English bulldog, used to sit here together and watch the world go by."

"Citizenship is every person's highest calling. Walter H. Annenberg"

"David, Really. . . Maureen" (I could only imagine the story behind this one!)

"Margie's Bench: Please use this bench to tell someone how much you care, kiss, hug, cuddle, canoodle, touch, smile, laugh, and do tricep dips and push-ups!"

"This above all: to thine own self be true." In Loving Memory of Dr. Barbara Stern (1937—2009)"

Whoa! I had to read that last one again. "This above all: to thine own self be true." How serendipitous. It was if she was speaking to me, so googled her, wanting to know her story. "… esteemed Professor of Marketing at Rutgers University…passed away peacefully…" her obituary read. Still teaching, I chuckled. Still teaching me.

I went through the photos, wondering what I'd put on a plaque if I had one. What message would tie up my life in just a few sentences and stand the test of time, years after I was gone. Like an obit, really, what in my life was most significant?

I'd mention my kids, of course, because they are my heart. Or maybe the five of us, as a family, my little circle of five. I'd probably include something about the career that was such a big part of my life, and a hint of how important my faith is to me. Just like Shawn Byers did on her plaque, I'd be tempted to mention this time in New York, but I doubted there'd be room.

Hers was the very first plaque I saw yesterday, I noted as I reread the inscription. "In honor of Brook Byers who allowed Shawn her Manhattan Fantasy." I felt a bond with this person named Shawn and was dying to learn more. Was Brook her husband? Had he given her a trip like mine, as a gift? Had she walked all the neighborhoods, and done it all alone as I was doing? But it was the appearance of my own word "allowed" that stumped me. So many of my friends claimed they needed permission, "Oh, I'd love to go on a trip alone, but my husband would never let me." It was hard for me to imagine. Jim had always been supportive of any time I needed to get away, and certainly of this trip. I typed "Shawn and Brook Byers" into Google.

"… Brook graduated with a bachelor's degree in electrical engineering from Georgia Tech …" How wild is that?! Stunned, I read on that he was raised in Atlanta. "A VC giant," "a lead donor at Stanford University…" and in his bio were listed his favorite websites, one of which was www.newschools.org which was Parsons! Whew, the synchronicity spooked me. It very definitely felt like a sign. "I should reach out to Shawn one day," I coached myself, but I knew I probably never would contact someone so out of my league. My fantasy of meeting them would remain exactly that.

It was almost 10:00 a.m. and a bit crisp outside when I finally left the apartment and started down Greenwich Street at quite a good clip. *I've got to get in a good long walk, plus a blog post, before*

Michele comes tomorrow! I'd almost lost track that my sister was coming the next day.

Just a few blocks down the road, I found a sweet little garden hidden behind a beautiful Episcopal church, St. Luke's in the Fields. I pushed through the gate and found a man sitting on one of the stone benches that curved alongside the lines of the grass. His head was head hung low, his clothes disheveled, like he'd been in them for days. His shoes were old and dusty. He didn't acknowledge me nor even seem to sense my presence when I passed beside him. I found my own seat, plugged in my earbuds, took in a chest full of fresh air, and lowered my head. I clicked the iTunes icon on my phone and as George Winston started stroking the keys of his piano, I closed my eyes and started rocking my body and tapping my toe as he played "Joy" on his piano. It took me no time at all to disappear into oblivion.

Before I left Atlanta, Trey taught me how to load songs from my CDs onto my computer, then into my new iPhone. I'd only had time to load one CD, one full of Christmas carols. I'd since learned how to buy other songs, and the first one was Frank Sinatra's "New York, New York." Bittersweet, because it was not only the pretend theme song for my trip but also an anthem of sorts for Jim and me. It was the song we played at our wedding reception and danced to during our honeymoon. I chose that song because it best described our weekend in New York, the weekend when my feelings for Jim shifted from being more than just friends.

I sat there, still, very still, reflecting back on the demise of my family. My mangled mania ping-ponged back and forth from my deep love for Jim to disgust of his actions, and from "What are people saying?" to "Should I mention my problems on my blog?" "They need to know it wasn't my fault," I contended, but then countered with "What part did I play in it?" I sifted through each of the kids' physical and emotional states and wondered how I'd shepherd them through next steps, especially when I was so broken myself.

When the loop of songs began repeating, I got up and worked my way under the gnarled branches of an old tree and through a clematis-covered archway, then closed the delicate little garden gate behind me. I then stopped and glanced back at the man still sitting in the park. In that second it occurred to me that he might be the homeless man who set up his cardboard tent outside my apartment each night. I felt an urge, a duty even, to go back and talk with him, to get to know him, but of course, I didn't. I walked on, south on Greenwich Street.

I knew I was leaving the West Village because I could see a noticeable change in architecture. The lush cobblestone streets lined with brownstones were soon replaced with rows and rows of old warehouses, begging to be restored into vibrant, new loft spaces young people would inhabit. The streets were empty, except for a few delivery trucks that lurched in and out of what seemed to be a shipping center. I walked on, dashing across the busy Canal Street traffic, until I found myself in the area called Tribeca. I would later learn that the area got its name from using the first two letters of "Triangle Below Canal." Canal Street, I gathered.

It was there that I got in a long line of people waiting to order from a street vendor selling Halal street food, or what I learned later, was meat prepared according to Islamic law. I was starving! I could smell garlic and curry, maybe even cloves. It must be good, I reasoned, noting the length of the line. This type of food was foreign to me, so I randomly pointed to one of the plastic-wrapped photos the vendor had displayed at the top of his cart. Within minutes the man handed me a plate full of stringy meat—chicken, I assumed from its light color, a perfectly formed round scoop of screaming-yellow rice, plus a loose mound of shredded iceberg lettuce. On the side were two fried balls which, according to the sign, were falafels. Included were two packets of sauce, one red, the other white. I found a seat on a short brick wall where I could dig into my mystery meal in peace.

The initial impression was great: the meat was very spicy, just like I loved my food. As I continued enjoying my meal and the ambiance surrounding me, a cute little pigeon landed on the wall, his velvety gray body right next to me. His black beady eyes looked up at me, then down at my plate. Another came, then a third one, all bunching up next to me, cooing like sweet little angels. Closer and closer they inched, until finally they weren't so cute. They were after my food. No wonder I was the only fool sitting on this ledge. I steadied my plate with my left hand, and with the other I tried my best to shoo them away, but it was if they'd called in for backup. More and more appeared, finally outnumbering me. *Even the birds are aggressive in this city*, I mumbled to myself. I finally gave up, shoved one last scoop of meat in my mouth, wrapped the two falafel balls in my napkin, then dumped the rest of my lunch into the garbage. Exactly what the damn birds had hoped for.

I then headed south where it quickly became clear that I was in the Financial District: all the starched white shirts, women in high heels and dark suits, men with ties and their hair all in place. No tattoos and dreadlocks on this side of town.

They all looked corporate and so bright and young. It hurt to watch them; they appeared so energetic, confident, and at their peak. I felt diminished by the mere sight of them, like I was old and out of date, no longer viable, even cast aside. They were at the top of their game, at their professional best, just like I was in my twenties and thirties. I was envious. But even at 58, I told myself, I could still compete, if only given the chance. *If I could get up to speed with the new technology*, I tried to convince myself, *I could earn my way back into their club.*

I thought back to the friends I'd come to know in the kids' preschool days and others through their elementary, middle and high schools. In many ways it sickened me to think how strong, smart, and capable these women were, all well-educated and many highly paid in their previous lives. They'd put their vocations on hold and, instead, led so eloquently in other ways—like lobbying

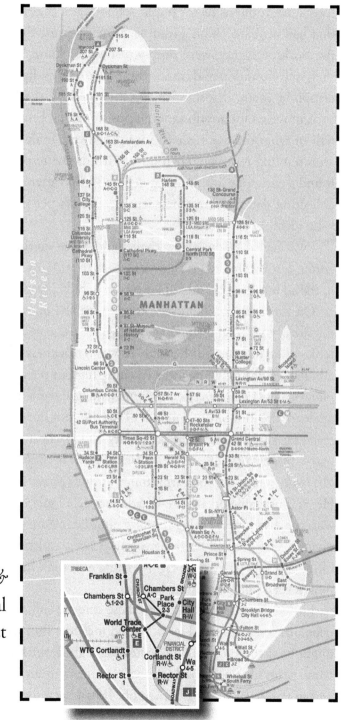

tribeca &
the financial
district

legislators, fundraising for public schools, and chairing PTAs, jobs that had little worth on a resume. When it came time to re-enter the workforce, they were simply cast aside. Some didn't even try, their self-confidence dashed, their fear of the digital advances crippling them. Those of us left strapped by the Recession of 2008 groveled for anything, even positions that brought less than half of what our younger counterparts were making. At age 57, after sending resume after resume with nary a response, I finally found a part-time job, walking neighborhood after neighborhood, collecting data for the 2010 Census. The $15 per hour wage did little to fill in the holes.

I was fueled by these new challenges I faced on this trip, I must admit, but I wondered if I'd ever fit back in with my old colleagues in the ad business. I doubted I'd ever match the wage I once earned.

On through the Financial District I walked until I approached the site of the fallen Twin Towers. The area was crawling with what looked like tourists. All I could see was a thickness of bodies and a bunch of skinny white arms reaching high in the air, all holding phones, all twitching in staccato form, jerking about to catch different angles of the monolith rising out of the ground. But the image that really caught my attention was a hefty, square construction worker with a bright turquoise bandana tied around his bowling ball head. His large, totally tattooed arms bulged from a sleeveless denim shirt. He sat, munching on a white-bread sandwich, looking totally bored with the Asian tourists surrounding him. I could only imagine him saying, "Get the hell outta here, you people, so I can do my job!" Oh, yes! I raised my own skinny white arm high into the air and took several photos of him.

I loved, loved, loved catching these colorful snippets of life and people around the city. I let my mind meander into what his story might be. I could only imagine hearing a gruff, thick Jersey accent come from his lips, a bark almost. I wanted to introduce myself and to talk to him, but I backed off. It had been such a long, long time since I'd let my mind go totally free like this, just wasting time, letting my creativity flow. Lorda mercy, in this very moment of time, I was sooooo happy!

I then turned east toward City Hall and after a few blocks, I began noticing that the streets were littered with trash. There were young people sitting under an overhang in makeshift cardboard houses. After asking a passerby what the ruckus was all about, I learned they were protesting budget cuts for the poor and working class. "Occupy Wall Street" was their motto, their cries were against business and income inequality. The scene was reminiscent of the '70s when we Auburn students staged sit-ins on the college president's lawn, protesting the Vietnam War, or when we marched for Civil Rights. Although I knew very little of the protestors' pleas, I was happy to see a renewed passion in politics, something I'd not seen in almost 40 years.

The scene was ripe with energy and full of visual appeal, so I decided to try my hand at videotaping a stand-up interview with one of the protesters. "May I interview you for my blog?" I asked the young man, even before realizing what I was about to do. Just as a reporter would do, I lobbed question after question at him, and with quite the resolve. I was stunned at my tenacity. "I've been here, on the same street corner, for 14 days," he began. "We chose our location because just across the street is where budget hearings are going on." Although I wasn't sure what I'd do with the video, if anything, I knew it was yet another skill I needed to learn. I had no clue I was recording history, the beginnings of a movement that would spread to 100 cities in the United States and more than 1,500 cities worldwide.

Later that evening as I struggled with my new YouTube channel, the old railway sign leaning against the brick wall in the apartment distracted me. The big white "3" painted on it took me back to the many classes I'd taken with Tavye. *Three, my Enneagram number!* The synchronicity spooked me in a comforting sort of way. "Focus,

Lisa, focus," I said out loud, forcing myself back to my task at hand. It was late and I needed to complete more lessons before Michele arrived the next day. After a full day of walking, it was hard to concentrate. I watched four or five more lessons until I could no longer absorb the material.

I then checked my Facebook page, where Debbie had posted a video of a six-year-old blonde girl who sang "Somewhere Over the Rainbow" for an audition on the TV series, *Britain's Got Talent.* "This song is perfect in describing your journey where 'dreams really do come true!!'" Debbie wrote. There were comments from Linda and Constance, my cousin Renee, my friends Janis and Patti and Glenda, and so many others who pushed me forward each day, their validation crucial to my confidence. Tonight, I labored through them. I was drained, hungry, and most likely dehydrated. I was nervous about going public with the notes I'd written earlier in the day, while sitting in the little garden behind the church. Even a tiny hint that my life was falling apart, my words would expose me.

> "I have a bad habit of trying to cram all I can into my days. Not just on this trip, but in my life in general. The more I can do, the more I have to mark off a list. The more lists I can make, the less time I have to delve deep into my soul. You see, I'm facing some new developments in my life at the moment and I need to dig. I need to deal with the confusion of what's behind and plan for what might be ahead of me."

18

"Day Seven - It shakes me up to write those words. My first week has flown by. I've worked very hard, not only walking, but also learning how to blog, how to maximize this iPhone, how to tag, add keywords, and basically learn the new language of SEO. Most days I get up by 6 or 6:30 to work on my paperwork and Atlanta clients. Then I walk for 5 - 6 hours, crash for an hour or so, and have a light dinner (usually yogurt or something from the deli). I plug away at the computer till 11 or 12 most nights — one night till almost 2 a.m. as my programming friend navigated me through the world of SEO. This focused time has been so good for me. It has allowed me to concentrate on learning as much I could, as rapidly as I can, about the new tools of my trade — social media."

I hit the "Publish" button on my blog post then powered down my computer.

I'd pushed hard my first few days in the city. My body, which arrived knotted and cramped and wound tight with stress and anticipation and unreasonable expectations, continued on autopilot, racing at its normal pace. I had conditioned it well to run on overdrive.

Michele was due in for the upcoming Fourth of July weekend, so I made a conscious decision to ease my walking schedule, to put aside my late-night writing and to forgo the tutorials.

When she first heard of my trip, my sister never once questioned my crazy 30-day scheme. Never during my marriage did she ever utter a single word of judgment, never asked for details about losing our home or how I was financing this trip, and she never questioned my leaving my family to come alone on this grand excursion. She did, however, tell me that I needed to climb to the crown of the Statue of Liberty, and she made reservations. The statue and surrounding park had been closed for years due to 9/11. Getting tickets was nearly impossible. Trust my sister, who loved researching and mapping out her vacations almost as much as the actual trip, to jump on the task and secure us two tickets — on the Fourth of July, no less!

I Googled the restaurants in my neighborhood, assuming reservations were required. They were all so much tinier than the ones back home, so I assumed they filled up fast. I was dying to try the Ethiopian and Moroccan restaurants I'd walked by, even the bistro around the corner whose menu board listed squid ink pasta, but I was still a bit squeamish about eating alone. I settled on a Cuban restaurant where prices were the most reasonable. I'd suggest to Michele that we eat there.

A couple of days earlier, after a long day of walking and then a good long nap, I woke up refreshed and with a new resolve. *I'm going out tonight, dammit, I'm going to do this!* and with that, I poured myself a glass of liquid courage. I would walk two blocks to the pretty little restaurant I'd passed a hundred times before. I hoped to meet people who lived in this neighborhood, someone like me, male or female, who I could talk with, just a simple back and forth, who was maybe my age or at least didn't judge me because I was Southern. I just wanted to feel like I belonged.

After showering that evening, I stepped in front of the mirror. Feeling uncomfortable and a bit silly, really, I pushed myself to stand at attention and face my naked body. I stood still, totally nude, focused on my wet hair. I watched a drip of water as it lingered on the lobe of my ear. I then moved to my eyes and my mouth, and down my neck to my shoulders. They looked broad and strong. They'd always been a point of pride. I pushed them back further, then lifted my chest as I took in a slow and deep breath. I was looking at a woman I hardly knew.

The woman in the mirror seemed a bit more svelte than the one who'd arrived here just a few days ago. A bit willowy, with a touch of elegance, I smiled at the confidence she held. She was exactly as I remembered her to be when she was young, in her twenties.

I took my time blow-drying my wet hair, rotating the brush around small strands, individually straightening it as I had been taught by my hair stylist. Emma had urged me to bring a straightening iron, but I scoffed at the idea. I won't have time for all that foolishness, I remember telling her. Tonight, I wished I had listened to her. "You're a pretty young lady, especially when you fix up," I could hear my Daddy say to the little girl I once was. I added a few drops of water into the bottle of thickened Max Factor foundation, then shook it vigorously. I smoothed it softly under my eyes and feathered its color under my chin.

Infused with an unfamiliar boldness, I felt a power bubbling up inside. I WILL, I started, walk in with my shoulders back, my head held high, and with a belief that even alone, I will enjoy myself and not feel lesser than the couples dining beside me. I even fantasized about meeting a nice man, but quickly trashed that thought. It frightened me, really.

In my long, flowery dress and with a steamy glow on my skin, I strolled down Perry Street. I headed toward the restaurant just two blocks away, the one whose sides opened to the sidewalk, the place I'd walked by time after time. I could hear young laughter drifting out onto the sidewalk, a faint song playing quietly under the voices. I could see the waiters, dressed in black with white aprons, navigating the sidewalk tables, wine glasses catching the reflections of the outside lights. Strings of green ivy hung from the rafters, swaying ever so slightly, dancing with the wind.

As I stepped closer, the internal chatter began. "Lisa, you're almost 60 years old. All the people in there are in their twenties and thirties." "You don't need to spend the money." I stepped closer to the front door and perused the menu posted outside. I tried to appear as if I was considering the food choices, but it was staged. I could feel the fear. I couldn't bring myself to walk inside. I could hear that cunning demon chip away at my courage, mocking me. "Poor thing, all dressed up and no date, no one to talk to." "Nothing worse than old people trying to act young." "Cougar!" I didn't want to be pitied. I didn't want to risk being judged. I just wanted someone to talk with. After a week, I was starving for a little human interaction.

As my dress blew in the hot wind, I could feel my hair thickening in the humidity. I wiped the beads of sweat from above my upper lip, then walked on. I was disappointed in myself. And angry, really. I passed by two other restaurants, each time talking to myself, trying to muster up the courage to stop and go in, but ultimately, I circled around a different block, where no one could see me, and then went home. Michele will be in town soon, I reasoned. We can go out then.

In her younger years, my sister was as much a risk-taker as I was. After 10 years as a successful attorney, Michele walked into her managing partner's office late one Thursday afternoon and quit to follow her dream of becoming a photojournalist. She did so without the security of another job, a huge no-no in my mother's eyes. But Michele was miserable in law. That very day, she walked out the front door of the law firm, clad in her lawyerly dark-grey suit, pantyhose, and pumps, mind you, and down the street into the local newspaper office where she asked to speak with someone in the photography department. "Okay, bring us a portfolio," the photo editor relented after she pressed for an interview. That was the beginning of her illustrious career as a photojournalist, with beats that included fires, robberies, and murders. She hung out of helicopters and maneuvered her way through Secret Service. The cops once awarded her with a bulletproof vest because she brought down a serial robber. A few years later, Nikon awarded her Grand Prize in their international photo contest, and her work earned her shots in Oprah's magazine, *O, Vanity Fair,* and *National Geographic' Traveler.*

The few times Michele and I traveled together, she normally

took the lead by doing all the planning, landing with a full itinerary securely in place. She became much more cautious when it came to travel, probably because she'd been robbed on a previous trip to New York. So, on this trip, Michele, the younger of us two, stepped into the shoes of the protector and instructed me to save the scary neighborhoods for her visit. "Wait until I get there so we can walk them together."

I was standing at the bottom of the escalator as Michele descended into the baggage claim area. For a second, I felt a bit smug, like a native welcoming a visitor to MY city. I took one of her bags and motioned her to follow me outside to the bus stand. "I've got us starting with Harlem," I announced.

As our bus proceeded toward 125th Street, I referred to my map, scoping out a route we could walk. Harlem was one of the neighborhoods on my list that had danger wrapped around it. Growing up in the South in the '6os, watching the six o'clock news, this north Manhattan neighborhood was portrayed as full of looting, murders, and the feared Black Panthers. The Riot of 1964 was still quite clear in my memory. My visual picture was one of trash-strewn streets, decaying tenement housing, and poverty-ridden youth hiding in dark alleyways, surviving through a life of violence. The names of the boulevards — MLK, Jr., Malcolm X, Frederick Douglass, Adam Clayton Powell, Jr. Boulevards — honored the civil rights activists who used Harlem as their podium. Nearly 50 years later, a sense of uneasiness remained inside both my sister and me.

Our bus rolled to a stop just past Malcolm X Boulevard. Michele and I shuffled to the back exit, following most of the others who were on the bus. I could see her move the strap of her shoulder bag across her chest, then secure it in close to her body with her right arm. I knew even without words that she was nervous. "Vigilant" was the word that came to mind to describe her demeanor.

As we stepped onto the curb and surveyed what was ahead, I could see the streets were wide and filled with light. The sidewalks were bustling with professionally and fashionably dressed people, name-brand coffee shops, and stores that painted the neighborhood as much more sophisticated than I'd imagined. The two of us strolled west on 125th, delighting in the many African handicrafts hawked by street vendors. We took photos of the iconic mosaic mural called "The Spirit of Harlem," and of course, the famous brass stars in the sidewalk at The Apollo. I made a mental note to return later in the week for Amateur Night but didn't dare tell Michele. I didn't want a lesson on why being out alone at night was unwise.

We jumped on the A train and headed south to Hell's Kitchen, another neighborhood on my list of uncertainties, mainly because of the ominous name. Except for a few trendy restaurants, it looked like a neighborhood on the verge of gentrification. Its red-bricked, nondescript buildings made it feel a bit sterile, its streets were fairly bare and subdued.

From there we walked over into Times Square where the body density changed dramatically. "Tourists!" I belted out, exasperated as if I were some bona fide New Yorker offended by the human clutter. I would no longer be caught dead holding up my iPhone in Times Square or wearing an "I (heart) NY" t-shirt in public. I'd only been in New York for a week and already I was copping an attitude.

Next, we rambled south through the Garment District, and on to one of Michele's must-see spots, the lush urban jungle called the Flower District. Crowding the concrete sidewalks of 28th Street, between 6th and 7th Avenues, were shrubs and trees, rows and rows of potted plants, and, of course, cut flowers in every color imaginable. We searched for a particular flower wholesaler she had found online but, much to our disappointment, we were too late to capture photos. Flowers were delivered before stores and hotels opened their doors, so all we found was an empty warehouse and a man who invited us back the next day at 4:00 a.m. "Come back and shoot then," he said to Michele, eyeing the fancy camera that hung from her neck. "I will if you will?" she threw at me and grinned. While I was quite

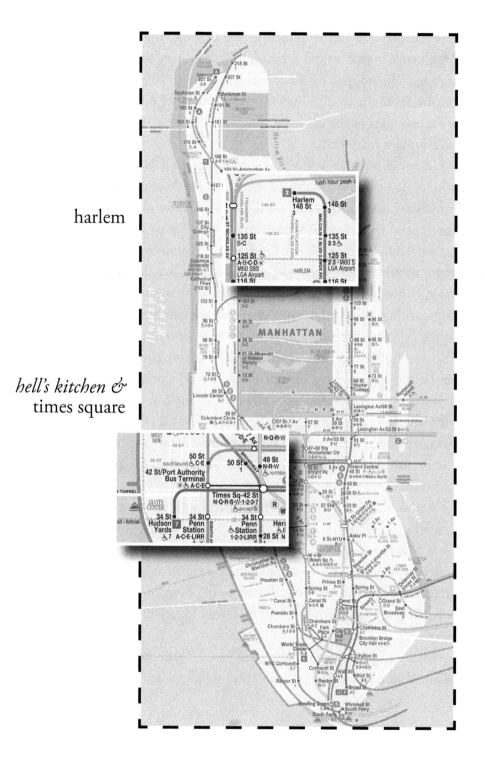

harlem

hell's kitchen &
times square

amused that Michele would even consider walking the streets of Manhattan at such an hour, I was fairly certain we wouldn't follow through. We stopped for a late lunch at a dingy little Cuban place nearby, sat at the counter and thoroughly enjoyed our tamales and fried plantains as the 40-something waitress flirted with her cute bodybuilder customer.

In some ways, it was a movie moment on a New York City kind of day, complete with soundtrack. As we descended down the 23rd Street station to head back to the Village, we melted into the murmur of the crowd. A slight rumble of trains passing along the tracks, the muffled sound of a loudspeaker announcing the arriving train, all wrapped in the notes of a sole violinist. This is my New York, I thought, as I motioned to Michele that our #1 train was approaching. After a short two-stop ride, we climbed the steps out of the 14th Street station and ascended back into my comfort zone. The storefronts and delis were familiar, the flower market around the corner appeared as I expected. I showed the neighborhood off as if it was mine. I walked my sister over a couple of long blocks to give her a glimpse of the High Line, the elevated railway park I'd bragged about, then another eight or nine blocks until finally, up the narrow staircase to my apartment. We crashed for an hour or so before venturing out to dinner.

As our maître d' escorted us to a table, I scanned the crowd, the laughter and smiles, the chatter. The energy felt so alive; I was fueled by it. Maneuvering through the tight aisles, I remarked that I loved how close together the tables were. It felt so intimate, even between strangers. *I've got to get past eating alone*, my thoughts wandered, as Michele and I sat down. I would be forced to talk to people at the next table, the voice of fear pushed back.

Michele interrupted my thoughts with, "I still can't believe you planned all this, and you planned it so well!"

I woke up the next morning, pumped, and in my usual can't-waste-a-moment! mode. Michele, on the other hand, was moving slowly. I had a momentary jolt, sensing my space had been invaded. I'd loved living such a freeing seven days up to this point, with no one's wishes to consider, no schedule to keep, and with time of total quiet, time to reflect. I began scolding myself for having guests; their presence would slow my progress, I feared.

I wanted to slip in a visit to the farmers' market at Abingdon Square, just a few blocks away. I had read a lot about the GrowNYC movement in New York and their Greenmarkets, plus I was curious to see firsthand how a big city with no farming space handled growing foods. I figured Michele would probably love the photo opportunity. So, we threw on some clothes and off we went.

The crowd was mostly young women, mothers, I imagined, out doing their weekly shopping. I watched intently as two women walked side by side, deep in conversation, without any sense of urgency. I wondered if they were career women. After all, the cost of living in Manhattan must certainly require two incomes for most people, I decided. Did they meet each other through their children's school or sports team, or maybe through church like many of my friends and I did in Atlanta? I'd not seen any swim clubs or YMCAs. There are lots of small parks scattered here and there in the Village, but none seemed large enough for kids to ride bikes or even host a birthday party. Do they have rooms large enough to make costumes and paint sets for their kids' plays? Do they go all out on big fundraising to-dos, like the spaghetti dinners and spring fairs in my neighborhood of Buckhead? Do their kids even go to public schools or are they all in private ones? How do the kids get to school, I wondered, having not noticed a single yellow school bus? Certainly not by subway, I hoped.

Duh, it's July! I chuckled when I realized it was summer and school was out. Even so, my curiosity heightened. I wanted to find a school and just see inside. I was dying to peer inside a real New York home and into people's workspaces, to get a taste of real life in this city.

Over the next few weeks I would return two or three times to this little Saturday market. I began to recognize the vendors and they me, and I loved that. Each time I came, I picked up on conversations that I identified with, whether grumblings about husbands or frustrations with a boss or motherhood. They were no different from me, really. It was here, at this simple little neighborhood market, that I felt most like a real part of this city.

My daughter Emma was due in from Atlanta later that morning. Although I felt ashamed that I'd been unable to pay for her plane ticket, I was ecstatic that she was coming. She'd insisted she had enough babysitting money saved to cover her airfare.

After showering, Michele and I headed to LaGuardia to retrieve Emma. She persuaded me to take the train, although I was still a tad unsure of the subway maps or how long trips would take. I was never good "at map," as my Daddy would say. "It's easy," she pressed, after researching it thoroughly. "At 14th, we take the eastbound L train. Two stops later, we switch to the F, which runs north and over to Queens." Once at the Jackson Heights/Roosevelt Station, we'd transfer to the bus that would deliver us straight to the airport. I knew how to maneuver that station.

Well, I thought I did. We exited the station and, once on the street, we had to re-enter and repay in order to get our bus transfers. While outside, though, I caught sight of a few women hawking something from a rusty grocery cart. In it was a huge silver can with steam billowing out of the top of it. "Tamales $1" was scrawled on a small piece of poster board taped to the side of the cart. I glanced over to Michele, caught her attention and grinned. "Do we dare?" We each bought ourselves two, and off we went, back into the station to catch the bus to LaGuardia.

Michele and I walked into baggage claim just in time to see Emma come down the escalator. I was a bit taken aback by the sight of her. It was my first time seeing her since Jim and I split, and I was nervous about how I'd address it, if at all. I was so confused about everything, and my emotions were still so terribly raw. As her parent, I felt so inadequate, totally incapable of offering any hope for the future, any stability. I was anxious to see her, to hug her, and to make sure she knew I loved her. That's about all I could offer her at this point.

Glancing at her, I saw my own self in her, back in 1977, on my first trip to the city. I was close to her same age. She stood tall and unashamed of her six-foot height and seemingly unaffected by her natural beauty. Her shoulders were back, her straight posture adding an air of confidence and sophistication. *I used to be like that,* I thought.

I grabbed her backpack as she spotted her suitcase rounding the baggage carousel. We then stopped to buy her a transit ticket, then the three of us headed for the M60 bus for our hour-long ride to the northwest side of Manhattan.

Our tour of the island started at Grant's Tomb in the lush Riverside Park neighborhood that overlooks the Hudson River, then we walked several blocks south through some of the most beautiful streetscapes I'd seen while in Manhattan. I felt as if I was in the rolling hills of Virginia, the streets and avenues undulating unlike anywhere else in Manhattan. The bell tower of the majestic Riverside Church with its Neo-Gothic architecture rose high above the other buildings, its stone carvings rivaled those I'd seen on Notre Dame in Paris. I remembered from my research that it was the tallest church in America, and that it was known for embracing political debate, which I found counter to any church I'd ever attended. "Separation of church and state" is what I'd been taught. I had to take a picture,

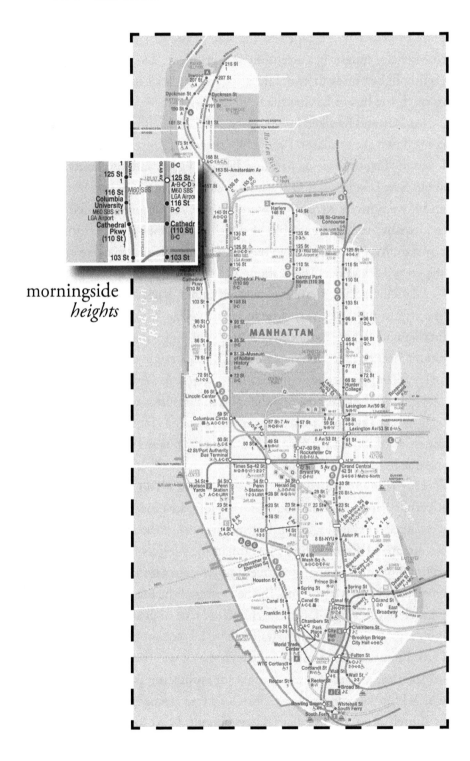

morningside
heights

though, of the church's parking lot entrance. It was the first time I'd ever seen a church charge for parking!

It quickly turned into a day of photo ops. Emma posed on the sundial that centered the impeccably manicured South Lawn of the Columbia University campus; the 14-columned Butler Library served as her backdrop. "This is as close as any of us Weldons'll ever come to getting in THIS school!" she added, and with that the three of us sunk down into the 116th Street station and made our way to the lower east side of the island, to a restaurant Michele was intent on trying.

"I'll treat," chimed Michele as I pushed open the doors to Katz Deli. "I've always wanted to see this place where Meg ..." She caught herself before recounting the "I'll have what she's having" scene made famous by Meg Ryan in *When Harry Met Sally*. Emma was with us, and I knew my sister well: We were raised by the same mother, and the word "orgasm" was certainly NOT EVER to be uttered, acknowledged, much less discussed in public. Even for the topic to come up between Michele and me was uncomfortable. Honestly, I was quite shocked she even brought up the scene in the movie, as I pictured her as much more private and hesitant to discuss anything related to sex.

It made me realize how little I knew about my younger sister and her current life. Michele and I fought like cats and dogs growing up. I left for college and those tensions disappeared, but as soon as she arrived at college, I graduated and left. Never did we live in the same town, nor visit each other more than a time or two per year. In the days before email, we hardly phoned each other because long-distance calls were expensive. Our lives had taken such different paths, our relationship a bit private and formal. Neither of us was good about divulging personal thoughts and feelings, not with each other, or anyone, really. But hey, that was par for the course in our family.

The three of us entered the mammoth deli and took our number, lining up behind other tourists. The place was loud and crowded.

When our turn came, we walked down the serving line, perusing heaps and heaps of kosher pastrami, brisket, tongue, and corned beef. Chopped liver and liverwurst. Giant mounds of chicken and salmon salads, latkes, knishes, and matzo ball soup—so many things I'd never seen before, much less tasted. The man behind the counter barked, and with a firm grin, pushed us to quit gawking and holding up the line. "This is New York," I winced and mumbled under my breath to Michele. It was all part of the ceremony and she seemed to love it as much as I did. With trays in hand the three of us edged our way to a table and waited for a young man to wipe his damp rag across it. I glanced down at the sandwich on my plate, piled ridiculously high, spilling over with luscious red meat wedged between two plump slices of rye bread.

My mind began to tiptoe away. The clacking of the dishes and voices receded to a background rumble, the smells dulled, my senses were elsewhere. I sat across from my daughter and thought about how differently she and I were at her age. I was deathly afraid of the wrath of my mother. Because of that I was the perfect child in high school, seldom attending parties, and certainly never experimenting with alcohol or cigarettes like many of my friends. One boy French-kissed me, but I quickly rinsed my mouth out with soap, thinking it was dirty. I would never confide in my mother about things going on with my friends. If she asked, I lied. She was stern and unwavering about what she thought was right and wrong. I had made myself a promise before Emma was born. *I will have a healthy relationship with my daughter. She will be able to talk to me about anything,* I vowed.

"I'm not sure she even loved us," I had once said to Michele about our mother. "Oh, she loved us, but I don't think she ever liked us," she retorted, trying to soften the hurt of such an inconceivable statement. We agreed that our mother loved the successes we had. She bragged about my sister's career as an attorney but hardly said a word when she quit to become a photographer. Similarly, my mother was always disappointed I never finished school as an architect. Visual design was "like painting pictures of Elvis on velvet," she barked when I told her I was changing my major. "Michele got the brains," she recited over and over again. Michele aced school and I eked by with Bs and Cs. I, on the other hand, got the curly hair, she said, which I think was her way of saying I was the pretty one.

Growing up it felt like my mother was most proud of my appearance, my pretty face and Twiggy figure. The same with her grandchildren. Prettiness, I assumed, was associated with class in her mind. She loved to brag about our accomplishments, not who we were as people. She often embellished the stories, to the point where Michele and I had to correct her. She was so proud when I got elected as Azalea Trail Maid, a hostess of the city, or chosen to model for the teen board at our local department store. Or when I pledged the right sorority in college. Or when I started dating Grady Lucas, whose family owned a telephone company, or Jeff Greenberg, a transplant from New York whose father had a business on Park Avenue. Those items were all worthy of her attention, my sister and I agreed. There were times we felt like trophy children.

Oh, I was a terribly strict and rigid mother, much more than many of my friends. I'd certainly made a lot of mistakes, but there's one thing I did right. I raised a daughter who could speak her mind, who was confident and not afraid to be different. Plus, she knew I loved her, liked her, and was in awe of her.

And of that, I was damn proud.

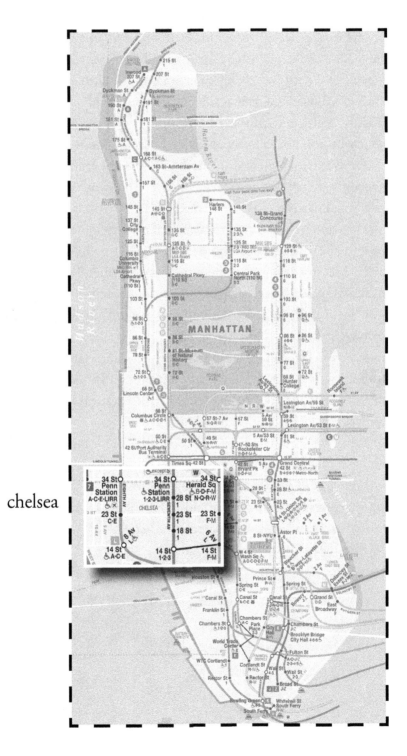

chelsea

20

The next day Emma and her friend Caroline, Michele, and our cousin Megan, a dance teacher in town for a conference, all met up in front of a store on Fifth Avenue. From there we spent a good part of the day strolling up the great thoroughfare considered one of the most expensive and fashionable streets in the world. We toured the famous Eataly, the enormous Italian market that houses restaurants, a wine store, a pizza station, and kitchenware department—all under one roof. Circulating through the expanse of pastas and cheeses, with our cameras clicking, we were the obvious tourists amongst the well-seasoned New York gourmands. The prices were a bit steep, so we each settled for a gelato, then walked on up the Avenue, sticking our heads in Saks and Bergdorf Goodman and gawking at the bling in the Tiffany's window. We found a trendy little donut shop, its walls adorned with 20 or 30 donut-shaped pillows, all in different fabrics and adornments. We agreed to split a green tea doughnut, but after having varying opinions about its taste, we felt the $3 per doughnut cost was a fair price to see the artwork on the walls.

Megan had to get back to her young dancers, so we hugged and said our goodbyes, then walked over to the 53rd Street Station, where we caught the E train south to the Meatpacking District. Our first stop was at the corner of 13th and Washington, where I asked Michele to take a shot of me in front of the wall painted with black and white graffiti. I had seen it on my first day, and I wanted it as the background for my new Facebook profile photo.

Next, we made our way to Chelsea Market. Caroline, a foodie, raved about its restaurants while I piped in about the unique architecture. Located between 15th and 16th Streets, it's a cross between a food court, a shopping mall, an office building, and a television production facility. Until 1958, this structure was home to the old National Biscuit Company, or Nabisco, bakers of everything from saltine crackers to Oreos. Today, the upper floors are home to the Food Network, The Oxygen Network, and Google. The developers and architects boast its "industrial archeology"—an unprecedented blend of the old and the new, old rusty pipes and wide-planked floors plus red, shiny handrails and hot-orange neon signs. "A harmonious balance," I remarked to my group as I played tour guide through the halls. "Just like when we old folks are equally honored as young people," I finished, trying to slip in a life lesson for the young ones.

Just a few days after arriving in New York, I'd taken a call from a woman in Auburn's Office of Development. When she asked for an appointment the following week, I got right to the point. "I can't. I'm in New York for a month." She then pressed for a later date, and I resisted again, this time with an emotional plea. "I have two in Auburn right now and another starting in a few weeks. I have zero money left, as I'm sure you can imagine!" Of course, she saw my answer as an opening to ask about the kids' fields of study. "Emma, my oldest, is majoring in art and photography. She'd like to work for a magazine." It was then that the woman told me that the executive editor at *Food Network Magazine*, located in Chelsea Market, was an Auburn grad. She offered to facilitate an internship for Emma if she was interested.

Oh, I couldn't have designed anything more perfect for my daughter! She was a real foodie, so I envisioned my daughter as maybe a stylist or a food photographer. "Would this not be THE most incredible place to work?" I posed to her.

I had always urged Emma to step out of her comfort zone, to move somewhere like New York. She was less enthralled with New York than I was, but here was the perfect opportunity to stretch her boundaries, I pressed. It seemed the perfect internship that would lead to her dream career, and in such a creative work environment!

As the others went ahead, I sat on one of the benches in Chelsea Market and Googled the internship guidelines required by the magazine and found that the deadline was only a week or so away. I then remembered that a friend's daughter had done a similar summer internship at a Conde Nast magazine. Excited about this new possibility, I rushed to catch up with the girls and to share the details with Emma. I offered to call the girl's mother for more details, but Emma stopped me with an eye roll. "I'll do it, Mom, I know Paige. I'll Facebook her." With that the girls split off from Michele and me for the rest of the afternoon. We agreed to meet back at the apartment at six, in time for dinner.

"Baby, if you want me to help you do this, you know I will," I said to her later that evening as we sat on the back porch of the quaint Cuban restaurant under the night sky, enjoying our cocktails. "If you don't have time, I can get you a website up and running in about two hours. I can load your portfolio onto it … if this is something you want to do. I just hate for you to lose an opportunity like this." She went on to explain that she was overloaded at school and just didn't have the time to think about it right now. "Mom, you just don't understand. I even slept through my job yesterday afternoon. I just can't do another thing." And with that she added, "Caroline's signed up to be au pair in Paris and already has an apartment lined up. Maybe I could find an internship there," Emma said, "especially since I'm fluent in French." Her words stopped me cold.

It was then that I realized she had no interest in living in New York. I had to face that I was trying to re-live a dream of mine through my child. I had to let it go. After all, it was her life, not mine.

My days as a mother were winding down. My first little chicken had begun to flap her wings and was about to permanently leave the nest. I wanted a daughter who felt comfortable talking openly with me, one who'd even stand up to me and be confident in making her own decisions. I never had the courage to do so with my own mother, and it was important that I change that. As I glanced across the table at my daughter, I knew I had succeeded.

"When are you moving here, Mom?" her voice sliced through my silence, the muscles in my throat tightened as I fought to stop the flow of tears. My God, was she giving me permission to step outside my role as mother and to embrace my own dream?

After dinner, the girls went their separate way, off to some cool, hip place with kids their own age. Michele and I ended our day with a nighttime stroll on the High Line, fast becoming one of my favorite spots in all of Manhattan. This mile-and-a-half-long elevated park wove through the frenetic streets of the west side, offering a respite from urban jungle below.

That night as I pulled the dark sheets over my tired body, I went deep into reflection on my day. It was such a rare and special gift that my sister and my daughter and I had this sliver of time together. It was a time of both laughter and openness, in a space where we all felt free to share our true selves with each other, maybe for the first time ever. I wondered if we would ever have this chance again. Or would we ever make time for it again?

I also began to understand how running away to New York, and removing myself from the familiar, had opened space for healing. My chaotic life back in Atlanta had left me frazzled and emotionally drained, and although I had an army of friends to help me, it felt fundamentally wrong to ask them to leave me alone. As an introvert I needed to reserve every single ounce of energy I could muster, and within the solitude I needed to renew it. For 26 years, from the time I married Jim and then had kids, I never stepped out of the rat race, never long enough to even see the path I was headed down.

A sound in the next room interrupted my thoughts. I chuckled, lightening up as I remembered Emma's remark at dinner. "This is the very first time I drank wine with you, Mom!" Her memories of this day would always be quite different.

21

It was July 4th, 2011. Our tickets for the Statue of Liberty were for 10:00 a.m. sharp. We would lose our entry if we were a minute late, the fine print on the back of the tickets warned us. Michele suggested we take the quick and direct route—the subway. She was the one who always arrived on time, even early. I, the one who always pushed the envelope, wanted to meander through the streets and parks and shops along the way. I was so afraid of missing something. "My app says it will only take us 49 minutes to get to Battery Park," I pressed, noting that our final destination was only 2.4 miles away. I was anxious to get back on my regimen so I could mark off my list the areas I'd not yet walked. "I have a duty to fulfill," I joked with my sister. And with that, she reluctantly agreed.

We took off down Perry Street a few minutes after 8:00. As we neared the corner of Hudson, I suggested we take a small detour to the quaint little cupcake shop, Magnolia Bakery, which was made famous by the TV series, *Sex and the City*. Michele shot me a glance, seeing right through my antics, but I knew she'd relent. When it came to sweets, neither of us had much willpower.

We were lucky; only five people were ahead of us in line. Michele ordered a carrot cupcake; I went for something a little less healthy, one with a double shot of chocolate. After checking out, I glanced at my app and saw that we had a 51-minute walk ahead of us. With sweets in hand, we took off down Bleecker Street and got back to our route. Michele led at a feverish pace.

Just as we crossed over Seventh Avenue, Michele turned her head back to me and smiled impishly. She then darted her eyes over to the red and yellow sign. Murray's, the famous cheese shop she'd mentioned wanting to visit, was just ahead of us. "Quickly!" I reprimanded her with a smirk. I wanted to go in as badly as she did, of course. In and out in just a few minutes, we took a right onto Sixth, then veered onto Church Street, which in my mind, put us within an easy shot of our destination. "Twenty more blocks," I assured her. "Easy!"

We passed by St. Paul's Chapel, the "oldest public building in continuous use in New York City," its sign read, which served as a place of rest and refuge for recovery workers at the World Trade Center site. I had read that the 9/11 exhibit inside the chapel was quite moving, but time was clicking away and we still had another six or eight blocks to go. Michele and I both were wearing out, and we hadn't even gotten to the base of the 354 steps that we had to climb inside Lady Liberty.

Battery Park was crawling with people: young and old, from here and from abroad, all wearing red, white, and blue. An older man was wearing an American flag tie-dyed T-shirt that I imagined him buying at a Joe Cocker concert. A young German-speaking teen was carrying a red, white, and blue knitted handbag. A little kid licked a popsicle that dripped red and blue down his little white outfit, his dad was too distracted to even notice. The family behind us in line was from New Hampshire. All six of them—grandma and grandpa included—proudly wore navy shirts that featured Old Glory. Michele, the photographer, had a field day capturing their patriotism on film.

We made it just in time to hand over our IDs to the guard whose eyes looked at us with laser intensity up one side and down the other before he searched our purses and then waved us through the metal detector. I hadn't added it all up until just now. It was not only the Fourth of July and the 125th anniversary of the Statue of Liberty. It was also the tenth year after the attacks on the World Trade Center. "Sitting ducks" were the words that flashed through my mind, but

I pushed the thought aside as I began the strenuous climb that had been described as 27 stories in height. The tight and claustrophobic stairwell had no air conditioning. At almost 100 degrees, only fools climbed on.

Once at the top, in the cramped space inside Lady Liberty's crown, it was just Michele and me for the first five or six minutes in the hot and humid chamber. The only sounds I could hear as I peered through the slits in her crown were the faint clicks of Michele's camera. All the street noises were gone, the honking taxis and hawking street vendors. All my worries of back home, all the responsibility to my followers had disappeared into thin air. For a moment, all I could hear was my own heartbeat saying to me, "You did it, Lisa, you did it!"

Our next stop was Ellis Island. All around me I heard a babble of languages—German, French, Spanish, Chinese, some I couldn't identify. My mind floated through all the sepia-toned photos that hung on the walls, while imagining myself being among fellow immigrants who were in line to be questioned, checked for diseases, and processed. It struck me as strangely ironic that just as my forefathers had done, I too, had come to New York in pursuit of a dream for a better life. I remembered hearing about a distant relative who came through this massive Registry Hall, a Scot named Angus Campbell. I scanned the lists they had available and found hundreds of Angus Campbells, quite a few from Scotland, so I simply made a mental note and promised myself I'd do the research. *So many stories left untold,* I thought, as Michele and I boarded the ferry back to Manhattan.

As we stepped off the ferry onto Battery Park, we were drawn to a large crowd circling a cast of street performers. Five young men, all shirtless, their ebony skin glistening with sweat, performed acrobatic feats that seemed impossible for a human body. For ten solid minutes, their bodies contorted to drumbeats, the crowds going wild. One performer stopped suddenly, pulled a young boy from the audience, and checked his pockets for money. The audience roared.

battery
park

"I know what you're thinking," one of the men yelled to the audience. "Why are these good-looking Black guys out here?" the cast yelled in unison. "Could it be for money?" one asked, then paused to a quietened audience. "Yeahhhh! This is how we make our living!" They roared, "Obama wants change. WE WANT DOLLARS!" and with that the audience howled as they went from person to person collecting contributions. *God, I love this city.* There was a surprise on every single street corner. Could I ever get enough?

We finished off the night in Chelsea, on the banks of the Hudson River, crammed alongside thousands of people watching a spectacular array of fireworks. Although New York always seems to do everything in a grander style, tonight's show in honor of the Statue of Liberty's 125th year promised to be beyond anything ever done before. Michele and I secured our spot on 34th Street. Emma and Caroline, who'd been doing whatever 20-year-olds do, met us an hour later. Police presence was heavy, patrolling cordoned-off areas, trying to control the crowd. The crowd hushed as the show began with a flyover of F-15 Eagle jets and NYPD helicopters. Six different synchronized bursts of color exploded again and again, illuminating the sky for almost 30 minutes. Later that night while back at the apartment, reading about the event online, I was not surprised to learn that over 40,000 shells of fireworks were shot in all.

"What do you think this might be?" Michele asked later that evening as she walked in from the bedroom. I could hear concern in her voice. She turned her back to me and showed me the back of her legs. The area from her lower shins to her ankles was covered in a hot red rash. There were several streaks that seemed to be shooting upward from the inflamed area. "Streaks are never good," I thought. I laid my hand on her leg and immediately felt the heat.

My mind quickly catalogued everything we'd eaten that day, fearing an allergic reaction. Only once had I experienced an episode, eight or nine years earlier, when I ate scallops. My entire body broke out in hives, my face swelled, my throat closed up. I couldn't breathe.

I vividly remember the doctor telling me I'd gotten to the emergency room just in time. Was Michele in danger?

I moved calmly into management mode. My mind traced the steps I'd taken just recently. Although I had walked much of the neighborhood, I had only a slight recollection of a hospital near 12th or 13th Street, somewhere near the 14th Street station, but I certainly couldn't pinpoint its exact location. I couldn't even remember seeing a doc-in-a-box. A moment of panic shot through me. I didn't even know who to call.

"I think we ought to go get it checked out." I suggested we call a cab, "they'll know where a medical center is," I said to her.

"Let me look online," Michele answered calmly as she walked over to my laptop, oblivious to the panic I was feeling.

After a few minutes, she read: "It's called The Disney Rash, also known as exercise-induced vasculitis." Broken capillaries caused by the heat that reflects off hot pavement. People who walk too much, like all day at Disney or Epcot, often get it, she reported. "Or fools who walk all the way to the Statue of Liberty!" We both got a chuckle out of it, but at the same time I realized I had no one here I could call on if an emergency arose. No one.

Our next morning started with a flurry of activity, as if a sergeant had just entered the barracks. I jumped up to fix a quick breakfast, a bowl of fruit and muffins. Michele pulled the sheets and pillowcases, and poor, bleary-eyed Emma was instructed to hurry up and shower. "No time to dally," my sister commanded. Clothes were packed into suitcases with military precision and within a few minutes, the vacation was over, and it was time to move on! Emma had a noon flight and Michele's was soon thereafter. Although I felt there was little need to rush, Michele insisted they get an early start toward the airport. I had offered to call a driver, but she had carefully plotted out a train route and was comfortable with it, plus I knew her. She didn't want to spend the extra money.

My sister led at an anxious pace, with Emma and I following, down Perry Street toward the Christopher/Sheridan Square station. There the two of them would take the train up to Times Square and connect with the #7 train, then get on a bus to their terminal.

We hugged and bade our farewells and, as my sister and daughter disappeared down into the station, I felt flushed with emotions. I stood there still, blocking the entryway, as if lost in a trance. I could feel commuters detouring around me, but I needed the pause, and I took it. For just a few days, I had unleashed myself from work and responsibilities. I'd subdued my drive and allowed myself the joys of laughter and companionship and for that, I was proud. I'd been able to step aside and see myself, and my role as a mother, through a clearer lens. It was all a step forward for me and I knew it. It was a shift, and it felt healthy.

Coming back into consciousness, I turned and walked a few steps to the newsstand where I treated myself to a *New York Times*. With paper in hand, I started back down Christopher Street heading toward Bleecker, then Charles and Greenwich, and finally onto Perry Street. Passing all the stores and shops and brownstones, I saw them differently than I had in the days before. No architectural details jumped out at me, no interesting characters caught my attention, no blog stories popped in my head. The colors of the landscape blended into a muted familiarity. The frivolity of the weekend was over, the vacation aura dissipating. Sensing the cloud of duty move back over me, I felt my body tighten. I began to rifle through what work lay ahead of me, as I often did most Sunday nights. Today was no different.

Once home, I climbed the old, narrow staircase up to my second-story apartment, tiptoeing on the treads I knew would creak the loudest. Once back inside, I booted up the computer, started a second pot of coffee, stripped the sheets off the sofa bed, then started the washing machine. I walked back into the bedroom and laid down flat on my back. I closed my eyes, drew in a slow chest full of air and relished in the fact that once again, I had quiet, and the place all to myself. I dreamed of falling back asleep, simply wasting the day, but I eventually shamed myself into tackling the tasks at hand. After a couple swigs of hot coffee, I slid my unwilling body—and spirit—into that lime green plastic chair.

Before my trip I made a fairly complete list of all the skills I needed to learn, and under each skill I listed sub-categories. First on the list, for instance, was "Website Design," and under it were: (1) WordPress, (2) user experience, (3) functionality, and the list went on. I fell short, however, in identifying the tasks I needed to complete in order to re-brand myself, the end goal of this trip. I had no idea how to parlay my talents or where my experience was most useful. How did I want to be labeled, or what should my job title be? I'd been an advertising art director all these years, but now there were titles and competencies I had no idea even existed.

I put off having to make that decision by turning my attention to all the new media outlets now available to me and my clients. I'd grown up in a business whose marketing tools were limited to newspapers and magazines, TV and radio, brochures and billboards. Now there were a plethora of platforms on which to market, and many had a real person connected to them, which I found fascinating. I could see who I was engaging with or advertising to on Facebook, and their instant feedback—in likes or shares—was intoxicating. I loved peeking at the "About" section on people's blogs to determine whether I had anything in common with them. All this was like candy to me, and it led me down a bunch of online rabbit holes. One such was a consortium of female bloggers called BlogHer. Being a new blogger myself, I was curious to see how it worked. I opened an account, then began loading the information they required: "Location: New York City + Atlanta, Perry Street, United States." Oh, you can just imagine how much I loved typing *that!* I then uploaded my photo, the title of my blog, but I quit at the next request, one asking for a few words about myself. I then wandered into another area listing the most widely-read female bloggers across the U.S. I'd learned that bloggers have a camaraderie between them, and often help each other cross-promote. I jotted down the URLs of ten who seemed most similar in age and interest area and committed to reach out to them. MidlifeBloggers.com topped my list. I scrolled through Google and found another site listing bloggers who lived in the immediate area of my apartment. I made a separate list and promised to connect with a few of them over a cup of coffee. I was on a roll this morning!

Then I jumped over to a tutorial on emailing, another piece of the marketing puzzle. Once finished I set up a basic YouTube account and tweaked my LinkedIn page. Although this ate up most of my afternoon, time flew by. Learning all this was invigorating. I felt empowered, my creative mind having a heyday with all these new tools.

I learned a lot online, but I really missed face-to-face instruction. I wanted to sit in a classroom where I could stay singularly focused. I needed to ask questions and get answers from a real, live teacher. Plus, I was curious about other students, so I searched online and found a corporate training firm that specialized in marketing. I registered for a two-hour course on social media, and then locked in two classes at the Apple Store and another through MeetUp.

Last on my day's to-do list was to try my hand at PR, or public relations. I researched instructions on how to prepare a press release for publications that might find interest in my midlife reinvention story. This is where it got tough. I was forced to define myself and this journey of mine, and to make decisions about my goals. More importantly, I had to find a way to disguise my age, or skew dates of graduation and employment, those previously redlining my resume and viability. "Lipstick on a pig" were the words that came to mind. After much chagrin and many hours, I settled on:

Atlanta Woman Remarkets Herself by Walking Every Square Mile of Manhattan

July 5, 2011 — Lisa Weldon, a 30-year veteran of the advertising business, landed in NYC this week to walk one square mile per day until she has covered the entire island of Manhattan. On her walks she will Facebook, blog, and tweet about people she meets and experiences she finds—all in an attempt to remake and remarket herself as a viable marketing professional, one who understands both traditional advertising as well as social media.

Ms. Weldon devised this plan to force herself to learn first-hand the tools of social media, the new platform in the market-ing business. "I know print, radio, and TV like the back of my hand. Social media is the most exciting thing to happen to our business and I want to know as much as I can about it," says Ms. Weldon. "It's hard to find folks who can bridge between the traditional and the new media; I plan to be that person."

Ms. Weldon attended a PR conference two years ago and heard many participants voice frustration about the great divide in this new world of advertising and marketing. CEOs said they recognized the need for social media but communicate with Blackberries, emails and fax machines. The new hires text, Facebook, tweet, and Skype. The two sides don't even speak the same language.

"After that conference, I decided to become a bridge over that gulf. 'I've spent the last year learning everything I could about the new media. I'm walking the walk to prove to clients, or a possible new employer, that I know what I'm talking about.'"

The instant I pushed the "Distribute" button, I panicked. I started second-guessing myself, overanalyzing the words I'd chosen. *Screw it,* I quickly corrected myself, and with that I shoved myself away from the table and walked toward the huge front windows. Knees locked in place, I bent forward at my waist, slowly reaching down until my palms lay flat on the floor. As I sucked in my stomach, the back of my waist burned with pain, but it was exactly what I needed after eight hours slumped over a computer.

Just as I stood back up, the phone interrupted my reverie. I saw that it was Jim and stopped myself. I decided not to answer. I felt a world away from him, so removed. I missed him, but that's the way it was supposed to be. I had made the cut and now had to accept the consequences. I let it go to voicemail.

"The check didn't come," were the only words I heard as the message played. I panicked. I had calculated the very day each of my payments was to arrive, and this client cut checks only on Fridays. They arrived on Mondays, religiously. I would deposit it, then have funds by Tuesday. If, for some reason the check didn't follow those strict guidelines, it would be an entire pay cycle before it would arrive. Since this Fourth of July fell on a Monday, I was prepared for it not to arrive till Tuesday. It was Tuesday afternoon and no check. My bank balance was down to $16.

His message sent my mind spiraling. *I have no safety net. Do I tuck my tail and ask Jim for money? How much food do I have in the refrigerator? How long can I survive on $16? I can refill my plastic bottles with water.* As I catalogued all my possibilities, I could feel my face pulse with heat and a burning sensation building in my chest. *Go for a walk, Lisa! Walk,* I coached myself, knowing good and well that this news would paralyze me.

The sun was beginning to dip into the horizon when I left the apartment and headed toward the river. I pushed myself for two and a half miles until I reached the island's southernmost tip. I then turned around and pushed myself another two and a half miles until I reached my home. I took a long, hot shower then crawled into bed, turning on the air conditioner beside my bed. *I can survive a week off Campbell's soup*, I convinced myself as I tossed and turned. I had done it before; I could do it again.

The next morning, as soon as I came into consciousness, fear gripped me. My back stung with stress; my head throbbed with worry.

I reached for my phone to check the time, then did the math. I'd slept only two or three hours. I sat up, then brought my knees up to my chest. Dropping my chin, I rolled my head back and forth, back and forth, my neck muscles groaning like a fraying rope. The sun tore through the shades and I could feel its rays lash across my chest. Pulling the black comforter over my face, I hid in the safety of darkness.

Nothing in my life paralyzed me more than the fear of running out of money. Jim and I had been through so much financial crap that I had become hyper-vigilant, almost obsessive about my every dime we spent. And I'd certainly suffered panic attacks over the lack of it. *I should've never come to New York with so little, I hammered away at myself. I'm smarter than this. I should go home now.* But of course, I didn't have enough to cover the change fee on my airline ticket.

I mentally rifled through the few client invoices that were still outstanding, praying one would get paid sooner than it was due. I could hardly concentrate, feeling my panic spiral wider and wider. *How will I pay the mortgage if the house doesn't sell? How will I afford to move? Will anyone give me credit ever again? Where will I live?* Fear, anger, hopelessness all took turns with my psyche.

I thought about the homeless man who I'd seen night after night, sleeping just outside my window. Although I never imagined myself so desperate, he became almost symbolic of the future I was facing, a constant reminder.

I'm not even safe in this apartment. If anything happens, I have no one to call for help. I have no family here, no friends. No one. If I need medical care, I don't even know where there's a hospital or a clinic around here. I don't have a credit card, nor the cash to cover my deductible. If I had to call an ambulance, do I even remember the address of this place?

I panicked, hydroplaning out of control. *Get up, get up out of bed,* I could hear my inner coach. *Just move, Lisa.* But my body began to tremble, sweat coated my palms. My heart raced, pounding as if trying to escape my chest.

And then, the feeling of inadequacy. *What kind of parent am I?* I wanted so badly to treat Emma to a cute top or a pair of shoes, or God, just anything she could say she got in New York, to remind her of her trip, but no, I didn't even have the money to pay for her plane ticket.

I grabbed a pen, scrawling on the pages of my journal:

What a failure I am. I should've asked Michele to lend me some money, but I would rather die than do that. I'm the oldest, I should be the responsible one. How incredibly immature I must seem to the world. To even be here, in this financial state, is ridiculous.

I am too old. No one wants me, no one will hire me. How will I make enough to live off of, much less pay for the rest of my children's education? Or their weddings …

And Jim. Why did he do this to me? Why did he take us to such depths? Why did I allow it? I am such a fool. When we married, I was more financially healthy than I am 26 years later. How did I let it happen? Where did it all go wrong? Why couldn't he talk to me and be honest?

I need to be strong for Emma and Witt and Trey.

I need to go home.

I felt like the hopeless target of a firing squad. With each problem I shot at myself I could feel the life bleed out of me. "I can't sleep, I can't get up, I feel pinned," I continued scribbling furiously on the lined pages of my notebook, my efforts more and more strained. I could feel myself fade further and further away, a paralysis beginning to set in.

I recognized this all as the onset of a panic attack. I could hear the words from the counselor who'd helped me through Jim's first business loss, and again when Jim was diagnosed with cancer. "Just breathe, Lisa, just breathe," her calming voice coaxed me out of my emotional noose. "When you feel these tingling sensations begin, when your heart starts racing, take in as much air as your lungs will hold. Then exhale slowly." I started with short, quick breaths. That's all I could manage. "You're not going to die from this, not going to die from this …" I whispered as I exhaled deeper.

"Get up and try to walk just a block or two," I remember her saying, but it seemed an impossible task. I felt light-headed, almost delirious with the lack of air.

I sat still for a few minutes, then stood up and slowly rotated my torso. Breathe, breathe deeper. Deeper, I willed myself, and as I felt the air travel deeper and deeper into my lungs, I felt an ounce of strength return. I reached for yesterday's jeans, pulled them up to my waist, tucked in the T-shirt I'd slept in, then zipped them up. I walked into the other room, grabbed a half-empty plastic bottle from the refrigerator, and topped it off with tap water. With my keys and a book in hand, I locked the door behind me.

It seemed an impossible goal to walk just one block to the Hudson River, but I made it. When I hit the river, I turned and walked south another two blocks, then slumped down on a bench, physically and emotionally exhausted. I opened my book to where I had left off, in Chapter Four, the one titled "Barriers to Transformation." In his book, *Finding Meaning in The Second Half of Life*, author James Hollis explained that the unconscious is a mighty force, and not until we dig deep into it and wrestle its power will we be able to face the fears that govern us. It was if these words were written for me to find on this very morning. They felt like a challenge, a dare of sorts, and I was fully aware that I'd been given this month, this time and space to do the work.

I could quit and go home. Or I could stay in the apartment until the check hit the next week. Or maybe call my client and ask her to push through the invoice. How embarrassing it would be to look so desperate. "As scary as living can be," I read on, "stop and think how you will feel if, on your deathbed, you look back on your life and conclude that you never really showed up because you were afraid."

After finishing the last few pages of the chapter, I got up and started back home. I remembered I had about twenty or so dollars in my wallet and another $100 or so in gift cards that my girlfriends had given me as going-away gifts. I had enough leftovers in the fridge to get me through another day or two.

With a new will, although it was terribly weak, I climbed the steps up to the apartment, laid back down in my bed and pulled the sheet over my face. I needed some more sleep. After wrestling around for a few minutes, I got up, wrapped up a leftover half sandwich, and stuffed a five-dollar bill, my Starbucks and McDonald's gift cards, plus my subway card into the pockets of my gray vest. Before leaving the apartment, I shot my client a quick email, asking if the check had gone out. Even as embarrassing as it was, it at least gave me some hope.

I took the #1 Uptown train all the way up to its last stop on the island, the 215th Street station. Once outside the station, I crossed the Broadway Bridge over into the Marble Hill neighborhood. Although that area wasn't on my to-do list of places to visit, I was very curious about it. My research had taught me that when the Harlem River Ship Canal was dug in 1895, it severed this little neighborhood from the mainland of Manhattan. But even today it remained legally part of the borough in which it originally stood.

I eyed a Target to my right as I came to the end of the bridge. I desperately needed another pair of shorts and a fresh pair or two of socks, but I didn't have the money to spend. I circled through it, making use of its bathroom and refilling my water bottle, then crossed back over the bridge. From there I walked through Columbia's athletic complex and down a few blocks to a neighborhood called Inwood where I came upon some really intriguing graffiti. I stopped to take some photos.

I questioned my newfound fascination in this outlaw art form. I thought back to my visual design major at Auburn, where I was required to take long, very boring semesters of art history. I hated every minute of those classes. I felt a duty to revere the great masters—Rubens, Matisse, Monet and, good Lord, forgive me, even da Vinci—but as hard as I tried to differentiate them, they all ran together in my mind. I much preferred the artists who bucked the system, those who, in their times, were viewed as irreverent, like graffiti artists. I was fascinated by Picasso, Kandinsky, and Lichtenstein. Andy Warhol was my hero. Maybe it was their spirit of experimentation that I was drawn to. Or maybe it was that those artists had the courage to be true to themselves and be different, no matter the cost. In my mind those were the ones who moved the needle in art, and I identified with them. That's how I wanted to be.

At the next block, I walked through a thicket of overgrown weeds to get a closer look at an old crumbling wall spray-painted with symbols. I was enthralled with the big bubbly letters, in weathered shades of oranges and yellows, reds and greens. I was curious about their messages, all soon to be hushed by ivy. Interspersed with the lettering were PAC-MAN-type characters, robots, and dark-skinned human forms making hand signals, none of which I understood. I wondered if they were gang-related symbols or at least something the younger generation might understand. Some of the writings dripped in blood. Others were simple letters like SUR, or numbers sprayed randomly, scribbled nonsensically in black. My instinct told me I shouldn't be here, but I couldn't help but go in further. There could be snakes or rats, derelicts or drug dealers in this building.

inwood

I felt a razor-sharp thorn tear through my skin as I pulled back a wall of weeds.

Enough, Lisa. Move on, I coaxed myself, turning toward a small cemetery next to an old, grayish-colored stone church. Nearing the small plot, I could see a tall rusted I-beam rising out of the earth. Behind it was an angel carved on the wall; I was moved by her sweet face overlooking the ground below. I moved closer to read the plaque: it identified the beam as a remnant of 9/11. It stood as the centerpiece of a plot dedicated to church members or neighbors who lost their lives that fateful day. There was a sun-weathered American flag stuck in the ground and brightly colored plastic flowers peppering the egg-shaped tombstones, each with a small color photo and name of someone whose remains actually lie elsewhere, forever in the ruins. I read each one of them, one by one. "Timothy Manuel Del Valle, Jr., John Hargrave ..." They were policemen, firemen, hard-working heroes who lost their lives trying to save others.

Tears filled my eyes as I witnessed this community's apparent sense of pride, by the honor they'd shown their loved ones. Their cemetery was modest at best, no handcrafted marble headstones, nothing fancy or expensive. But it was obvious that it was built, not with hired hands, but with suffering hands and with the little money they had. I turned around and surveyed the structures around me. It certainly wasn't a rich neighborhood. On the buildings hung a dusty tint, many in need of a pressure-wash to remove layers of age, exhaust, and grime. There were no Mercedes driven by chauffeurs, no grand planters plumed with colorful flowers. No tourists in sight, only hard-working-class folks busy on the streets. I felt a pervasive sense of harmony in their simplicity, but then again, maybe that's what I wanted to believe.

Clearly, this Church of the Good Shepherd was the anchor for many folks. As I came up on the front of the church, I noticed on their signboard that they held mass at noon, ten minutes later. I walked in timidly, intending to catch only a peek, but instead decided to stay. I slid my sweaty body into the very back pew. Fifty or so people, mostly older women, filed in quietly from three sides of the sanctuary. They walked at a slower than normal pace, their heads bowed as if in quiet prayer. One by one they filled the wooden pews near the altar. I'm not really sure why I focused on the plain, outdated dresses the women wore. Maybe because they were so different from the dresses in my church, maybe because it didn't matter to their God. Or perhaps because their simplicity made me feel accepted.

The reverence of this place shook me, then challenged every bone in my body. Would I ever find peace? Will my insatiable spirit ever settle down and be satisfied with the many gifts I have? Why must I continually push for more and more? Why can I not let go of the house peacefully, and move somewhere cheaper, where I can settle down and live more simply?

As the priest began his chant, I could hear the needle stick, the same questions playing over and over and over in my head, this time reminding me of the push and pull between Jim and me and our differences in parenting. *Was I so terrible to want more for us as a family and for my kids? To want them to travel abroad and learn about other cultures? To be able to attend the same university we did, even with the additional out-of-state fees? Our parents provided all this. We certainly should do the same or better for our kids! Did I contribute to this financial mess? Was it my fault, too?* I got angry just thinking about how often Jim dismissed me with, "Oh, Lisa, we're so much better off than most." But was he right?

Why can't I slow down, I continued, flogging myself for the 12-, 14-, even 16-hour workdays that had become my norm. *Why must I write a blog post every single night? What am I trying to prove? Why does it have to be so perfect?*

I thought back through the thoughts I'd penned in my diary the previous night:

"When will I ever be at peace with this place of mine?
When will I stop and just smell and look and feel?
When will I be satisfied with the sound of birds and the smell
of coffee? Or the feel of wool on my hand? How do I calm this
unsettled spirit?
My world is wide. Yet my curiosity begs for more.
Help me, God. Help me embrace the mystery."

As I focused back on all the women lined up in the pews at the front of this little church who, in my mind were seemingly content, making their little dent in this huge universe, I had to wonder if they had it right. The offering plate came around and I deposited my five-dollar bill, the five dollars I didn't think I could part with just hours earlier. I knew I would be okay.

When the service was over, I left the serenity of the church with a new peace. I turned south on Broadway, passing Fort Tryon Park and Fort George, then veered over into Hudson Heights.

My face was beet-red, my head throbbed. The 90-degree heat was dehydrating me. I didn't feel it was safe to walk much farther but couldn't find anywhere to sit down. The smell of hot tamales and enchiladas, which normally tempted me, nauseated me instead. My spirit worn, all I wanted was to be home. I stopped at a street vendor and, in my rusty Spanish, asked him for directions to the bus station.

He answered in a rapid string of Spanish, too fast for me to understand. I asked him to repeat himself, but to speak *más despacio, por favor,* or more slowly, please. But instead, he tugged at his son's arm and motioned him to take me to the station. I insisted I could go alone, but he wouldn't hear of it. That sweet young man walked me two or three blocks to George Washington Street Bus Terminal where I found a bathroom, water to fill my bottle, and a safe ride home.

As low as I had swung on today's roller coaster, I rode equally as high. I realized that no matter where I was, there were people who would help me if I needed them. Even strangers. A street vendor and his son, or a church full of Franciscan friars and worshipers.

All I had to do was ask.

24

I spent the entire next day inside, slumped over my laptop, squinting at instructional videos and wrestling with software that refused to cooperate. At 7:00 p.m. that evening, I stood up and rubbed my bloodshot eyes, then rolled my shoulders back and forth, back and forth again, to knead out the knots. I was desperate for some fresh air.

The river.

At this time of the evening, the Hudson River Park was usually jammed with after-work joggers and cyclists, but even with all its congestion, I felt pulled toward it. When it was full of people it held a dynamic force, an infectious energy that I needed to lift me out of the worry that consumed me. I could lose myself for hours in this five-mile strip of land, sitting on one of its park benches, allowing the sun to warm my face or the gulls to lullaby me. It was a place where I could feel the hope of young lovers and the serenity of sunbathers or the laughter of little children. This had become my sanctum.

I reached for my old ratty grey vest that hung on the back of my chair. It held my innermost protectors close and safe. Tonight, as I'd done so many times before, I slid my debit and health insurance cards, plus my driver's license, into the top right pocket. My phone went into the one on the bottom right because it was the easiest for me to reach. Into the bottom left pocket, I tucked my subway card, even though I had no plans to use it. And the top left pocket? It held the door keys. After this silly little ritual, which I did each time I left the apartment, I secured all four compartments with industrial-strength snaps, and along my way I went. I loved not having to carry a purse.

Because I'd been sitting for the past ten or eleven hours, I pushed myself to walk. I also needed to process my next steps. My friend Annie was due in tomorrow afternoon and I had to deal with the fact that I only had $16 in my bank account. She would expect to go out, of course. How embarrassing it would be to admit I couldn't pay.

It was a relief being in New York, away from my friends for the last two weeks. In a weird sort of way, I felt released from the pressure I'd put on myself, the pressure to dispel the rumors, to spin the gritty details, and to lie about how well the kids were coping. Although my friends certainly meant well when offering condolences or help in finding me a new home, I felt I had to dress my raw wound with an air of resiliency. I couldn't face the truth, nor could I reveal it; it just hurt too badly. Being with people took way too much energy, and I had so little left.

When I announced I would be going to New York for a month, a slew of friends said they wanted to come for a visit. I thought I'd made it clear it was no vacation, but apparently not. Before Parsons cancelled my class, I had a good excuse: "I'll be in class all day and from what I hear, I'll be pulling all-nighters on homework." "…and weekends," I would add for emphasis. But now that I appeared to be simply loping around The Big Apple, I struggled to find a polite excuse. I got annoyed, really, not with them, but with myself. I was horrible at saying no.

"I'm not sure I'd be great company," I'd practice telling them, when what I really needed to say was, "I can't afford for you to come. I don't have the money to split tabs in fine restaurants, or to go to a Broadway play," like I'm sure they wanted to do while in the city. I couldn't spend money I didn't have, and I didn't want them paying for me, either, like some charity case.

On the other hand, I did fear I'd get lonely. Thirty days is a long time. I finally relented and settled on having the four I felt most comfortable with: my sister and Emma, of course, and Annie. To that list I added my childhood friend Debbie, who was the wild card.

I'd seen her only once since Jim and I got married 25 years ago, so I was quite surprised when she posted on Facebook, "If you want company, I'd love to come see you."

That night I found myself incapable of composing another rosy blog post. I wrote:

I need time to withdraw from all society ... to process my shit by myself. I am worn out trying to handle all the opinions of my failed marriage. You deserve better, Lisa. "It wasn't healthy." "You'll come out of this just fine." Even the unspoken ones, I could hear them loud and clear... I don't have the strength to pretend. I'm so tired...

I couldn't go any further. It was just too hard.

With each word I wrote it was if I ripped the scab off another wound.

Our home.

My marriage.

My days of motherhood. Gone.

My heart: my family, my circle of five, ripped from me.

The loneliness and fear, the sadness and desperation, anger and helplessness, all burned inside my chest. I couldn't bear it. It was too much. I had finally come to the realization of how much I was losing.

My days as a mother. I was having to let go. How could I explain how desperate it felt to watch Emma and Witt, and now Trey go off to college, and probably never return. There was no way to put into words how sad I felt, knowing they'd never need me in the same way they needed me before. It was a rite of passage, I know, I know. It all made sense. But the thought of no more breakfasts or dinners and no more birthdays together, all sitting around our table...

And my marriage, my lifelong dreams of having someone love me forever. Taking care of each other until death do us part...

My little family unit, the five of us. I just couldn't bear the brokenness.

Oh, Lisa. The days of having three small children, the exhaustion, being broke ... those were such tough days, I reminded myself as I kept writing.

I remember like it was yesterday lying on the hospital prep bed, waiting to have my tubes tied on the day after I had birthed Trey. At 41 years of age, I was old, and my time for having children was over. I even remember the taste of those salty tears as they streamed down my face. The doctor leaned close in and whispered to me, "We don't have to do this, you know." Of course, we did. My time was over. This phase of my life has passed; I must move on.

Why do I have such a hard time passing onto the next stages of life? Why do I hold on to my youth, to my family, to my career? Why can't I gracefully let go and look forward to what many describe as the best years of their lives?

I put down my pen and closed my diary feeling like such a failure for not doing everything in my power to keep the house. I could have re-educated myself sooner, maybe found a good, safe corporate job, and saved our home and family, like my mother had done.

Maybe if Jim and I both left Atlanta and started somewhere new, maybe we could make it work. I sat there, wanting so badly to cry it all out. If only I could get this pain out of me. Instead, a hardening began to set in. A numbness, a cold. Instead of feeling, it had become much easier to cut off all my friends, my church, my neighbors, anyone and anything that might require me to appear happy, to seem in control. To be strong.

"What's the real purpose of life ..."

... I started typing on my blog, feeling a momentary push to produce for my audience. But I couldn't go on. I was depleted. I hit "delete" then powered down my computer and headed into the bedroom. As I pulled the black sheets over my bare shoulders, I heard a faint, "Hoohoo-hoo-hoo. Hoohoo-hoo-hoo," an owl outside my window, or so I thought.

I would later learn it was a mourning dove.

25

My friendship with Annie dated back to 1978, some 30-plus years, when our two ad agencies merged into one. She worked in the media department and I was on the creative side, on two separate floors. Our paths crossed most frequently on the softball field. The Atlanta ad community had a very active softball league, and our team was highly regarded, not so much for our skill, but for our infamous after-the-game celebrations at the Beer Mug. I remember those days in my mid-twenties as some of the most fun of my life, and even after Annie and I went on to other firms, we traveled together with a wanderlust group of ad folks who were known to jump on a plane at the drop of a hat.

Her plane was due to arrive at 3:00 and I promised to meet her at the airport. Before leaving, I quickly scanned the comments on my latest Facebook post and unfortunately one of them stopped me cold. It incensed me. I could feel anger rise up through my face as I read it again, looking up to find who this jerk might be. "Oh, I wish I could afford to go live in New York for a whole month," it read. *ARE YOU SERIOUS?* If only he knew how I ate everything in our cupboard back home, down to the out-of-date mushroom soup, anything to save from buying groceries. Or that I worked the Wednesday night dinners at my church, so I could take home leftovers to feed my family for the next few days. Or the time I had to decide between paying the electric bill or the gas bill, enduring cold showers.

Why do I need to defend my decision to this jerk? I worked hard to get here, and I deserve it, my heart argued as I walked with a feverish gait down along 14th Street toward the station. I steamed all the way to the Roosevelt Avenue station in Queens where I hopped out and rushed through the crowd to find my connecting bus. I could hear my phone ping, but I was late and couldn't stop to check messages. I needed to laser-focus on getting on that next bus. When finally seated and on my way to the airport, I glanced at the texts. They were from Annie. "Am in Pittsburgh. Plane rerouted. LGA closed for weather. Will call when I know more."

I was puzzled. There was not a single drop of rain, nor any heavy winds. It was a beautiful day in New York. I stepped off the Q70 and got back in line to catch the M60. Without even looking at my map, I knew which bus would take me home via the westernmost stop near Columbia University. There I could catch the #1 train home.

By the time I got off my bus at Columbia, I had the full story from Annie. All planes due into LaGuardia been rerouted. The airport had completely shut down, the passengers were told, supposedly due to weather. "Seriously, I think it's a terrorist threat," Annie opined in a tentative tone. It could have been; it was New York, after all, the bullseye for anyone wanting to make a political or religious statement. My reaction surprised me: I felt annoyed by it, not fearful at all. *Guess I'm now a real New Yorker*, I posed, smiling at my own joke!

Annie's next call was to inform me that she would arrive the next morning, at the crack of dawn, via a bus Delta had rented.

Back at the apartment I threw together a leftover dinner of sorts: a drumstick, half a cucumber, some cherry tomatoes, and for dessert, half a banana. After having leg cramps on one of my first few days, I ate them daily for their potassium. I finished my makeshift dinner, cleaned my dishes, and put on my tennis shoes. I splashed some cold water on my face, stuffed my keys and phone into my vest pockets, then headed downstairs. It was nearing sunset when I walked toward the river, heading toward a finger of land that extended out into the wake, one I'd seen on the map. It was labelled, "Football Field."

Imagine someone just plopping a huge rectangular piece of land

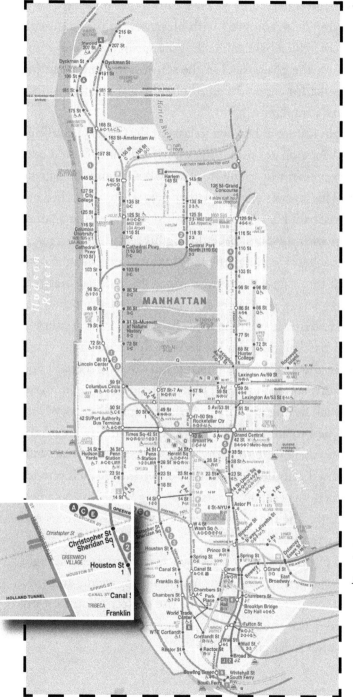

hudson river
park

right out over the water. Only in New York! They'd chalked off a big green playing field, complete with bleachers. In the summer it became a soccer field, a baseball field in the springtime, and in the fall, they roll out the goalposts. On the south side I found batting cages and kayaks for rent. On another side, a man swung on a trapeze. Yes, on a trapeze.

A sign caught my eye as I turned to leave: "The Greenwich Village Little League." As soon as I read it Jim's spirit filled me. I could only imagine his excitement in seeing this baseball park and the batting cages. Some of his favorite years as a father were when he coached our two boys in baseball. He was good at it. Just like he was as a father, he was patient with the boys, never losing his temper like so many of the other coaches. He put all the kids in the game, even the poor players, which oftentimes cost him a win. Oh, he loved bragging about his weak players, sometimes even more than his first-draft hot shots. I often joked that when he died, I would spread his ashes in the Buckhead Baseball outfield. He loved it that much.

Standing in this place, remembering Jim's days as a coach and a father, my heart softened toward him. As hard as I fought not to allow myself such feelings, as hard as I tried to uphold my newly set boundaries, I had to admit that I missed him. And my kids. Like this slice of life, there were so many things I wanted to share with them. So often I'd call the kids and they'd not answer their phones, their mailboxes not yet set up. I missed my dog Frank, my own bed, even my bathtub. The high I'd enjoyed for the last two weeks was now beginning to wear thin.

I was tired of performing. I no longer wanted to work all night wordsmithing the perfect blog post that would engage my audience. Or download, crop, retouch, and post the perfect photos on my Facebook page. I was tired of selling myself for another Facebook like. I just wanted to let go and be me.

26

It was almost 5:00 a.m. when the ring of my phone awoke me. "I think I'm at the right place," Annie said in a fragile voice. "I'm outside."

I pulled on some socks and tiptoed quickly down the steps where I found her sitting in a cab. She was visibly exhausted.

Once we hoisted her suitcase up to my apartment, I drilled her about why her flight had been rerouted. I'd found nothing online about a terror threat at LaGuardia, and she added that neither Delta nor the bus driver offered any concrete answers, so with that I insisted my weary friend take my bed. "This couch is fine," she countered, but I was wide awake now. There was no way I would be able to go back to sleep.

"I have to finish yesterday's blog post," I countered with a not-so-truthful excuse, and with that, she acquiesced. "Just pull the bedroom door to," I went on, "I don't want this light to keep you up." I knew the purr of the air conditioning unit would lull her to sleep, giving me a couple more hours to figure out what to do about money.

Why I couldn't be honest with Annie, I don't know. She knew my situation intimately. Two decades earlier, shortly after Jim lost his first business, a bunch of us advertising gals took a weekend trip to the beach. I barely scraped enough to cover my portion of the house rental, but when it came time to go out for dinner that first night, I chose to stay back. "With no little babies to interrupt me, I'd rather stay home and take a long, hot bubble bath," I pronounced to my friends with a big smile. Annie shot me a look, her eyebrow arched in suspicion. She knew good and well why I wasn't going. Annie always chose her words wisely and had never once been judgmental of my marriage to Jim. But unlike me, she lived her life firm in her convictions. On that day her silence spoke volumes. "Why are you allowing this?" Her body language told me to set boundaries for myself, to demand more. But I didn't. And now here I was again, 20 years later, allowing it to happen again.

As she closed the bedroom door, I tiptoed over to the table and opened my laptop, its blue light filling the dark room. I typed in my password and as the screen filled, I noticed an email from Jim. "The check came today, and I rushed it to the bank and got it in just as Sue was about to close out the day. She promised to get it posted today. Things are good here. The boys are working in the backyard. Realtors showed the house again today. Traffic's been good. I hope you and Annie have fun. Frank says hello!" He knew how much I missed my little dog. Then he closed it by saying what he always said at the end of a phone call, and what he'd taught each our kids to say. "Love you!"

A huge sense of relief washed over me. My entire torso slumped, and my muscles surrendered. I checked my online account and found the money had, indeed, been credited to my account. I wouldn't have to reveal my situation to my friend. Jim had been so thoughtful. I knew the postman came late in the day. I knew Jim had looked out for him, maybe even chasing him down a few streets over, hoping he could make my deposit before the bank closed. I'd seen him do that before. *He's really trying;* his actions softened me. At that moment I felt raw and terribly conflicted. Maybe I should invite him up. I'm so happy here, and I'd love to share my euphoria with him. We could take long walks by the Hudson River and finally hash through what happened. Maybe he'd open up to me here. We could walk the High Line, and I could show off the graffiti I'd found.

With that I stopped. Jim never really liked New York. "Too damn liberal!" he would bark. He would see nothing at all worthwhile in graffiti, and I knew that, really. I'm not sure he ever got my artistic side. "Thank you," I began typing, then added, "so much." I wanted to make sure he knew I appreciated his efforts. With that I closed my laptop and stretched out on the sofa and collapsed into something just short of a coma.

It was nearing 10:00 a.m. when the sound of running water woke me. Annie was taking a shower. I gathered my senses and hopped up to start a pot of coffee. I woke up craving some oatmeal from my little 11th Street Café, one street over, so when she emerged from the bedroom, I suggested we grab breakfast before going to the street festival I planned for us to attend.

The tone of the Village streets was idyllic on this Saturday morning and I could feel myself lightened, once again seduced by the energy on these cobblestone streets. Annie and I chuckled at the young 20- and 30-something women, many wrapped in oversized shirts thrown over their jeans or leggings, sitting at crowded tables outside quaint little restaurants. Their partners, sitting across their breakfasts, with unshaven faces and hardly a hair in place. Some couples giggled and cuddled over their eggs Benedict and bloody marys, while others barely spoke, their faces buried in *The New York Times*. "A few hangovers," I shot at Annie, the two of us smiling, remembering those carefree days of our youth.

We'd hardly reached the fringes of Washington Square when we heard children giggling and squealing as they splashed in the fountain. Pigeons waddled out of our path, flocking around old men engrossed in their games of chess. A pianist tickled the ivory keys, his beautiful melodies filling the park with romance. Then, to Annie's delight, we came upon a fenced-in area full of small yappy dogs. She, the ultimate dog lover, of course had to stop and take photos. On the fence was posted a sign that read, "Chihuahua Meet-Up," and with that I fell out laughing. It made the perfect blog post, which I published later than night:

"Dating has gone to the dogs. We saw the smoothest move ever today. A single guy organized a MeetUp group of single

Chihuahua owners this morning at Washington Square. There are hundreds of MeetUps all over America—a common way for singles to meet. But I've never heard of doggie play dates. This stud had no less than 20 women show up—just in the 10 minutes we were standing there. Ya gotta give the guy credit for his creativity."

We strolled on to our next destination, the Arab-American & North African Cultural Street Festival in Little India, just east of NYU. It was an area I had not yet walked. Crammed on top of each other were tiny little ethnic enclaves with their own distinct personalities. Little Italy and NoLita, short for "North of Little Italy." A bit south was Chinatown. There was a Russian Orthodox cathedral nearby plus a Ukrainian Museum, which painted the area as a true melting pot.

Some news articles I had read spoke of crime in this area; others heralded its richness in diversity. Of course, the gourmands bragged about the cuisine. Even though I encountered nothing at all that made me question my safety, I was glad to have someone accompany me through the neighborhood. Annie was right for this adventure because she was worldly, well-traveleled, and curious and open to other cultures and foods.

The one block between Broadway & Lafayette Street was blocked off to car traffic, but there were so many people spilling over, the police were having to extend their boundaries. As we rounded the corner onto Broadway, I could hear a single drum beating what I assumed was an African rhythm, accompanied by what sounded like poetic spoken word. Flags of predominantly green, red and black—Tunisian, Syrian, Yemeni, Algerian, and Palestinian—flew overhead. The crowd was mostly dark-haired, olive-skinned young men and women: many of the women's heads were covered by hijabs, while the men wore red Moroccan flags that fluttered from their shoulders like capes as they danced. I got caught up in their regalia

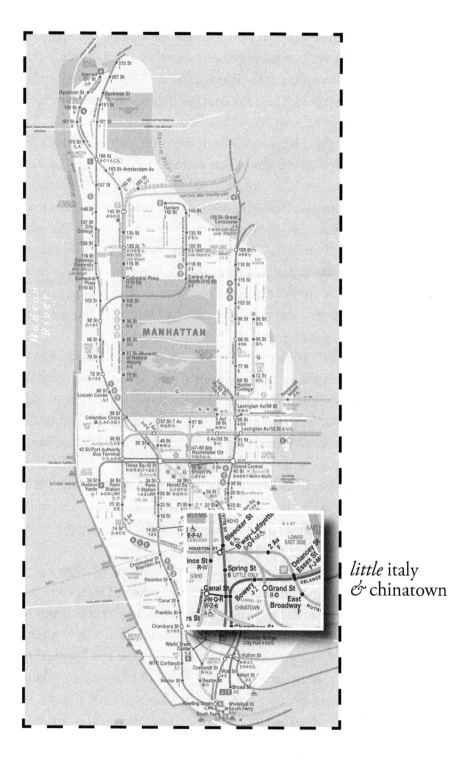

little italy
& chinatown

and admired their cultural pride. It then dawned on me that they danced on the very streets where lives were forever changed by 9/11, exactly ten years earlier, at the hands of fellow Muslims, people who looked just like them. That took courage. Not sure we would've been as hospitable to such an event back home.

Booth after booth on each side of the street displayed books on injustice and revolution and t-shirts written in Arabic. They hawked jewelry, masks, and "We love Egypt" bumper stickers. Hookahs billowed with smoke. "Smoking limited to 30 minutes," the sign read.

As we neared a henna tattoo artist, Annie dared me to get one and of course, I obliged. "Only if you get one, too." I chose a large, 8-inch ornate floral design and instructed the artist to apply it to my left leg. I could only imagine the kick my kids would get out of their old mama, who time after time had warned, "You're out of my will if you get a tattoo!"

As the woman painted the dye onto my skin, I wandered off into theoretical thought. In the very deepest part of me, I had come to believe in the progressive ideology that diversity—not only skin color or sexuality, but religion, as well—stretches our minds and could enrich us as a society. It made logical sense to me. The different foods, the dress, even the ways in which each of us come to know God, or Allah or Buddha. I was proud that I'd worked through what I had been taught as a child and although I was strong in my conviction, and even fervent about it, I would rarely admit it among my peers who felt differently from me.

Years earlier I had gotten especially excited when Emma had a comparative religion assignment in middle school. I jumped at the chance to take her and a friend to the Hindu temple just south of Atlanta. I chuckled under my breath, remembering also stopping in at the Jewish temple in our neighborhood. She and I walked in the back door where we found a kitchen full of women cooking for an upcoming event ... EXACTLY what you'd have found in our own Methodist church. After explaining why we'd come, one of the women laid her pan on the counter and insisted we tour their sanctuary where she pointed out the ark that held the Torah, and the significance of the eternal light, the menorah and other ritual objects on the altar. Then she very graciously answered our questions. For me, all this new knowledge was very exciting. It was especially freeing to learn how similar we were. I was equally excited for my kids, but most of all, I was proud that I had changed my mother's narrative.

But then, why had I winced when I witnessed two women kissing just weeks earlier? If one of my boys announced he was gay, would I be able to accept it? Of course I would. But would I hold my head high and brag about him as I would if he'd fallen in love with a cute little blonde who was white and Christian and from a respectable Southern family? Would I be okay if Emma married a man of color, and how would we in-laws come to deal with each other? I can assure you my Black friend Mary would be asking the same questions if the tables were turned.

At that very moment it dawned on me that only in recent years had I come to know any Black children and their parents and know them intimately. Never growing up did I mingle with anyone outside my lily-white bubble, nor did I at college, and only two or three times in my career. It wasn't until my late 40s that I came to work alongside Black moms on school projects where I learned about their lives and their challenges and the goals they held for their children and how much they aligned with mine. It was such an aha moment for me when I realized Mary and I were bitching about the very same issues, and our hopes and dreams for our children were all the same. It brought me great relief and comfort and joy in knowing how similar we were. Finding our commonalities had allowed me into a special sanctum.

With my attention back on the celebrants, I asked: *If people continue staking claims in their origins, and boasting their religious differences, or contrasting their sexual preferences ... won't the divide continue? Perhaps we should be talking about our commonalities. Wouldn't* that *bring us together?*

I'd worked with a gay woman on school board issues. I had great respect for her and her intelligence and her fervor to right issues across the different schools in our city. I felt so comfortable working alongside her, but never had I had a drink with her, nor shared a meal. I didn't really know about her wife, or the children they adopted. Likewise, I never had any friends who were Muslim or Buddhist or agnostic or ... or immigrants from other countries. No, not one. My world had been so narrow.

I was challenging myself. How true was I at my core? Would I ever move into a neighborhood that was predominately mid-Eastern or Muslim? Would I have the courage to openly refute the way my religion interpreted the Bible? No, and I didn't dare divulge how I had begun to redefine God and Jesus. No, of course not! Even as right as these thoughts felt, it was safer to stay silent—but I felt like a coward.

Reeling me back into the present, the woman painting my leg explained in a heavy accent that henna was applied for luck, as well as joy and beauty. She finished by promising that the art would darken over the next three days. Exactly what I did not want to hear. All I wanted was a photo for Facebook.

So, off Annie and I went to lunch at a little Cuban luncheonette that was famous for their grilled corn. We wrapped up our afternoon by walking through Little Italy and Chinatown, getting big laughs as the street wares transitioned from statues of the Blessed Virgin Mary to fake Chanel sunglasses and Gucci bags. Just as we laughed about their tacky trinkets, I'm sure all the merchants got quite an eye-roll out of us, two middle-aged gals sporting big ole henna tattoos up our pasty white legs.

Back at the apartment after a nice Italian dinner, I was not at all alarmed when I saw that Annie's legs, like Michele's, were also covered in the Disney rash.

27

The next morning, I maneuvered Annie's suitcase down Perry Street, its wheels jumping and skipping over the cobblestone streets. We hotfooted our way over to 6th Avenue, where we found our places in a long line outside the iconic Murray's Bagels. As we inched closer, the scents of garlic and onion and of freshly baked dough floated through the sluggish line of detoxing 20- and 30-year-olds, most clad in wrinkled tees and yesterday's jeans. Annie ordered the cinnamon raisin bagel, toasted, with regular cream cheese, and I, the plain one with lox and cream cheese. When I asked for a few capers on the top, the gruff, overweight man behind the counter barked, "Fifty cents extra!" I nodded a begrudging okay and paid the upcharge. There was no bargaining here, much less sweet-talking, like we get away with back home in the South.

After breakfast, we walked up to Hudson Street where I hailed a cab to get my friend on her way to the airport. Because of the Friday night screw-up it had been a very short visit. I hugged her goodbye, and as I watched the cab pull away, I reflected on how she'd always stood beside me and when I fell, she was always there for me. I was really sad to see her go.

Just as soon as I headed back to my apartment, the mental negotiations started. What neighborhood is next? *No, Lisa, you have work to do.* Walking would have to wait. I needed to get a client's job finished so I could bill it. Billing = eating!

Before sitting down at the computer, I pulled out the manila envelope that held all the pieces of my Manhattan map and dropped them onto the wide-planked floor in front of the windows of my apartment. I then sat down beside them. One of the windows was cracked open, and I could hear car tires skipping over the cobblestones of my street. Almost daily I heard the sounds of the men working on the building across the street, their drills humming and their hammers pounding, their conversations in Spanish. Their familiarity was comforting.

Like a child, I began sorting through the cut-up pieces of my map. Almost ceremoniously, I moved the areas I had walked to the left. The ones remaining went to the right. I took the pieces I'd walked and began fitting each of them into my homemade puzzle of Manhattan. I knew, without even thinking twice, that Chelsea was to the west, Washington Heights was above it, and Harlem to the north and east. I knew where Central Park (at least the southern part) was supposed to go, and the Upper East Side to the right of it. Little Italy and Chinatown would be to the right and south of the West Village. I felt quite proud of myself that I'd come to know this city so well. It was Day 17 and I was more than half finished with the 20 pieces. I made a mental assessment of the areas still left to cover and gathered them back up and put the pieces back into the cubby I called my map room. I opened both windows wider to allow fresh, albeit hot, air to flow into the already-steamy apartment and sat down at the computer to start my work. It was all I could do to keep myself inside.

First order, I read a comment on my blog from a friend from back home. "As much as you love graffiti, you might be interested in this," Kym's remark read. What followed was a link to a *New York Times* article titled, "Street Art Way Below the Street," written nine months earlier by arts journalist Jasper Rees. *Graffiti underground? In an old abandoned subway station? Whoa!* One hundred and three artists from around the world spent 18 months painting its walls. There was something very cloak-and-dagger about the whole operation. "The gallery's existence has been a closely guarded secret," Rees reported. It closed on the same night it opened, but not before this sole reporter was allowed a two-and-a-half-hour tour of the dark, cavernous gallery underneath the streets of the city. His entrance was conditioned on secrecy: no revealing facts of location, no names, not even the equipment needed for entrance. It wasn't just that the artists feared prosecution; they also were conscious of the "anxiety about terrorism in the subway."

By this time, I had become almost obsessed with graffiti, urban art, murals—this art form of so many monikers. Graffiti, most believed, spawned from gangs, the dangerous, the feared "underworld." One notch above that were the delinquent teens and vandals, those who ruined sides of buildings and bridge girders just for the fun of it. They were followed by those who painted political statements or provocative visuals with their aerosol cans. The more I read, the stronger I felt the tug to learn about these artists themselves. I was particularly struck by a quote from one of the artists who led Rees on his tour. He said, "Where else do you see a creative person risking themselves legally, financially, physically, and creatively?" I had to re-read that line, slowly, to take in its full meaning. "Where else do you see a creative person risking themselves ..."

When was the last time I believed in my own work enough to risk financial loss? Had I sold myself out? Of course, I had to make a living, but at what cost? Had motherhood and marriage choked it out? Was it even possible they could co-exist? Had I allowed my own self to die? The questions challenged me, but I brushed them off and bent to my workday ahead.

I left my apartment a little after 6:00 that evening and meandered my way to 14th Street where I jumped on the L train, riding east to its last stop in Manhattan, 1st Avenue. Straight out of the subway, my first view was a massive apartment complex called Stuyvesant Town, or as residents called it, "Stuy Town." Thirty or so aging red-brick buildings surrounding an oval park. There were trees in full leaf, young people on tennis courts, and kids kicking soccer balls—all activities atypical of what I'd seen so far of New York life. It was unusual to see this much green space around Manhattan's buildings.

I left the massive Stuyvesant neighborhood and headed southeast toward the East River where I found myself tangled up in what seemed the bowels of the city, an industrial Con Edison power plant. I wove around the plant, my bearings complicated by dead-end streets. I redirected myself, and my frustration calmed when I came up on yet another Little League park, this time with a game in full swing. Intertwining my fingers through the diamonds of the chain link fence, my face pressed in, I watched each boy step up to the plate, just as I'd done so many times before with my own boys. I had to chuckle, though. The dads and coaches looked so different than those at our ballpark. Some had ponytails, others had tattoos, but just like ours back in Buckhead, they, too congregated behind the dugout, slipping their six- or seven-year-old sons signals. The moms sat on the bleachers, deep in conversation with each other, oblivious to the game was exactly as it was back home. *We're no different!*

The sight was yet another bittersweet visual reminder of my own Witt and Trey, and of Jim. Baseball, and the kids' sports in general, claimed such a huge chunk of our time together as a family. I couldn't deny that our days involved with the kids' sports had forged deep friendships and left the kids with wholesome memories, but I sometimes felt a tad cheated by it all. I desperately wanted simplicity, more dinners together, more family time. It seemed out of whack when we had to skip church in order to make a practice, or when we had to forgo a summer vacation because one of the boys made All-Stars. My mother had warned that we were over-committed, that we needed to simplify our lives, but I scoffed at what I'd latter recognize as wisdom. *Maybe she was right.*

I moved along another block or two where I watched a long line of little girls pile out of what must have been the community pool. Their little round bodies bulged in one-piece suits, and the towels around them were soaking wet, their goggles dangling around their

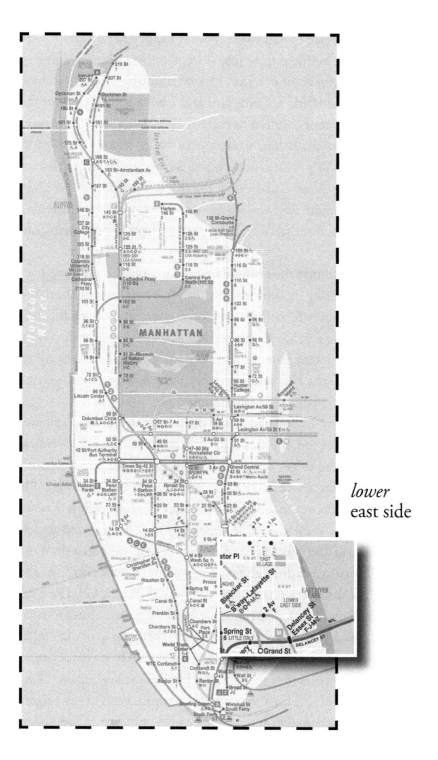

lower
east side

necks. One peeled off her swim cap and flapped her ponytails back and forth like a little puppy, just as I remembered Emma doing so often after swim team practice. I sat on a nearby bench, watching this scenario unfold, realizing Jim and I both had fallen into the trap. "Expose your children to everything you can" was the mantra of our generation. Ballet, scouts, gymnastics, swim team, soccer, basketball, choir practice, homework, themed birthday parties, art club, science projects ... My God, the chaos. What I would've given to have spent more time simply reading with my children, listening to them talk about their day, lying next to them in bed, saying our prayers together.

As I stepped into the Lower East Side, it appeared the bohemian crowd was moving in, bringing gentrification, yet the neighborhood still had a leftover fog of poverty and crime. Even the graffiti, the toothy vultures and blood-dripped skulls, seemed angrier than what I'd seen in different parts of town. I took a few photos, but they didn't portray the brilliance of the actual painting. It was getting late and my available light was disappearing.

With the sky getting darker and darker and the streetlights fewer and farther between, my air of curiosity and reflection began fading. My gut told me to get out of this area. No one was around; nothing was moving except a stray cat who darted under a huge pile of construction equipment. My thoughts started racing. *I could get mugged ... if I screamed no one would hear me.* I found myself at a dead end and was forced to turn back and walk on a dimly lit sidewalk that wove through tall, red-brick tenement housing. The pitch-black shadows loomed in front of me like massive Grim Reapers. I imagined that inside these massive, foreboding structures of what seemed like thousands of tiny boxes, all stacked on top of each other, each apartment holding people who I imagined to be hardened to the crime that was surely in their area. I pulled the keyring out of my vest pocket and slid the different keys between each of my fingers. My hand clenched tight into a fist, the keys fanning out like spikes, my knuckles whitened by my grip. My weapon was ready if the need should arise. I steeled myself and started race-walking.

Bolting through the area, I began challenging my fears. *The people who live in these public housing buildings are hard-working souls, moms and dads who care about their families,* I reasoned. *Just because they are poor, it doesn't mean they are criminal.* But I kept my pace.

After passing under the first two bridges which spanned the river, the Williamsburg and the Manhattan, I finally reached the third, the Brooklyn Bridge. Underneath the monumental struts of the concrete bridge, I could hear the deep, hollow clunking sounds of cars passing overhead. It sent a chill up through my already-tensed body, but I had no choice but to dart across four lanes feeding from several directions.

Safely on the other side, I finally caught a glimpse of the Pace University sign and saw people walking through streets that were better lit. Just past City Hall Park, I descended down into the Chambers Street subway station and picked up my pace when I heard a train approaching. Once inside the nearly empty car, I slumped down in a seat, laid my head back, and closed my eyes for the next few stops. My limp body followed the lead of the rhythm of the train as it hopped and skipped along the tracks. It was after 10:00 and I was physically drained.

My stand-by neighborhood deli had already taken up its salad and hot bars. There were a few leftover packaged sandwiches I could eat but they looked cold and unappetizing; besides, there was enough leftover pasta at home to hold me over till tomorrow. Laying my tired body down and sleeping were more important.

I climbed up the steps to my apartment at almost 11:00 that night. I peeled off my dusty socks and went straight to my laptop to check emails and for any feedback on my blog posts. I answered the Facebook comments, then pushed through two more hours of cropping photos, designing that day's blog header, and penning my day's blog post. At around 1:30 a.m., I took up where I had left off reading about the graffiti artists who participated in The Underbelly Project. I then went to Google for more information and came across several books by a woman named Martha Cooper, a photographer who was famous for chronicling street art. The further I dug, the more it became apparent that she was widely respected by artists all over the world. *Surely, she knows about The Underbelly Project.* Meeting her, and seeing The Underbelly Project, soon became my focus.

Instead of crawling into bed, I reached for my diary and began writing:

> *Alone describes the place where my physical self sits. Quiet is a state of being, but typically we think of it as relating to only one sense, that of sound. However, I'm learning that quiet can be found in a place full of visual clutter, smell and of taste, of feelings even. It's a decision to find quiet. If I can find quiet in New York City, certainly I should be able to find quiet when I return home.*

The nighttime air around me was so empty of people and cars that a faint caw of a lone bird flying over the Hudson cut through the darkness. No planes, no laughter from the bar next door, no air conditioning units to muddle the air. A luxury really, yet so uncomfortable. How often have I prayed for this emptiness, a day alone, a day of pure solitude? Time to think, to ponder, to simply wallow in simply being?

… and the space to hear my own heart.

28

I awoke this morning feeling a bit fitful. I could feel my body wound tightly in the sheets; my arms bound to my side like a mummy. I felt a bit exhausted, like I'd thrashed about during the night. I was terribly hot, but I didn't dare move. I needed to recapture my dream before it disappeared:

I stood in the den of our home, watching as my mother worked frantically to extinguish the flames lapping the rafters of our roof. I can't remember if she was fighting them with an extinguisher or throwing water on them, but they'd temporarily die down, then reappear with a vengeance, twice as strong. I was not a child, but an adult instead. "Let's call the fire department," I said, remaining calm as I watched the roof shingles burn wilder and wilder. My dream ended as the siren rang louder and louder, coming closer and closer to our home. Then, I woke up.

God! When was the last time I'd dreamed? What was the significance? A house burning. I sensed there was a message directed at me, one I needed to decipher. I was curious about its possible meaning but instead of delving into it, I untangled an arm from the sheet and reached for my phone to check the time. I'd planned to walk over the Brooklyn Bridge at sunrise, to view what was purported to be the grandest view of Manhattan. When I saw it was half past five, I kicked away the covers and shot out of bed so fast you'd think there was a roach under the blankets! Yes, I'd set my alarm for 5:00, but unfortunately, I'd forgotten to change the PM to AM. Afraid I'd miss my chance, I scrambled to get dressed, swished my mouth with mouthwash, stuffed everything I needed in my gray vest, grabbed a piece of my map, and tiptoed down the steps in a manic pace.

Just as I opened the front door, I caught a tiny hint of the morning's first light. The humidity hung thick in the inky blue sky. A high-pitched "he-who, he-who" flew through the stillness overhead, as if to announce the new day. I tapped the HopStop app on my phone and was disappointed to learn that a 32-minute trek to the Brooklyn side of the bridge by sunrise was indeed impossible. *Maybe tomorrow.* Since I was awake, dressed, and outside, I turned toward the river instead. A mist was rising off the water as the rays of the sun twinkled on the tiny ripples. It was a gorgeous morning, still in the 70s, crisp and fresh. I felt myself disappear slowly into a morning meditation.

I was getting tired of Frank Sinatra and the continuous loop of Christmas carols I'd loaded up from my CDs, so I sat on one of the benches on Pier 45 with the goal of expanding my selection of music. On Pandora, I set up a Jimmy Buffett station, another of Mannheim Steamroller, and one of George Winston tunes. I set up a '70s station, one with the Carpenters, Carol King, Lynyrd Skynyrd, and Queen, all songs from my college days. Each song, one after the other, took me further and further down memory lane. Led Zeppelin's "Black Dog" brought back memories of Friday night band parties at the Fiji fraternity house. I could almost taste the Red, White "and Barf" beer or the "hunch punch," with whiffs of weed tied to these tunes. Or Seger's "Old Time Rock and Roll." Gyrating bodies so thick, all moving in sync, sweat dripping from person to person at The Plaza, the dive bar known for its upside-down sign. How did we stupid college kids ever survive the SAE house party in Sunnyside, Florida? Tanked on Boone's Farm wine—green-apple flavored—singing off-key to "Hotel California" as we sat on the beach, watching the sun lower down into the dark blue ocean, our shoulders blistered because of the cocoa butter we'd lathered on. Youth, what a magical time, and oh, how I missed it.

Once I got the channel selected, I turned up the volume as loud as it would go—and kick, clap, backward, one, two, three, four—danced myself down the riverwalk like I was 20 again, humming just loud enough to embarrass myself. I didn't give a damn. I felt good, I was happy, I had a little money in the bank, and it was another glorious day in Newwww-Yorrrrrk-Citeeee!

I hopped on the subway a little past 7:00 a.m. and took it to the last stop on the island, South Ferry. Once out of the station, I could see that I was in the right place. American Express, Chase, J.P. Morgan, Moody's: all the signs spelled Financial District. Men and women moving at a fast clip going somewhere that seemed important. Lots of polished wingtips and starched white shirts, sidewalk vendors selling power ties. I ventured six or seven blocks over to Wall Street where, I'd read, our Atlanta mayor Kasim Reed would be ringing the Stock Exchange opening bell.

As I waited for an entourage to usher in our mayor, I Googled the history of the J.P. Morgan building, the corner landmark which faces the door of the New York Stock Exchange. Built in 1914, the address of this "House of Morgan," as it was called, was once acknowledged as the most important in American finance. In September 1920, a bomb exploded in front of the bank, killing 38 and injuring 300. Though a warning note was found in a nearby mailbox, after 20 years the FBI had rendered the case inactive without finding the guilty. I found it eerie that heavily armed police were stationed in front of that very same building, every single day, as a result of a similar incident — 9/11. And in the 21st century, the once iconic House of Morgan now flies a China Sonangol flag. It was ironic that a Chinese flag was flying over this historical American building, but then nowhere else in the city have I seen such a large concentration of Asian tourists.

Neither Mayor Reed nor a limo ever appeared and later I read that he was scheduled to ring the closing bell, not the opening one. As the activity subsided, I headed north on Wall Street to Trinity

Church, where I strolled through the old cemetery and found myself intrigued by the fonts and ligatures used on the old headstones.

From there I walked to St. Paul's Chapel, where I caught a sign that read: "During the post-September 11 ministry, volunteers lined the perimeter of the Chapel with cots. Recovery workers stumbled into the Chapel after grueling shifts at Ground Zero, looking for a place to rest for a few hours before returning to 'the pit.' After arranging a wake-up call at the volunteer desk, workers fell asleep on the cots. During the wee hours of morning, snores from the sleeping workers softly echoed throughout the Chapel. Each day, volunteers changed the sheets and blankets and placed a stuffed animal on the pillows. They worked diligently to make sure the cots were always ready for tired workers."

As I read, I recalled bringing Witt to New York just three months after 9/11. It was his 10th birthday, the one when I surprised each of my children with a trip of their own. When I told my friends of my plans to take him to the bombing site, they warned against exposing a small child to such horror. They felt it might scare him. Even at ten, Witt was a history buff. I felt strongly that one day it would be meaningful for him to see the effects of what would probably become the most significant event in his entire lifetime. I remembered Witt and me standing in front of a chain link fence that surrounded the immense hole in the ground, the dust still swirling around, permeating our skin. We saw hundreds of dried flower bouquets and weathered teddy bears and angels and handmade crosses which people had attached to the fence surrounding the devastation. We saw thousands of notes, in all languages, that children and adults from all over the world had sent New Yorkers. We read letters from Muslims apologizing for the acts caused by those claiming to share the same religion. "We are a religion of love," one read, "not of hate." The number of prayers in a myriad of faiths showed me a spirit I'd never seen before. *This is a defining moment,* I thought, *the closest I'll ever come to seeing the power of man's collective love.* I doubt Witt

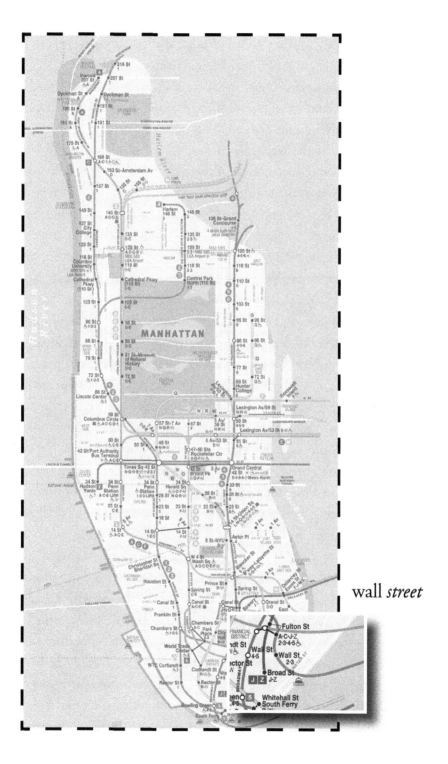

wall *street*

remembered this spiritual tomb in quite the light I saw it in, but I hope, at least, he got a hint of what his world could be.

My day was beginning to wear on me. It had started shortly after 5:00 a.m. and I had plans for the evening. My Atlanta friends, Julie and Randy, had invited me to dinner at the Tribeca apartment they'd rented for the week. Both were in the advertising and PR business; I'd worked with each of them over the years. Randy was raised in the New York area and kept up with old friends. Each year they returned to visit and hosted a dinner party. I was delighted to be included.

I went home, took a nap, then got myself together, putting on the only top and pair of pants I brought that were in any way presentable for such an affair. I walked down to the Hudson Street, bought a pinot noir, and then hailed a cab downtown. The night sky was clear, all the building lights twinkled, and there I was, sitting in the back of a New York City cab, zipping through the streets of Manhattan, heading to a nice dinner in a fancy Tribeca apartment. I couldn't believe I was living in this picture, the one I had painted in my mind for years. Silly as it might seem, I reached down and ceremoniously pinched my leg.

When I arrived the doorman opened my car door, and as I stepped out, he welcomed me, then asked my name and the names of those who I'd be visiting. He then led me to the elevator where he punched the button to the 22nd floor, waited for the doors to open, and bid me a good evening. *Ooh-la-la!* I felt like I was in the movies! As Julie opened the door and hugged me, I could see behind her a long table perfectly set with china and crystal and centered with a huge bouquet of fresh blue, white, and pink flowers. The savory smells from the kitchen mingled with the flowery scents that rose from the candles flickering throughout the dimly lit room. Bordering two sides of the apartment were floor-to-ceiling windows. "I must go take a peek," I told Julie, who took my drink order, then motioned me to make myself at home. I stood there as if in a trance, peering out into the dark indigo sky, a panorama of lights twinkling like a huge Christmas tree. *Whoa!* was all I could think.

Most of the guests had already arrived. Feeling uncomfortable not knowing anyone, I ducked directly into the kitchen and offered to help Julie with the meal. Randy handed me a gin and tonic and introduced me to the couples already there, and finally, to the only other single person, a man whose name I didn't catch right away. I re-introduced myself, then apologized for not catching his name.

Hal, a New Yorker, was tall, with dark hair and tanned skin. An open-collared crisp white oxford cloth shirt and tightly tailored houndstooth jacket covered his broad shoulders. Hal knew Randy from when they worked together years ago in the ad business. Apparently, the agency Hal ran had an office in Atlanta. "I'm there often," he claimed, turning his attention more directly to me. His eyes felt friendly, his demeanor warm and engaging. I was intrigued by his confidence and apparent intelligence. Oh, it felt good having such an attractive man be attentive. I could feel a confidence rising up in me. For the first time in almost 25 years, I found myself actually being swooned by a man other than Jim.

It was quite unsettling at first — my willingness to go along spooked me—but I allowed myself to continue the conversation. I knew that in the future, I would have to re-learn how to speak to men, how to date, how to re-wardrobe myself to look attractive. My body had changed, my history was tainted, my self-confidence weak, at best.

Despite my thoughts, I was pleasantly surprised to feel a physical attraction. That little tingle and the fluttering heartbeat felt good. Hal seemed as interested in what I had to say as I was in him. Our hostess walked over to us and asked if I'd told him what I was doing in the city. Julie, known as probably one of the best public relations professionals in the Southeast, was adept at spinning a story and laid out my tale quite eloquently, fluffing me up into some cutting-edge media maven. Hal smiled and nodded several times as she spoke, seemingly intrigued by my walking adventure. The conversation focused on me, which made me terribly uncomfortable, but just then the doorbell buzzed, and Julie left us alone to go greet her new guest. A woman stood at the door, a cast on her leg. She limped in slowly then headed directly over to us. As she came closer, she reached her hand out to shake mine. Hal introduced her as his girlfriend. She seemed very nice, but of course, I was disappointed. Or, perhaps a little relieved.

We moved on to dinner, dessert, and rounds of old stories from the good old days of advertising. It was a lovely night filled with a lot of laughter, but it was no surprise that I was the first to leave after we all cleared the table. "I've been up since 5:00," and with that I thanked my hosts and excused myself. The doorman offered to fetch me a cab, but I joked that I needed to burn off some calories after a big meal. I walked west a couple of blocks through darkened streets then decided walking at this late hour was not wise. So, as soon as I got to the West Side Highway, the four-lane roadway paralleling the Hudson River, I turned toward the northbound traffic, hoping to snag a cab. Unfortunately, traffic was extremely light, and I didn't see a single one pass by. There were no people around, and I began to feel scared and vulnerable standing in the foreboding shadows of the buildings. I turned north and began walking briskly.

I had no choice but to keep going.

The next morning I took my sweet time reading through a tour book my friend Katy had given me. I was particularly intrigued by the neighborhood I planned to walk that day, East Harlem—or as it's often called, Spanish Harlem or El Barrio. I was curious, of course, because of my love of anything Latin. My interest was piqued by others' descriptions, "a soulful fusion of cultures," and "a hidden gem." One noted that their schools were among the most innovative in the city. I had worked long and hard to get more creativity in my kids' schools, so that totally spoke to me.

I skipped my usual station at 14th Street and walked the extra blocks to Union Square, where I boarded the #4 train headed north alongside the east side of the island. It was nearing noon when I finally arrived at my destination, the 125th Street station in East Harlem. Eager to see this colorful neighborhood, I trotted up the subway stairs with a great gusto—but, just as I reached street level, my eyes instantly locked onto those of young man standing in a group hovering at the edge of the entrance. I immediately looked down, trying not to acknowledge him. Pretending to be unfazed, I continued up a few more steps, then glanced back up and he was staring at me, his icy gaze intentionally tracing every part of my body. My heart began to race. *I should go back down inside. Don't be stupid, Lisa,* I heard my rational self say. I pulled the thin strap of my small travel bag over my head, securing it across my chest, then carefully slid my phone into my vest pocket and zipped it closed. He was inside my head; I knew he knew what I was doing.

I climbed the last step onto the sidewalk, then hesitated. I quickly scanned my visual field. Across the street a group was forming around two guys screaming obscenities at each other, I sensed a fight about to break out. To my left a black van, its windows blackened, pulled in front of a building where two men stood sentinel at its front door. I could only imagine a drug deal. Beads of sweat formed in my palms. I could feel the force of the adrenaline raging through my veins as visuals of my children appeared. My heart begged God to let me see them just one more time. Even though it was broad daylight, this was the most scared I had been. *Go back down into the station, your life is more important than this silly project,* I reasoned.

But the voice of duty shot back: *You can't default on your goal. Walk at least to the next station.* All I needed was a flavor of the area to write a blog post, I reasoned, and a few photos to make my audience believe I'd walked it. So, with my shoulders back and my chin artificially held high, I marched forward, trying my best not to appear vulnerable or afraid. I didn't dare look back.

Halfway down the block I was distracted by a large painting on the side of a red brick building. I walked to the curb, and pretending to check traffic before crossing, I looked behind me and was relieved to see that no one was following me.

In the mural, I recognized a bit of Picasso in the artist's misshapen figures, their arms and legs tangled amongst animals and devils. A mother held her limp child, its body painted blue, a haunting shade of death. Centering the mural was a Christ-like figure hanging from a cross. His body was a deep green color; his face, wreaked in anguish. A dagger was thrust into his back, its gruesome meaning puzzling me. I held up my phone to take a wide shot of the painting, then crossed the street to capture its detail. I zeroed in on words painted just to the right of Jesus, leveled my camera just perfectly, then clicked a tight shot. They read: "Life's path is not always clear. Many of us look, but still don't see. We hear but still don't listen. This doesn't mean that slavery does not exist. Jesus struggled through great obstacles

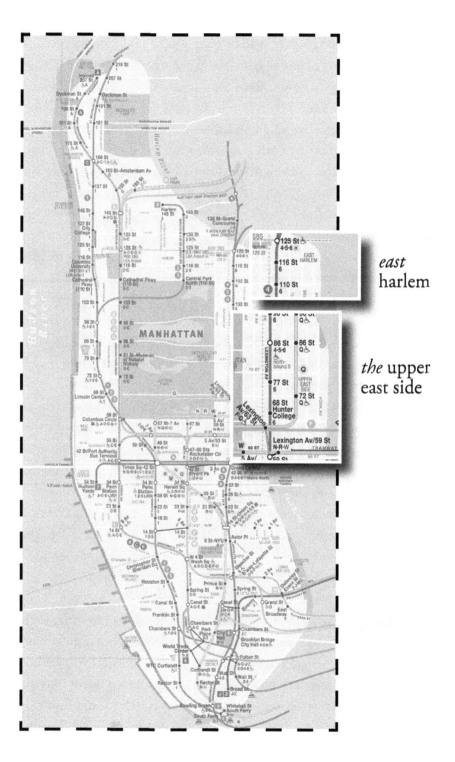

east
harlem

the upper
east side

so that we could learn how to be free; how to find our way through darkness. Many of us will continue down a path of destruction like chained slaves moving toward their grave. Be free, my friends, be free. —De La Vega"

I read the passage again and then again, its relevance spooking me. I sat down on the curb and tucked my legs up against my chest, my feet anchored in the littered gutter. I began questioning the tormented Christ figure, the dead child, and the biomorphic figures. *Was that me, a slave chained to my past, to generations before me? To my religion and to society?*

Why the dagger? I struggled for a meaning. *Has humanity stabbed Jesus, or the lessons he represented, in the back? Was he anguished because we didn't get it?* I felt myself getting dangerously close to my wild imagination. *Am I overthinking all this? Am I going places it shouldn't go?* I stood up and pulled myself out of my heady place. I brushed off the back of my pants and slowly started forward, bring myself back into the present.

I meandered down the street, pausing to photograph details of intricate mosaics or of stone gargoyles that hung from soot-covered buildings. As I went on, I lost myself in the music and in the Spanish conversations I heard, all colorfully braided together, floating out of open windows along my way. I walked past tiny slivers of stores and cafes, inhaling scents of coffee and spices and cigars, all bringing up sweet memories of my childhood days in El Salvador. The murals hung with me, spoke to me like no other art had ever done. Nowhere, no other place that I could remember, had I seen, felt, heard, tasted, and inhaled such sensory richness.

As the day went on, raw blisters on my feet began to sting; I was hot and dehydrated, the vessels in my temples throbbed. I pressed on, not stopping for water or food, not even to sit down. I had walked far enough. It was time to get home. As I descended down into the Lexington/59th Street station, its number registered, and I quickly calculated that I'd walked almost 70 blocks that day. Although I still had other pieces of the map to cover, my gut told me I'd rank "El Barrio," as the locals call it, as my favorite neighborhood on the entire island. Plopping down into a seat on the train, I chided myself for feeling afraid at the 125th Station. *I almost let SOME KID rob me of all this? I'll be back,* I promised myself.

I got home and Googled the artist whose work had made such a powerful impression on me. James De La Vega was apparently one of the most revered street artists in New York. With further research, I found that he was raised in East Harlem and graduated valedictorian at his prep school, then summa cum laude at Cornell. All this time I pictured graffiti artists as gang members! I was fascinated to learn that in 2003 he was charged with vandalism for a mural he painted, and the courts offered him a year's probation in exchange for a guilty plea, but he refused. He'd have to admit that he had to caused "damage" to the property. Instead, he was found guilty and sentenced to 50 hours of community service. "It's the animal in me, the animal in all of us that I paint," De La Vega explained.

The more I read, the more I wanted to know. The bond among these secretive artists felt like a spiritual fraternity: they have a drive to change social injustices in the world, and they take great risks to make a difference. They are change agents. There was something so very real that drew me to this cadre of artists—a pull, a camaraderie I couldn't explain. Perhaps they represented the real me who was dying to be released, to be freed from all the rules I'd always obeyed.

Late that afternoon, after I posted all of my graffiti photos online, my friend Kym emailed me again about a place in Brooklyn called "5Pointz," an entire block of old dilapidated warehouses which a developer had "lent" to the art community. Although it was in Long Island City, way off my grid of walking, I made plans to see it. While there, I could also go through MoMA PS1 which was reported to be the "largest institution devoted solely to contemporary art" in the U.S.

"OH, CRAP!" I belted out loud, as I sprung from my chair. I had forgotten about my class I had scheduled for 7:00 p.m. I changed my shirt, grabbed a banana, then bolted out of the door, racing frantically through the neighborhood toward the 14th Street station.

After registering for the class, I spent several hours researching what SEO, or Search Engine Optimization, was all about. I'd read about keywords and metadata, and organic versus paid searches, but my knowledge was merely surface level, and I knew that. I began to feel a bit insecure as I stepped into the school's lobby, smack dab in the middle of 10 to 12 people in their twenties.

The teacher, who appeared to be barely thirty, opened the session by asking each of us to introduce ourselves, then share what we did for a living and what we hoped to get from the class. I heard titles I didn't even know existed, much less what they entailed. "Content Manager," "UX Designer," "Interactive Designer ..." Some wanted to learn how social media integrated with their present job; others were out of work and wanting to expand their resume. When it came time for me, I recited my name and hometown. I told them I was an "old advertising art director" and was in the city for 30 days, walking, and learning to blog. "How cool!" one of the young kids remarked. His two little words instantly gave me the boost of confidence I needed to hold my head up for the rest of the class.

The two-hour class went too quickly. I soaked in every tidbit of knowledge the teacher offered us, and I took copious notes for later. This new knowledge was like candy. I wanted more and more, so I set up a two-hour private tutoring session for later that week. I walked out with the young teacher, firing more and more questions at her over the five or six blocks we covered. She decided to move here on a whim, I learned, shortly after her 28th birthday, leaving a good paying, but dead-end, job. She sold her car and her furniture—everything she owned. With no job, no apartment, and knowing no one, she packed a small suitcase to chase her dream. "Best decision I ever made," she said with a smile.

As we split and went our separate ways, I thought back to how fearless I had been at her age. At 28 I bought a condo plus another piece of property with no worry about how I'd cover two mortgages. I accepted a job offer across the country with nary a qualm. I signed a $75,000 lease on an office suite for my fledgling company and hired employees without hardly a second thought of the responsibility of others' livelihood. My old gutsy spirit, I so badly wanted it back.

I remembered getting pregnant without ever considering how much a child would cost, and how I'd feed her and keep a roof over her head, get her through college. The emotional costs of children never dawned on me either. When I married, it never occurred to me that I might get hurt, that two people's societal and financial genetics could destroy a family. I had no clue how embarrassing it would be for neighbors to see a sheriff pull up in my driveway or have our car disappear in the middle of the night. I never imagined the shame I, as a parent, could feel when my child would ask why we didn't have hot water. Or the isolation I would one day feel, unable to meet girlfriends for dinner because of the fear I'd come up short when splitting the tab. Or how filthy I felt walking into a pawn shop or one of those check-cashing places, and how afraid I was for the baby I carried in my arms. Or in a collection attorney's office, pregnant and denied my basic needs—I'd never in my life imagined hearing, "We don't have public bathrooms." The looks from the bankers who didn't give a shit that you'd been a good customer for 20 years, or a cashier saying out loud, "your card was denied" while you held up a long line at the grocery store, leaving behind the groceries your family needed. Nor could I imagine the the intense pain of knowing the physical foundation of my family—our home—the place where my children always felt safe, would come so close to being auctioned off on the courthouse steps.

Had I known all that in my late twenties, I would have never taken a single chance, not a one; I would have missed the gifts that come with being a wife or mother, even an entrepreneur. I would've never come to understand the incredible power in the words, "hope" and "faith," or the power of my own strength.

That night I struggled to write even a single sentence for the day's blog post. I was physically and mentally wrung out. It had been a long, hard day, and I wanted permission to simply fall into bed and quit for the day. I poured myself a glass of wine and pulled up a piece my friend Gala sent me right before I left Atlanta. "It's from *A Course in Miracles*," she wrote, "and was used by Nelson Mandela in his inaugural speech."

> "Our deepest fear is not that we are inadequate. Our deepest fear is that we are powerful beyond measure. It is our light, not our darkness that most frightens us. We ask ourselves, 'Who am I to be brilliant, gorgeous, talented, fabulous?' Actually, who are you not to be? You are a child of God. Your playing small does not serve the world. There is nothing enlightened about shrinking so that other people won't feel insecure around you. We are all meant to shine, as children do. We were born to make manifest the glory of God that is within us. It's not just in some of us; it's in everyone. And as we let our own light shine, we unconsciously give other people permission to do the same. As we are liberated from our own fear, our presence automatically liberates others."

Reading through to the last word, I felt a heat rise up through my face, my chin began to tremble. A tiny hint of triumph filled me. I sensed a newness, a courage to edge into my own self, to who I really wanted to be, and I had come to realize that there was a freedom in that.

A freedom I deserved.

30

I began my day by planning for tomorrow's arrival of Debbie. Because she'd never been to New York, I held off walking several neighborhoods that included two of Manhattan's most iconic spots— Midtown, the area in which The Empire State Building stood, plus the site of 9/11.

I had only four more pieces of my map to cover in the nine days I had left. I was ahead of schedule, but not by much. Tavye was arriving in the city next week, and although she was staying with friends in Brooklyn, I wanted to see if I could steal an afternoon with her. She'd been one of the driving forces behind this trip. There was so much I wanted to tell her.

In my remaining days, I also wanted some downtime, some time off the clock. I was dying to walk through one of the hoity-toity boutiques in Soho and into a leather shop that had gorgeous one-of-a-kind purses in its window. And certainly, the fancy vibrator store just down the street—my curiosity had gotten the best of me. *Oh, if only I could go back to East Harlem.* I wanted to visit El Museo del Barrio, plus I was craving some REAL plantains and tamales, and papusas like I remembered Rosa making back in El Salvador.

Then there was Martha Cooper, whom I was hell bent on meeting after reading her bio online. She graduated from high school at 16, earned an art degree at 19, then went to teach English in Thailand. I was totally intrigued when I read that she rode a motorcycle all the way from Bangkok to England, where she earned yet another degree, this time from Oxford. She interned at *National Geographic* and was

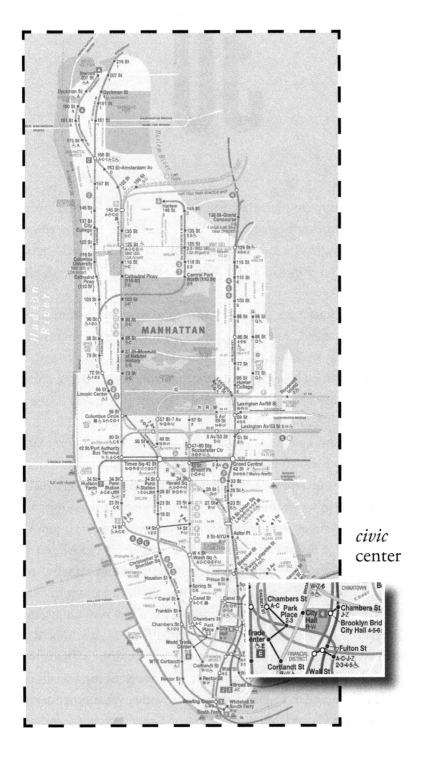

civic
center

staff photographer at the *New York Post* when one of the street artists she came to know broke protocol and allowed her to take photos as he painted. At almost 80, she continues to fly all over the world to shoot. I was dying to know this woman, plus I felt sure she could get me into The Underbelly Project.

I dug around online until I found a contact for Martha. I scripted a quick email on the off chance she would agree to meet me for a cup of coffee. I then closed the computer, grabbed one of the pieces of map, and took off toward my destination, the Civic Center area.

I could see an immediate change. The marble-clad municipal area in lower Manhattan was exactly as I'd imagined, with beautifully manicured hedges and lawns, centuries-old marble-columned edifices, and various statues of famous New Yorkers sprinkled about. I strolled up one of the wide promenades that bordered a triangular green space known as City Hall Park.

This was clearly not a tourist area as most folks in the area were dressed professionally, appearing to be taking a lunch break, or maybe waiting for a trial, I imagined. I took a seat alongside four or five others on a stone ledge that circled the fountain and found that the area was the backdrop for the many scenes in the TV show *Law and Order*. I then noticed a young man wearing dark sunglasses and a bright red tie under a long, black judge's robe walking briskly toward me. His hands flailed and his energetic gait was quite the antithesis to the other lawyer-y types slugging around. I was a bit taken aback as he handed my neighbor a card and began selling some cartoon about a blind judge. "You want to follow THIS judge. He does a lot of crazy things …," he went on, tailing the poor fellow down the street. I had to laugh at this guy's moxie and his boundless energy. "Only in New York!"

I read that this area housed Homeland Security, Immigration, the Police Department, the FBI, and Justice Buildings. It wasn't particularly exciting, one more area to check those off my list.

As soon as I got home, I took off my shoes and pulled a chair to the front window. I cracked it open just an inch or two, just enough to hear the laughter from the young people at the bar next door. For a moment, I considered joining them, but instead I sat alone, by the window, just listening.

31

I should've been on my way to meet Debbie but was a bit too shaken to face a guest quite yet. Trey had called to tell me that he and Witt had laid a new front walkway at the house, as the realtor suggested. They'd also cleaned up all the sticks in the yard and pulled some weeds. I told him how proud I was of them, but it took every single ounce of strength in me to combat the feelings of selfishness and guilt for abandoning them. I felt compelled to apologize for not being there for them, but instead I kept quiet. Jim was with them, but not me, their mother.

I could hear in my child's voice that he was searching for approval. Perhaps he thought his work in the yard could possibly save the house and ultimately the family. It was if he'd stepped into the shoes of the protector, the man of the house, and the mere thought of it broke me. I hadn't done my kids right, especially not him. He was the one born just months after our first major financial downfall, when the arguments between Jim and me began, when the stress began eroding our family. "That's all he ever knew," Emma would tell me years later. I'd not taken the time to bond with Trey like I had Witt and Emma, I was too much of a wreck myself. But that's no excuse, I would remind myself over and over.

Neither Jim nor I, nor the two of us together, had ever sat the kids down and laid out what happened. Neither of us had the courage to admit to them that we had failed, that we were losing our home and why. He and I never told them why we were separating and if it would last, or end in divorce, but, of course, I didn't even know myself. After he left, the only words we exchanged dealt with the kids' college or of splitting up the contents of the house. Those were tangible items and easier to address. But the abstract matters, like the future of our family, where the kids would call home, or where we'd spend Christmases, neither of us could handle.

Inside I was terrified, but being brave, strong, and assuring my kids that everything would be okay was the only way I knew to be. "A strong woman" was the goal I strove toward but unconsciously, I sensed that I was teaching my children that showing emotions was unacceptable, that asking for help was a weakness, and that being authentic was not valued. I wouldn't come to realize that until years later, and what a disservice I did to myself and them.

Putting all that aside, I splashed my face with cold water and shifted my attention to Debbie. I quickly moved about the apartment, "pretty-ing" up things. Our mothers had taught us from the same playbook—Emily Post, of course. I chuckled at the flashbacks of my mother who worked herself silly getting ready for visitors. Sometimes she seemed too worn out to even enjoy the guests once they arrived, and here I was doing the same thing!

Just as other girls in Mobile, Debbie and I were trained to be the perfect hostesses, not only by our mothers, but also by Girl Scout leaders. By age ten, I could set the perfect table. I knew the difference between a red wine glass versus white, or the one for sherbet. I could spot a luncheon fork versus a dinner one and I knew to place the butter knife diagonally across the butter plate, and to serve the ladies first, and from their left side. And although I'd never admit it today, publicly, I was proud that my daughter, and even my sons, knew the rules of etiquette; that they opened doors for ladies, and they never picked up their forks until the hostess lifted hers. I was most proud of the fact that all three of my children still wrote thank you notes in longhand, all on "informals," or cards with their names printed on them. And, although I thought it all was ridiculous growing up, I was glad my mother drilled those things into me.

As I wiped the dust off the windowsill, I thought bac. perfectly groomed I was in Southern etiquette, yet how equally ill-equipped to negotiate the strong social class system that existed in my Southern hometown. Debbie's visit was reigniting that insecurity in a weird sort of way. In Mobile, where we grew up, you were either an Old Mobilian—usually defined by who your daddy or granddaddy was—or you were a nobody. The secret Mardi Gras and debutante societies full of people of "prop-ah" lineage, all seemed impenetrable to me, especially as a sensitive and insecure nine-year-old. Although my father's diplomatic stint in El Salvador came with a lot of societal perks, like hosting the social and political elite, neither of my parents had the lineage to afford them a place back home. My mother returned from Salvador a different person, much savvier and sophisticated and certainly more socially self-confident. But that didn't matter: we weren't "*Old* Mobilians."

As I moved my clothes to one side of the closet, I reflected on how the friendship I formed with Debbie, as the two new girls in fifth grade, grew to encompass both our families, including our sisters, Michele and Laurey, and our mothers as well. In fact, throughout the next six or seven years, the two pairs of us kids were almost inseparable. We considered each other's parents and siblings as our second family. We spent Christmases together, shared summers at their aunt's Dauphin Island beach house, and it was Mrs. Hartwell who kept me when I was home sick while my mother worked. Some of my fondest memories of growing up—dressing our Barbies, catching tadpoles in the creek, attending Girl Scout camp, crabbing and floundering at her grandmother's home on the Bay—were with Debbie.

It wasn't until our teenage years that struggles with our social differences surfaced. Peer groups formed and possessions became more important. Clothes were the status symbols. I stepped into my own social awareness when we all moved to high school. Hormones bubbled up and boys started sorting out the pretty girls from the plain ones. The fashion labels, Ladybug and Villager, Capezios, and

Bass Weejuns began to weed out the female haves from the have-nots. Some of my friends got cars. The rich summered over the Bay; others of us had summer jobs. For the first time in my life I began to digest my mother's words, "Her daddy's a doctor," or lawyer or owner of a shipping company. "She married one of the Delaneys" or they have "a house in Dellwood." I began to understand those words as important. I became aware that because our home in Country Club Estates was not within walking distance of the club, it was less desirable, according to my mother.

It was toward the end of tenth grade in high school that the big, painful lever came down, splitting Debbie and me, leaving me on the lesser side of the social equation. A sorority bid was the very first official piece of documentation of whether you were socially acceptable or not. I had been invited to all the rush parties, so I was confident I would receive an invitation to join.

On the culminating Saturday morning of rush season, late in the fall of 1968, I woke up early, made my bed, tidied up my room and put on one of my cutest outfits. It was Bid Day, and I was told that the senior Sisters would come to your door and swoop you away and take you to some unknown location. There they would lead you through secret handshakes and rituals, and you would become a pledge. I sat quietly in my room waiting for the knock on our door. Although my mother and I never discussed it, she was well aware of what the morning held, and she waited just as anxiously as I did. The anticipation built as the morning went on. And on and on. That knock on the front door never came.

I'm not really sure how the day ended, but I do remember my mother barking out some chores to take my mind off this very first assault on my social self-esteem. Taking my mind off it and pushing down my hurt was the way she dealt with my sister and me. Never a single word was ever spoken about it, not a hug, and certainly no discussion about feelings. Our hard luck was often brushed off with, "These things will only make you stronger." But that's just the way it was back then and I'm willing to bet that's the same way she was taught. She was proud that people referred to her as "strong-willed," and it was important to her that her girls be, as well.

That afternoon I didn't dare phone my best friend because I didn't want to have to face the truth: Debbie had not only gotten a bid, but she got one to the top sorority—Beta, the one all the rich girls were in. My mother didn't make me go to Sunday School the next day, which was highly unusual. We never missed church. The following Monday I toughened up as I was to do, pulled my little 15-year-old self together and walked into school, hurt, embarrassed and humiliated. As insignificant as this incident seems today, I'm sure these early experiences made me the steely person I am today.

A few weeks after the sorority dust had settled, Debbie was back at my house to spend the night. My mother was seated on the gold Naugahyde sofa near the far wall, watching the television, and getting annoyed by us girls disturbing her view as we came and went from my room to the kitchen and back. I can only guess that she suspected we were sneaking food back to my room, which was definitely against the rules.

I can't remember what triggered her, or the exact words that were exchanged, but I have a vivid memory of Debbie and I in the hallway as my mother came around the corner. Her temper ignited suddenly, flashing as if someone had thrown gasoline on her anger. It had obviously been building for weeks; she couldn't contain it. She lashed out at Debbie unmercifully, belittling her, and claiming all this sorority stuff was her fault. "You think you're too good for Lisa," she flared, her face throbbing with rage. Hardly a single breath came from either of our mouths. Michele and I had witnessed more than our share of these flare-ups, but never could I imagine her lashing out at a friend. I was horrified and terribly embarrassed that my best friend witnessed this behavior. And although I can see now that my mother was defending me, at the time it felt as if she was rubbing salt in an open wound, making the hurt even worse. All I knew to do was to shrink away and make myself invisible. I had no words in defense of my mother. Debbie gathered her things without saying a word, ducked out the front door, and drove home.

As I look back, I can only imagine that my being shunned by a sorority did something much deeper for my mother. It was yet another mark against her own social standing. All those deep, raw insecurities she had experienced as a teen, in the very same high school—her lack of enough clothes, her demeaning job at the butcher shop, the humiliation of living in government housing—must have resurfaced. Not only had Mobile society ripped open her wound, they had also wounded her child.

From that point on, our relationship with the Hartwells was different. Neither Debbie nor her sister Laurey ever spent the night at our house again. Michele remembers believing the same of Laurey, after she, too, joined Beta.

After graduating from high school, Debbie and I both went on to Auburn, joined different sororities, and, except for a few shared rides home, our paths rarely crossed. Upon graduation, Debbie married and moved to Ohio, where she flourished in her career of public health leadership. I moved on to Birmingham, then Atlanta. In the following three decades our only communication was through our mothers, or occasional Christmas cards.

Now, after all these 40-some years, Debbie and I had agreed to meet at Grand Central Station. I remembered how I had botched my carefully planned entrance into the city. Since this was her first time ever in Manhattan, I was damn sure going to get it right!

The minute she got off the bus, we picked up exactly where we'd left off so many decades before. After a big hug, we took off through the streets almost as if we were still just two little girls running through our backyards. "First stop, Bryant Park," I announced to her. Maneuvering her rolling suitcase through the crowded sidewalk, I led her confidently through what I now called "my" town.

From there we zoomed over to Times Square where we spent an

hour or so in and out of the touristy shops. "We'll come back at dark," I promised. I couldn't miss showing Debbie the light show that is so emblematic of New York. We then rode the train down to 14th and walked a few blocks west to Chelsea Market, where I walked her slowly from store to store, making sure to jam in every detail I possibly could.

Just outside the Market, we lugged her suitcase into an elevator and rode up to the High Line. "This is only a peek," I taunted her. I was planning a long, relaxing stroll for later in the weekend.

Late that evening after dinner, back at my apartment, Debbie sat on the couch and I on the big chair beside it and caught up with the years we'd missed. We reminisced about the countless hours we spent as nine-year-olds cross-legged on her bedroom floor, playing jacks or with our Barbies. Debbie reminded me of the time in my backyard when we pricked our fingers and exchanged blood to forever bind us as blood sisters. Or the bras we hand-stitched in the 5th grade. We were both flat-chested, so much so that our mothers saw no reason to buy us even the stretchy flat things. I reminded Debbie of how Santa brought us pieces of silver flatware—in the pattern we'd chosen—for birthdays and Christmases all through our childhoods. Good Southern mothers made sure we had a whole set when we married! Oh, and of course, the names for the babies we'd bear. "Mine will have middle names!" I exclaimed. She chuckled, understanding full well why that was important.

As the evening wore on, the conversation got deeper and heavier. It became dark and emotional at times. We shared some harsh realities we'd never known about each other's families. Even as close as we had been as children, there were certain things that we had known better than to expose. "There's no need to share dirty laundry" and "What will people think?" were rules we recited in unison.

I admitted to Debbie that I left Mobile in 1970 and vowed never to return, the social damage was too deep. Quite surprising to me, she hinted that she felt the same way.

But the crux of the evening came as Debbie began stumbling over her words as she recollected her encounter with my mother. She became visibly uncomfortable. She admitted to me that after my mother's explosion, that horrible evening when she was seared by my mother's rant, she and her sister were forbidden to come to our home unaccompanied. They were not allowed to spend the night with us ever again. Hearing her words explained so much.

It was becoming quite clear that this month in New York was much more than a quest of career reinvention. It had created something much, much larger. It was providing a space outside of the linear life I was living and the time to unravel each piece of my life. It was only a beginning. I would have to work for many more years to unravel it, understand it, and, hopefully, to see how the scattered pieces of my life might fit back together.

32

I didn't sleep well at all that night. I awoke agitated. As I reached for my phone to check the time, my mother's words jerked me out of my daze. "You think you're too good for Lisa." Where did it come from? What set her off? Even if Debbie was copping an attitude, a grown woman should've certainly shown more restraint. We were 16-year-olds, for God's sake. I remember feeling so sorry for Debbie, wanting to fight back for her, but I couldn't. I was afraid of my mother.

Debbie would witness my mother's explosive temper again on the eve of my wedding, as did several other girlfriends who were celebrating with me at my condo. Mommy was climbing the stairs to go to bed when she overheard me say that Jim and I had travelled to New York together, assuming correctly that we'd stayed in the same hotel room. In a flash, she whipped her body around, lasered in on me and snapped. "WHORE!" My cousin shot back in defense but that only fueled her. "I will NOT be part of this wedding!" and with that she stormed upstairs to book an earlier flight home.

Jim and my children witnessed her fury, as did many of her friends and neighbors and students who absolutely adored her. Most would dismiss it with, "Yeah, well ... Liz speaks her mind," and would go on and on about her sense of humor or her kindness or her love for Michele and me. "She brags about you two all the time," I would hear over and over again.

As for me, her rage silenced me. I felt much safer confiding in Debbie's mother or Pam's. Or when in Detroit, as I was losing my baby, I instinctively called Jim's mother for help, not my own. Whenever I took my kids to visit her, I felt myself revert to being a child again. It was safer to respond with an obedient "Yes, ma'am," than to challenge her with my views or wishes.

At 58, I still felt resentment; I was angry that I'd been robbed of what other mothers and daughters shared, but I was sad, too. My mother had endured a hard life, and I knew it. She'd grown up without a father and lived in extreme poverty. She'd worked 8-hour days, then gone to school at night to ensure a better life for Michele and me. I was sure of it, and it made me feel terribly guilty that I wasn't grateful. How selfish of me. I was supposed to love my mother no matter what, or at least admire her for all she'd accomplished.

"That's all Trey knew," Emma's words interrupted my thoughts. Out of nowhere came scenes of Jim and me. The anger. Me yelling, just like my mother. "I had to work night and day. I was always tired," my psyche defended me. Yet the similarity struck below the belt. I had mimicked my mother, and the realization gutted me.

My emotional spiral halted when I heard a faint rustling in the other room. I quickly bolstered myself then climbed out of bed while calling Debbie's name. Not another word was said about last night's conversation.

After coffee and showers, my friend and I took off toward the Abingdon Square farmers' market. I couldn't wait to share the magic of *my* place and to tempt her with quiches and croissants, flowers, and crafts. The morning air was thick and muggy; it weighed on our skin like a gooey custard. I apologized for the heat, explaining that, in this city hot air gets trapped between the tall buildings. The concrete pushes temperatures even higher, and there it lingers, no breezes allowed in to cool it. As my friend and I neared the subway station, I suggested we walk instead. "Underground stations are even worse when it's hot," I explained. "It's like entering a pizza oven, one that smells like slow-roasting urine and mildew."

I led Debbie east on 12th until we reached a beautiful little garden that bordered the First Presbyterian Church. "We are now officially on Fifth Avenue!" I announced to my friend, and on that famous street we frolicked all day long. We took a train home late in the afternoon and snuck in a quick nap in preparation for what promised to be a very out of the ordinary event that evening.

While doing pre-trip research, I found a company that designed audience participation events, or "unexpected performances" held in public spaces around the city. I signed up hoping one would occur during my stay. These events were shrouded in secrecy, so I was thrilled when I received one of the 3,500 email invitations. The instructions were explicit: Wear a black shirt, a watch, and bring a flashlight. We were to download an hour-long mp3 track onto our phones then meet at the Esplanade, a wide open, grassy area near the Hudson River. Once there, we'd press the play button on our phones at exactly at 8:30 p.m. I'd been really curious about this event, but now that it was time to go, I was exhausted and started making noises about backing out. Debbie insisted we go, and I knew she was right. I'd regret missing it.

We recognized our destination when we saw a small crowd forming, all wearing black shirts, carrying flashlights, and earplugs hanging from their ears. It was quite humorous watching all of us glance around, obviously wondering what the hell we'd signed up for. I asked a guy near me if he knew anything, but he just shrugged his shoulders.

At exactly 8:30 p.m., a hush fell over the crowd. From the simultaneous smiles, it was apparent that we were all were receiving our first instructions: "Welcome to the MP3 Experiment 8!" I glanced at Debbie with a what-have-we-gotten-ourselves-into face. "My name is Mark, and I will be your omnipotent voice today," the robotic voice continued. "Tonight is the annual celebration of the Lights Festival. In just a moment we are all going to take one big jump, all at the same time. ONE, TWO, THREE, JUMP!"

The entire crowd leapt in sync! Sheepish giggles broke the silence. "Great job," the mechanical voice continued. A few picnickers moved out of the way, up onto the bank away from mysterious activity. Joggers stopped and watched suspiciously. After taking the crowd through a few more exercises, our leader instructed us to proceed to the "Neutral Zone." Hundreds of us, all dressed in black, moved forward, slowly, murmuring like a flock of starlings. In the distance I could see another crowd, one seemingly as large as ours, come closer and closer toward us. They were all dressed in white.

Meanwhile, the sun had fallen, the darkness of night moved in. The event unfolded into a spectacular dance of lights. The folks wearing black shirts battled the ones wearing white, Jedi-style, waving their light sources in perfect sync. We danced, all stepping right, then left, our mp3s leading us through every step in perfect synchronicity. It was an amazing sight.

Debbie and I were smack dab in the middle of one of Charlie Todd's wild creations. After graduating from the University of North Carolina, where he was known as the class clown, Todd concocted a performance-based group called "Improv Everywhere." His slogan was "We Cause Scenes." Charlie and his troupe first became famous for his January 2008 "Frozen Grand Central" stunt, where over 200 actors froze in place for five minutes as commuters rushed by. Stunned by this unexplainable occurrence, commuters stopped and gawked, recorded videos and shared them online. Realizing the marketing potential, T-Mobile hired Todd to create a "Life's for Sharing" stunt in a Liverpool train station. Three hundred dancers, veiled as commuters, suddenly broke out in dance, and his first commercial antic went fire-hot viral. Todd was the talk of the industry!

"Two 60-year-old gals from Mobile, Alabama in a flash mob! Can you believe it?" I chuckled as we walked home. My mind raced in awe at the infinite possibilities with this new medium. I felt so fueled, so wide open, like my creative spark had been re-lit. *All this fun, new stuff I have to work with!*

The next day Debbie and I played tourist and I delighted in showing her all the wonders I'd once marveled over in my first visit in 1977. Her only request had been to see the 9/11 Memorial, but we were a few months short of the tenth anniversary of the attacks, when it was slated to open. Instead, we visited a temporary memorial center at 120 Liberty Street, which was near Ground Zero, plus the one at St. Paul's Chapel. While on the southern tip of the island, we also covered Wall Street and the Financial District, as well as the area around Chinatown.

We grabbed a quick bite and headed north to Times Square. From there, we walked on to the Flatiron and Empire State Buildings, back to Bryant Park and the stately New York Public Library. Even though they offered free hour-long tours of the library, I took her straight to the third floor to catch a glimpse of the Rose Reading Room, which was every bit as magnificent as in photos. In all, we'd walked almost 30 blocks, which I thought might be a bit much for my friend, but when I considered suggesting we hop a train, I realized that Rockefeller Center was close by. I certainly didn't want Debbie to miss that!

On we walked, past Radio City and St. Patrick's Cathedral. We oohed and aahed at the glitz and glamour in the windows of Tiffany's and Saks, then went underground into the famous Apple Store. I paraded Debbie through FAO Schwartz, up and down aisles of stuffed tigers and leopards and bears, then led her upstairs to their candy wonderland. We both got sugar highs just walking by the jellybeans and gummy worms, and the 24 colors of M&Ms. Out on the streets again, we wandered over to the famous windows of Bergdorf Goodman. Debbie read my mind as we both gawked at the fashion artistry adorning the toothpick thin mannequins: "We used to be that skinny!" We didn't even walk in. Instead, we stopped at a street vendor and treated ourselves to a hot dog and bag of roasted coconut.

AND THEN ... the quintessential Central Park, the inner sanctum of the city! As we deposited our tired bodies on a nearby bench, I felt satisfied that I had succeeded at cramming in as many

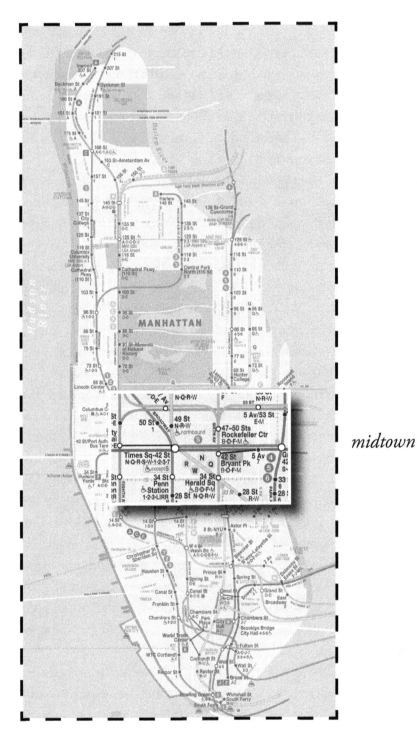

midtown

of Manhattan's iconic symbols as possible for Debbie's first trip. She seemed as mesmerized with "my" new city as I was and that pleased me.

I saved the Empire State Building for last. It was a Sunday evening, and I was hoping we'd not have to stand in line very long. Good call. Once there, we walked through the cold marble entryway and wove around the velvet ropes before stepping in front of the obligatory Green Screen to have our photo taken together. We then rode the elevator to the 86th floor, the Observatory, where the bell dinged to announce our arrival.

As the thick doors parted, I caught a hint of the inky blue sky, glittering with tiny white lights. I was almost giddy. I couldn't wait to show off the sights I'd marveled over 30-plus years earlier. Would it be as glorious as I remembered? Even before Debbie and I stepped out of the elevator, an intense, romantic sense filled me. I was in *Sleepless in Seattle*, watching Sam and Annie lock eyes for the very first time. Every little girl's dream played out right in from of me.

I pressed the silver handle of the door leading to the Observatory, but it didn't budge, the outside wind muscling against me. I turned my body, my shoulder up against the glass, and shoved my entire force against it until it finally gave way.

The minute I opened the door, wind slapped me in the face. The cruel reality of my love story unfolded as the movie scenes came to life. I could feel a tightness in my chest, my cheeks begin to warm. My love story had not played out as I always dreamed it would, but I now knew I'd power through it. *Get over it, Lisa.*

We inched around the observation deck, each of us stopping at the telescopes for closer views. Central Park was majestic tonight. It felt mysterious, all draped in a dark, moonlit texture. Circling the balcony southward we were able to see the two vertical towers of blue light that shone high into the heavens. Supposedly the most powerful columns of light ever projected from Earth, this tribute emanated from the graves of the 3,000 who died in the 2001 terrorist attacks.

"Go ahead," I told my friend. I wanted to linger a bit longer. As she walked on, I zeroed in on the vicinity I imagined was the West Village. I squinted, intent on finding Perry Street, or at least a larger one like Hudson that would help me identify my neighborhood. But of course, I couldn't. It was too dark. I searched for any identifying lights or buildings, the big billboard on top of the Apple Store or the High Line, or even the piers that stretched out into the Hudson River. I was desperate for even a hint of certainty, but again, nothing.

Who knows why I was so intent on finding my little home. Maybe I needed to lay my eyes on it, to touch it and feel it, to verify that the last three weeks were in fact, real. Was I being drawn to an altar where I had come to question my past, to understand why, and to accept and to forgive, and to ultimately move on? Perhaps it was my future I begged to see. The darkness, the void. I would never know.

The pitter-patter dance of raindrops on the windowsills woke me up. Oh, how apropos, my memory going directly to the glorious summers at Girl Scout camp, where we 8-year-olds, Debbie and I included, would huddle in our cots and tell ghost stories as the lightning and thunder roared and raindrops pelted our tin roofs. Today's rain and yesterday's memories were just the permission I needed to curl up tighter in my fluffy comforter and fall back to sleep.

When I finally got up, I couldn't hear Debbie in the other room, so I pulled on my jeans and scurried one street over to the 11th Street Cafe to grab us a quick breakfast. Coming back into the apartment, I saw Debbie making up the bed I'd slept in. "Always leave it cleaner than when you found it—where did we learn that?" I joked, both of us laughing, recognizing the source. Our mothers had recited the same lessons, word for word. "And you trying to feed me, putting some meat on my bones?" she shot back, and with that we both cackled, remembering the afternoons I would come home from school with Debbie, a hefty snack ready for us. "Y'all are too skinny," her mother claimed. "Because of your mom," I reminded Debbie whose mom was a great cook, "I still put a pinch of sugar in my cornbread—and, of course, nothing but Martha White!"

As I watched Debbie prepare to leave for the airport, I realized how intricately our histories were intertwined. The time we had traveled together on this visit was much more than a physical walk; it was a cathartic journey that refueled our friendship. We hugged, and Debbie climbed into the cab. My heart filled with gratitude as I realized the significance of our time together.

I had an appointment for a one-on-one social media tutoring session later in the day with the teacher from MediaBistro. I could only afford two hours, so I spent much of the afternoon organizing my questions to maximize our time together.

After our session, I hopped on the train, pumped with new info. In celebration, I would treat myself to a bottle of wine!

"Do you have any Spanish reds?" I asked the young man at the cash register who pointed to the cabinet in the back of the store.

"Where are you from?" he asked as I laid my Tempranillo on the counter, assuming my paltry six words were enough for him to know I was from the South. He was a nice-looking Black man, way younger than me. He had a warm, inviting sense about him and even though I expected some sort of snide remark about the South, I appreciated his warmth. It was rare that someone would start a conversation with me unprompted.

"Well, I'm from Atlanta," I started off. I usually claimed Atlanta as my hometown since I've lived there for 35 years, way longer than anywhere else. It has a big-city, young, and vibrant reputation, despite being planted firmly in the South. "But, I'm originally from Alabama," I added in an almost apologetic voice. As much as I love my home state, I knew there are stereotypes about its backwards ways of life, especially up here in the North.

"I knew it!" he belted out, grinning from ear to ear. "I'm from Greene County—you know where that is?"

A bit stunned, I answered with a resounding, "Well, of course I know Greene County!" I wanted to jump over the counter and hug him. With great gusto, I rattled off names like Eutaw, Demopolis, Boligee, Sumter County, Livingston, York, Ward. He smiled and nodded at each town I listed. "All my mother's people are from there," I boasted. "You probably know my uncle, Nathan Watkins. He's retired now, but he was the District Attorney there forever."

As soon as the words left my mouth, I stopped. I should've chosen my words more carefully. In small towns in Alabama, everybody knows everybody. Although he nodded, I sensed he probably only knew *of* him. Unless he'd been in some sort of trouble, which I doubted, there was no reason their paths would have crossed. The lines between the whites and the blacks were rarely crossed in his hometown and the office of District Attorney was reserved for white well-to-do attorneys. Memories flashed through my head from my most recent visit to Greene County, when a woman's words had jolted me back decades. "The Blacks eat there," she quipped, pointing across the street to the Sonic drive-in. Immediately I panicked. It was such an awkward moment for me, but he didn't seem at all fazed.

I complimented his home of Eutaw, gushing as Southerners do, over the gorgeous old antebellum homes that line the streets of his town. I told him that my cousin, Pat, Nathan's youngest, was now living in Brooklyn. "You look about her age. I'll have to tell her to come meet you!"

He went on to tell me how he ended up in New York, how much he loved the energy of the city, all the cultural events and restaurants. "I needed a change. But I miss my family back home, the wide-open spaces, the clean fresh air. I miss people asking about 'ya. You know what I mean?" Yeah, I got it. We had a common bond, an unspoken understanding. We'd both tried to escape our roots, each for different reasons. Now, it seemed, we'd both come to appreciate them.

As I turned to leave, I stopped and spun around. I reached out my hand. "I almost forgot! I'm Lisa Weldon. It was really great meeting you." He introduced himself as well, and with that I promised to be back.

Back home in my apartment I fixed myself some chicken plus some sliced-up carrots and green peppers. I poured myself a glass of wine and sat down at my computer to pen my day's blog post. It read:

"Now that I've spent a month learning how to blog, tweet and optimize my search, I am officially hot to trot. I've learned how to add keywords, and the right ones at that. How to tag my meta …

... and even though my class at Parsons was cancelled, I have accomplished exactly what I came to New York to do. I have taken classes, been tutored, stayed up all hours of the night trying to learn the new tools of my trade. I can't wait to get back home and start playing with my new toys.

I scanned over my writing hastily, then hit the "Publish" button with a laissez-faire attitude, spurred by a newfound confidence.

I ripped one of the blank pages out of the back of one of my books and dropped it and a pen on the floor. I poured myself another glass of wine, then walked over and opened the front window. Laughter from the little bar next door flowed in with the nighttime air. I stretched out on the bare floor, on my stomach, with my legs crossed in the air, then started an exercise my mother had taught me in my childhood. I drew a line down the middle of the small piece of paper, making two columns. At the top of the first column I wrote, "MY STRENGTHS," the other column, I titled "MY CHALLENGES." I would use this exercise to invent a new professional title for myself, especially now that I had learned so many new things.

"I make deadlines. I'm a quick learner. I understand my clients' needs," I listed in the left-hand column. "I'm best when being creative," I added.

The only thing I wrote in the other column was, "Money," but at that point I was well into a second glass of wine. Feeling a bit woozy, I decided to call it a night.

34

It was my 25th day, and I had successfully moved all 20 pieces of my map over to the "Done" column. I was quite proud of my performance and felt compelled to go out on the written stage and take an opportunistic bow. "I'm pleased to announce that today I completed …," my fingers flowed across the keyboard in a rote rhythm. "… my last square mile of the city." Well-trained to embellish the truth and paint the grandest possible imagery, I had carefully crafted my verbiage to lead my readers into thinking I had walked every single block of the island, but I hadn't really. Every neighborhood, yes, but I'd barely touched the tip of the iceberg and I ached for more, much more than my five remaining days would allow.

I was still curious about the commoners of New York, people like me. I wanted time to sit in on a school board meeting or attend a session of the City Planning Board. I wanted to return to East Harlem and spend more time photographing and understanding graffiti. I was dying to learn more about the artists, and oh, God, I reeeeeally wanted to meet one of them! I wanted to finagle my way into a writing lab nestled in a loft, where writers can go 24/7 for quiet time. I had made notes of upcoming Carl Jung meetings and a MeetUp of the NYC Women Entrepreneurs, the Speakers Bureaus at NYU and Cooper Union. The list went on. As silly as it may sound, I became obsessed with those little underground rooms tucked underneath stores and restaurants. I was dying to peek inside.

I wanted to know how New Yorkers held big family Thanksgiving dinners without the plentiful space we have in the South. How do kids get to Little League practice and how is mail delivered? And heaven forbid I'd need a new mattress—how on this earth would I get it up these skinny little stairs? Crazy, crazy little mundane questions I was dying to ask, but I was running out of time.

I replayed so many little life vignettes that seemed so different from those back home, the ones I feared were "too weird, too Bohemian" to post on my public blog. I was afraid I'd forget the dark, hole-in-the-wall grocery on the Lower East Side, the one filled with a ghastly fog of incense mixed with weed. I wanted to record my encounter with the mind reader who lured me in at a street festival, her price too steep for my budget. "You must write a book," she said to me with zero knowledge of my situation. "You have a story to tell." Duh … but then, doesn't everybody?

Or the afternoon I sat on the curb, watching kids at summer camp—their playground, a hot and steamy tar-covered street in El Barrio, cordoned-off to traffic but not to predators, I feared. And then there was the arthritic old lady who, in her thick Eastern European accent, bragged to me about her son, a soon-to-be doctor. We talked for almost an hour as she ambled her way through the tiny sliver of a garden she was weeding, a dusty little plot of dirt wedged between two faceless public housing buildings. I hung on to her every detail.

No, I didn't want to forget all these little moments. I knew in my heart that each one had a special value, a real purpose and a lesson to teach me. Yeah, my first instinct was to write about each one of them for my blog or share them on Facebook, but I'd finally gotten to the place where I didn't feel responsible to my audience anymore. I no longer felt indebted to them. It was okay to keep these stories for myself, in my heart.

For Day 25, I made plans to be a participant in the audience of the popular TV show, *The View*. I registered online months ago. "You must arrive no later than 9:30 a.m.," the instructions read. The studio was located at West 66th. Although I had become quite good at assessing how much time it took to get from one place to another, on this morning I was running late. I walked up a block to Greenwich and hailed a cab.

When I arrived I could see a young woman was making her way down a long line, a clipboard and pencil in hand. With each person she approached, she asked their name then marked it off her list and gave them a printed sheet of instructions. When it came my turn, I gave her my name. She scanned the list, and scanned it again, flipping pages and pages of names. Looking puzzled, she then asked me to repeat my name. "Your name's not on the list; can I have your confirmation number?" she asked. I reached for the paperwork I'd printed off the reservation page on their website but, unfortunately, she explained, if I'd not received tickets in the mail, there was no confirmed spot for me. I was stunned, my temper lit. But before I could say anything I'd regret, the young assistant producer handed me a numbered "waiting list" ticket and encouraged me to return at 11:45, when standbys would most likely be called. I left in a huff, but I returned and got in with no problem.

It was quite surprising to see the set, the studio, and the atmosphere in which these famous actresses work. They were quite stark; the table and chairs they sit in looked like something cheap out of IKEA. Not the luxury you'd expect to see for such famous people. I found a weird comfort in knowing that these five women go to work just like the rest of us, in normal surroundings, with normal people, with normal deadlines. They just make a helluva lot more money doing it, and they do it with a lot more people watching.

I got to see Barbara Walters and Whoopi Goldberg, Joy Behar, Sherri Shepherd, Elisabeth Hasselbeck, plus their featured guest Wendy Williams, who lit up the audience. I was struck by how friendly and gracious—and have I mentioned how normal—they were when they came and spoke to the audience.

I came to learn that most studio audiences are prepped by either a comedian or an employee of the studio. They warm you up, tell you when to clap, when to ooh and aah, and how to perform other actions needed to tape a show. They also tell you over and over—and over again—to turn off your cell phones, because, apparently, the phone signal wreaks havoc with the hosts' wireless mikes. Of course, I turned mine off.

Or so I thought.

You guessed it. Right in the middle of the taping, when all was very quiet, I hear crickets chirping, my ring tone. Every single eye in the studio turned to me. I grabbed my purse, punched the button, punched it again and again but the chirping continued. My phone was new, and I'd never had to turn it off, so I handed it to the young girl beside me and said, "Do you know how to turn this thing off?" Of course, she did and I'm sure she wondered why old people were allowed to have them. As I wrote in that night's blog post, "This will go down as 'The Most Embarrassing Moment of My Life.'"

And yet, after finishing the taping, the production crew invited everyone in the studio audience back for a make-up taping. "No, no," one of the production assistants assured me when I went over to apologize; my phone ring had not ruined the taping. They were simply trying to squeeze in an extra show so one of the hosts could go on vacation.

I crawled into bed that evening a tad more weary than usual, and for the first time, I wanted to be nowhere but home. I desperately wanted to be with my kids, to hug them, to look into their eyes, and to assure them that our family would survive.

I visualized my own bed, my tub filled with hot water, the scent of sea salts. I longed to cook a meal in my own kitchen, to cut flowers from my garden, and to sit on my porch with a glass of wine looking over the treetops, listening to the crickets and cicadas. Oh, and my Frank; I couldn't wait to see him, the constant "happy" in my life.

Day 25 marked some sort of shift. I felt stronger now, and a bit more prepared to face the enormity of the task ahead of me. I was ready to take a bow and step off my public stage and go home. Home, to the ones I loved.

Tavye was in town for a couple of days visiting with old friends who were now living in Brooklyn. When I mentioned going to see my second taping of *The View*, she jumped at the chance, and we agreed to meet at the studio at 9:30 a.m. The same young producer was making her way down the line when I nervously looked back to see if Tavye was coming. A minute later I caught sight of her, race walking around the corner, a bit winded. A grin on her face, she rolled her eyes at me, in apology for running late. This time we were escorted right in with no problems.

Once inside the studio, we were seated dead center on the front row. As I settled in my chair, I reached for my phone and turned it off, even before being asked to. I'd learned my lesson. The handlers recited the same rules I'd heard just two days before, then out came Whoopi, leading the show's hosts out onto the stage. The crowd roared. I'd seen this same show only two days before, but it was still as electric as my first time.

The headliners were Davy Jones, Micky Dolenz, and Peter Tork from The Monkees, the '60s band that at one time were hotter than the Beatles. As Whoopi questioned each of them, I mentally calculated their ages. "They must be older than ME," I whispered to Tavye. At first glance I winced, surveying their wrinkles and sagging jowls, thinking that they were too old—how foolish—to be touring again. But they were clothed age-appropriately in mostly black, nothing kiddy, their hair not dyed or poofed up, no glaring plastic surgery. I backed down from my initial thought, rather disappointed in my prejudices.

I listened intently as each was interviewed. Micky Dolenz had moved on to producing and directing in England, doing some musical theatre here in the States and in London. Davy explained how they had enjoyed reworking their old music for the last six weeks, but he struck me between the eyes when he said, "Enjoying it more, I think, than anything we've ever done ... You know we've been through a lot of personal changes ..." They were all three healthy-looking, quick-witted, and relevant. They seemed to be enjoying their continuing careers as musicians. I loved their confidence and learned something by it, wrinkles and all.

After the show, Tavye invited me to attend a party her friends were hosting the following evening. She sweetened the deal by saying her friends had offered to show me all of the graffiti in their neighborhood. "Apparently, Brooklyn's got the best murals," she pressed. "There's a really cool place, a huge old warehouse called '5Pointz'..." I took her up on the deal.

The only thing I scheduled for the afternoon was a meeting at 3:00 p.m. with a woman I read about online a few months earlier. Nicole Kenney, who with a partner, conceived a project called "Before I Die I Want To." Their idea, as stated on their website, was "inspired by a combination of factors: (1) the "death" of the Polaroid, (2) a psychologist's tool called safety contracts, and (3) a passion to get people to think about, and act upon, what is really important in their lives through this simple, straightforward question."

I was moved by the emotions she'd captured in her subjects' faces and the dreams those people had scribbled on the glossy face of the Polaroid. A Brooklyn-based artist, Nicole's byline was, "Enjoy life, you only have one shot!" She'd photographed people, young and old, across the United States, in India, even in hospice. Feeling a kinship with her project, I dug deeper and was shocked to find that her work had hung in a gallery in Mobile, and another in Atlanta. *The synchronicity!* I was moved to reach out to Nicole, to hopefully meet her so when I finally emailed her, she wrote back. "I've got a photo shoot that morning, not sure how long it will last. If you could stay flexible ..." she bargained, and of course, I agreed.

I was curious about the neighborhood called "Dumbo," an acronym for Down Under the Manhattan Bridge Overpass. It was the area of Brooklyn wedged in between the Manhattan and Brooklyn bridges and bordered by the East River. Touted as one of New York's emerging arts districts, I'd heard raves about its gentrified warehouses and chic stores and restaurants. It had become, I was told, the place where young people were moving since Manhattan had become too expensive.

I hopped on the A train early in the afternoon for a 15-minute ride to the High Street station. From there, I decided to simply wander until I heard from Nicole. Since I'd completed walking each piece of my map, I had become lax, giving myself permission to turn at street corners without checking my map and with no destination in mind. I had foregone writing on my blog for the last four days. I began to care less and less about answering readers' comments and checking my social media traffic. I was still hoofing it through the streets of Brooklyn, but I guess you'd say I was pushing a little more gently.

My face was beet-red and my shirt drenched in sweat when Nicole crossed the street to meet me. "Please excuse the way I look," I apologized to this bright, young woman who immediately felt like a daughter. In no time, I learned she attended the Catholic high school in Atlanta where Emma and Trey had competed in swim meets. Her project was inspired by a college professor at Notre Dame, she admitted. "And I've loved the travel, meeting so many different people..." and with that she stole my heart. I could *so totally* relate to her passion and her curiosity and her motivation. I felt an instant camaraderie.

"Smile," she said as she hoisted her Polaroid camera, then clicked.

As the glossy paper emerged from the camera, I apologized for my unkempt hair and sweaty face, and the lack of make-up, but really, I hardly cared. I was more worried about what I'd write on the front of the Polaroid, the goal I'd commit to meet before I died.

"I want to change the way we teach our children," I scribbled on the front, just under my photo. I'd given so much of my time and heart to public education the last few years, but now that my children had moved on, I doubted it would continue being a priority. What I really wanted to write was, "Before I die, I want to see my family healthy again," but at that moment, I couldn't find the words. And I certainly didn't want to make it uncomfortable for Nicole. Nor did I want to explain.

After our meeting, I hurried home, took a shower, and headed back to Brooklyn for a dinner with my cousin Pat. Our two families spent a great deal of time together growing up, but I had only met her once or twice as an adult. She was an enigma in our family. We'd always thought of her as a star-struck ne'er-do-well who, at age 48, was still hopelessly chasing dreams. She'd never had "a real job," according to my mother. Any line of work in the "dream" category, or in something other than a 9-to-5 with guaranteed paycheck was not acceptable by my mother's standards. She felt quite sure Pat's life was subsidized by her parents, which was totally irresponsible and immature in her book.

"You know Ruth always wanted to be on stage," my mother would say of Pat's mother. Convinced Ruth was living her dream life through her child, my mother ridiculed her cousin. "Ruth finds every excuse go up to New York to visit Pat." I sensed in my mother a tinge of jealousy. Ruth had married Nathan, a prominent attorney, a man who could support her, not like my mother who was forced to go back to work in a "stable" line of work when my father lost his business.

That evening Pat and I spent three glorious hours gabbing like long-lost friends over our pastas and red wine. "I've got to let you eat," I remember saying, apologizing for all the questions I lobbed at her. She asked about each of my kids and I pressed on about her son. The public schools in New York—I wanted to know all about them, even how her son got to school, did he ride the subway, and did he play sports like my kids? I asked for details about her husband and his work in audio recording. When she asked about Jim, I skimmed over our situation quickly and maneuvered the conversation back toward her parents, whom I loved dearly, and her siblings and their children and their lives back in Alabama. She shot back, wanting to know about my mother and Michele, all our back-and-forth stories sweetened with remember-whens. Then we delved into our careers. She's spent most of her career producing in the movie business, but her love was writing screenplays. "One got very close," she admitted with a tinge of disappointment in her eyes. I found talking with her so stimulating and her work projects so inspiring. I'm sure she viewed many of my questions as mundane, but to me, each little tidbit of information was like candy.

I loved every single minute of our time together and was in total awe to hear how a girl from a tiny town of 3,000 in west Alabama broke out and landed in New York City, doing what she loved, and making a good living out of it. I was quite envious, really. I was sorry that I'd based my reality on my mother's description, that I had not made the effort to really know her.

As I entered the subway station, I turned back and yelled out to her, "Pat, wait!" I'd almost forgotten to share my chance meeting with the young man at Imperial Vintner. "He's from Eutaw!"

Back down in the station, as I waited for the train, I quickly scanned my emails and voice messages, and saw one from a number I didn't recognize until I clicked to hear it. "I've been following your blog, Lisa," the familiar voice started. "I've got a beer client in Singapore who is asking for a social media campaign to help promote one of their brands. I'd love to get a proposal from you." WHAT?!!!! This was a man I knew from Atlanta, a highly respected marketing

On my next-to-last day, I awoke slowly and peacefully, my body melted motionlessly into the streams of dawn that warmed me. I wanted to bask in this glorious emptiness, to steal this moment of beautiful completeness, and to keep it for a long, long time, or forever.

As my time in the city was dwindling, I started to understand that, so too were the days of my own life. Perhaps for the first time, I laid bare my own mortality. How do I create my last years? Do I carefully plan and tightly schedule items on my bucket list to ensure I get them all done? Or should I get off the subway at a random stop and just wander aimlessly through whichever avenues open to me, through the magical mysteries of life?

Just as I began slipping into a meditative state, the air conditioner kicked in, interrupting my tranquility. The sloshing of water, the click, click, click of my internal master. "It's your last day, make the most of it," I heard her say.

I threw off the sheet that covered me, as well as the plans I'd laid out for myself. I stepped into the same clothes I'd worn the day before and took off through my little neighborhood to roam randomly, one last time, in this sanctuary I'd come to call home. I knew I'd come back from time to time, but deep in my soul, I knew I'd never be able to replicate the curiosity, the awe, the inspiration, the courage, and ultimately the awakening I'd come to experience these last few weeks.

I began at *my* little market in Abingdon Square. *Just one more time,* I whispered, fighting the tears. I would buy no vegetables or fruits nor indulge in a loaf of sourdough bread or a tiny quiche. I was leaving the next day. It was almost as if I simply needed to say goodbye, and thank you, to the place where I'd come to find my sustenance, the one place where I was most connected, my little corner where I felt most like a real New Yorker.

It was early yet and several of the vendors were still setting up when I arrived. As I wove through the aisles just one more time, I came upon a man I'd never seen before. He was lining up small cloth packets of freshly harvested lavender, each printed with a different poem or verse. With no hesitation, I went straight for the one that read, "All of our hopes and dreams are within reach if only we believe." I paid the man, brought the tiny sachet to my nose, drew in a deep breath of sadness, then bowed my head as I whispered my final farewell.

From there I meandered south on Bleeker Street, took a left on Charles, then a few blocks further I found a group of people waiting at a locked gate of a park. "Jefferson Market Garden" the sign read. "What's going on?" I questioned the woman closest to me. With a delightful Australian accent, she replied, "It's yoga. You should join us. The teacher'll have an extra mat." Well, one and a half hours later, my body had been stretched, pulled, and contorted in more ways than one could imagine, but I couldn't have set a more perfect scene for the ending of this, the last full day of my journey.

After class I milled around aimlessly through the familiar streets, crisscrossing through all the smells and sights and sounds I'd come to know over the last twenty-nine days. Early in the afternoon, I headed south toward SoHo, in search of Dean & Deluca, the famed gourmet market. Kelli, my friend back home, had given me a generous gift card which I'd purposefully saved to splurge on a celebratory dinner, one I deemed my "Last Supper." Once I found it, I floated through the aisles, choosing carefully a small container of shrimp and artichoke salad, a mix of fresh berries, a slice of spinach and tomato quiche, a blonde brownie, a bottle of British lemonade, plus one cranberry-orange scone for breakfast. Mentally tallying up my tab,

I then reached for a small bunch of pink roses to complement my dinner. I would leave them for Barbara and Seema to enjoy after I left.

Back at my apartment, I put my food in the empty refrigerator, then focused on going home. I chose the clothes I'd wear on the plane and left them hanging in the closet while I packed the rest in my suitcase. I gathered the few plastic bags and bottles that remained, the newspapers and glass. In the morning, I would walk across the street and deposit them in the neighborhood's recycling bins. I wiped the kitchen area clean, and broom swept the floor. I retrieved all the books and pamphlets from my little map room, rearranging them again and again until they all finally fit into the bulging pocket on the outside of my suitcase.

Later that evening and with a bit of pomp and circumstance, I laid out my feast, filled a wine glass with the lemonade, then held it high as if to toast myself for a job well done. I slid my body into that {damn uncomfortable} lime green plastic chair and pulled it in closer to the desk, then took my sweet time savoring every single flavor, rewarding myself with pure deliciousness!

When I crawled into bed that evening and reflected upon the previous few days, my mind took me to a place of questioning. Why had God so unexpectedly slipped Debbie back into my life? And why, after such a long time? What piece would she play in this puzzle of my life? I suspected the enlightenment she brought that night during our frank talks would possibly heal a very deep wound, but would it? As I began to release myself into sleep, I realized how, in the first part of my life, I had tried to escape my roots, even bury them. Maybe now, in the second half, I would learn to embrace them.

· · · · ·

I was awakened abruptly by the alarm on my phone. My heart raced. My body was clenched, paralyzed, knotted with fear. Confused, I groped my way into consciousness and finally realized I was reeling in the aftermath of a dream. To calm myself, I drew a slow, deliberate breath of relief into my lungs, then slowly worked to release the tension in my body, inch by inch. I untangled myself from the covers in which I'd thrashed, then lingered for a moment, trying desperately to understand what my subconscious was telling me. It was 8:00 a.m. "Write down your dreams immediately," I remembered Tavye teaching us in one of her classes.

"Met in Harlem 2 graffiti artists fr Underbelly Proj"...

... I scribbled as quickly as I could write, desperate to remember every detail. I immediately identified the mental images of my dream were those in the *New York Times* article my friend Kym had sent me, the one describing the graffiti project located in an abandoned subway station somewhere beneath the streets of New York City. The reporter noted its location was fiercely guarded. It had been sealed and no one was allowed in.

Getting inside this secret underground art gallery had become my mission since I'd learned about it a few weeks back. I had spent hours digging for details on its whereabouts and which artists participated. I found two, then contacted them via Facebook and Twitter, but of course, got nowhere.

"Martha Cooper called - Tues 2pm post office @ 110th Harlem"

It was a dangerous and illegal mission, I reasoned, flipping in and out of wakefulness. *What happens if I get caught?* I cautioned, the risks gruesomely apparent. *What if I died and the media reported my death as "she should have known better?"* The more I pulled on my sensibilities, the further my curiosity spiraled. My mind kept racing through my dream:

I rode the train to 125th. I was a bit ahead of schedule, and I wanted another peek at the murals that had captured my heart. I got so wrapped up in these graffiti-rich twelve blocks down Lexington that I foolishly let go of the vigilance I should have exercised. At 110th I turned left. The Hell's Gate post office was right there on the left. Five minutes late, I saw no one except a postman who disappeared into the building. I paced nervously back and forth. I knew I had made a grave mistake. I could feel approaching body heat; someone had moved close behind me. I've never in my life experienced such sheer panic. I was frozen, not knowing whether to yell for help, turn, or simply stay put.

Just six inches away were two men, one black, one white. The black man's face was mostly hidden in a dirty, ratty gray hoodie. His mouth formed a smirk, slightly open, revealing a chipped tooth. He had an unkempt mustache and week-old chin hair; his cheeks were pocked with signs of teenage acne; his eyes were hidden behind dark glasses. Out from under the hoodie hung long, curly hair which held tiny spots of paint. To this day I'll never forget the visual—a reflection of my face in his glasses. He was that close.

I knew my time on this earth was over. My entire life raced through my mind. "Please, God, don't let me die," I pled. An excruciating few seconds went by and the other man, the one to my right side asked, in a very quiet voice, "Lisa?" He sounded like a smoker, his voice raspy and hoarse.

I nodded. Not a sound would come from my mouth.

"Did we scare you?" and with that they both grinned widely, backed off, and I could feel the blood trickle back into my veins.

These two gentlemen of the night were actually quite enter-taining. I never felt 100% comfortable with the fact that I was where I was, doing what I was doing, but I was easing into believing these two characters were not going to rape me. They weren't going to kill me either, I didn't think, leaving my corpse hung from some wall, spray painted with a gang message on it.

They took turns drilling me about my intentions. "Why do you have this need to go down there?" Where did I come to appreciate graffiti? they pressed, listening to my answers in bewilderment, wondering how a nearly 60-year-old woman would feel about mixing with the rats, feces and mold to see the art they'd produced. I'm sure they suspected an ulterior motive.

"I want to go down there and see unleashed creativity, see what it feels like. I want to see the results of what artists do when not judged, when not paid or commissioned, when not told what colors to use. I want to see what it feels like to be totally free to be oneself.

"I heard about this Underbelly Project, and it's since become a personal journey for me." I was almost begging at this point, so my two comrades finally agreed to take me underground.

"Blunt," as the black man was called, explained to me the rules of the game. I was not to tell a soul where the entry point was located. I was not to bring a friend with me, nor allow anyone to shadow me for safety. I had to make a commitment to do this alone. If anyone got any wind of this, anyone at all, the whole thing would be called off, they warned. With great trepidation, I agreed to their terms.

Blunt's sidekick, the white man called "12 Tack," went on to explain to me that this was a very dangerous mission. "It's not for sissies," he warned. "Your face, your hands, your whole body will get dirty going down." They chuckled, saying they were still trying to wash the smell of crap out of their clothes.

I never saw Blunt's eyes, but I began to trust him. We agreed to meet at 11:50 that night. I can't tell you where. That hot July evening, as I walked alone through the nearly empty city streets, I felt a tightness in my chest, a drop of sweat rolled down my cheek. My jaw was clenched tight as the fear of death clutched me around my throat. My life raced through my mind. My children. I so wanted desperately to see my children just one more time. Even Jim. Please, God, stick with me, please.

Before leaving the apartment, I jotted down the street address—a clue if I came up missing. My driver's license was tucked in my vest pocket. I wanted to make sure someone could identify my body if the inevitable happened.

My mind was battling squarely against my heart, firing passion directly into a line of reason. I was foolishly placing my trust, my life in the hands of these artists I'd only just met, these painters of the night. In just a few minutes I would descend into the cavities of the city, deep into the dark unknown, and follow through with the goal I had set for myself. This I was doing for me.

As I arrived at my destination, Blunt was there waiting for me. He was by himself. He instructed me to swipe my subway card to get into a presently operating station. Instead of boarding a train, we waited on the platform until the last train had passed, until everyone had disappeared.

Not yet fully coherent, I tried to decipher what was my dream and what had been reported by Rees. The dream felt so real yet so entangled with the article. I struggled to see the meaning. *Why did I dream this,* I questioned as I drifted in and out of consciousness.

I followed my leader into a damp, nasty tunnel along the maze of tracks to the old station's entrance. It was pitch black in this underground world, lit by only a sliver of light from Blunt's flashlight. We approached a large open space where columns lined a platform. Between them ran track beds sunk below. The area was huge, what seemed to be close to the size of a football field.

My heart wouldn't slow down. Blunt's words kept ringing: "You understand that coming down here is a huge risk. If you fall no one's going to hear you scream. You could lay here and die." The risks of rats, murderers, the law were plainly obvious. But I had taken on this challenge and I had to finish.

And then, my first view: the words, "Get Up. Get God." From there we had to climb up twenty or so feet to see the main belly of the gallery. The walls dripped with creativity, angst and electricity.

Clear and vivid images from *The New York Times'* article flashed through my mind. Cavern walls filled with stenciled forms of creatures. A huge, impressive American flag with zigzagged stripes of red and white. An actual dining table clothed in white linen holding a bottle of red wine and a pink rose. Two mismatched chairs were pulled underneath, awaiting a couple for dinner.

A group of black and white souls shrouded in black. Their longing faces with an almost death-like stare.

A home, with sad eyes, walking away with all its belongings tied to a hobo stick.

"WE OWN THE NIGHT" written in imposing strength along the facing wall, claiming the space as their own.

I stood in the rotunda of this art gallery, the passion of the artists, their rage electrified me. Yet the stillness, the quiet screamed a message of death. I gasped for each breath as I swallowed what I had discovered, what took possession of my own self.

Nothing but the splashes created by our footsteps interrupted the peace.

My young imaginary comrade made some offhand remark about how cool I was, wishing his 53-year-old mother had the same respect for his artistic ability. Age reared its ugly head again, but this time it was wrapped with a bit of admiration.

Stumbling through this stench of sewage and mold, I could feel the soot and grime beginning to coat my skin. No natural light streaming through. No fresh air to inhale. This black hole was not for the weak of spirit.

As I re-entered the energy-filled streets of the city, I turned to thank Blunt. But he was gone. Vanished, it seemed, into thin air. I was alone. But oddly, I wasn't afraid.

It was clear to me that this nightmare was multilayered and complicated. It haunted me and stayed with me for years. Not until I began drudging through my own journey, way deep underneath the frenetic streets of my own life, did I come to understand that it was a metaphor for my life.

goodbye

For the next hour I washed sheets and towels and darted about the apartment, cleaning the bathroom with Clorox and stuffing the last remnants into my suitcase. Standing at the front window, I called for an airport limo. I glanced across the street and it hit me that the homeless man was gone; he had moved on. It was time for me to move on, as well.

As I hugged Barbara and handed her the keys, I felt the tears start to pool in my eyes. "Oh, tears of joy," I reassured her. "Thank you and Seema so much for allowing me into your beautiful home." I wanted to share with her that her city, its streets and avenues, its energy and its heart, had cracked me open, and had given me a peek into a much deeper place inside myself. I was leaving with a much wider dimension to life where I could find greater peace and purpose. I also felt an urge to share my sense that this 30-day pilgrimage was actually just the beginning of a much deeper search. But, of course, I didn't go into any of that. I hugged them both one more time, then pushed open the front door and lugged my suitcase to the street, where I clung to my last few minutes.

My time in New York was over. I can't really tell you what happened to me, or what those thirty days did to me. All I can tell you is that something deep down inside me changed. I would return to New York many times after that month in 2011. It was never the same, but neither was I.

epilogue

Just a week after my return to Atlanta, we received an offer on the house. I spent the next few weeks preparing Trey for his freshman year at college. I also took on the dissolution of our home, the heart of our family for 26 years. Knowing our kids would never again have a place to call home fueled every flame of failure in my being, but I soldiered through with an emotional numbness that shielded me from the trauma of each day.

Once the house closed, my dog Frank and I moved into a small rental house just a mile away. Emma and Witt settled into new apartments near the Auburn campus, Trey in his freshman dorm. Jim moved to Auburn as well, into an apartment not too far from the kids. He took a job selling cars so they could begin to qualify for in-state tuition. I felt cheated that Jim got to see the kids on a regular basis, that he got to be an integral part of their lives.

My career reinvention scheme began to pay off. A literary agent heard about my New York walk and insisted I write a book. My story caught the attention of business leaders in New Orleans and I was invited to come tour their city, then blog about their entrepreneurial rebirth after Katrina. The following year I spent a month in Paris, walking every arrondissement of that city. *The Huffington Post* offered to publish my Paris journey, posting my first submission on the front cover of their "Live Fearless" section. "That's a really big deal," the editor told me, sensing my naiveté. I got a call from a publicist in L.A. asking if I'd share my story on a CBS reporter and *The New York Times* best-selling author's website the month she was to release her second book. Then I hit the top: Oprah's network called and invited me to give Cindy Crawford advice on turning 50 on one of their online shows. I was a huge success story. At least in the public's eye, and by other people's measures.

Then, I signed on the largest client I'd had in twenty years, or since stepping aside when Emma was born. Once again, I had a budget that allowed me to assemble a team of the best in the business. I was challenged by the current requirements in my field, but I was armed now, so I met them with success and with confidence, just as I did in the earlier days of my career. I felt useful again, confident. And electrified. I was in sync with my newfound power, or the divine, inside me.

I had made room in my life for both of my passions, to be a mother *and* a career woman, and I was awed by how it unfolded.

⋅ ⋅ ⋅ ⋅ ⋅

The following year, my 83-year-old mother, still fiercely independent, made the decision to say a final goodbye to her friends and her home in Alabama in order to move closer to me. She turned over the keys to her car, sparing Michele and me of making the one decision children dread the most, and for that I am forever grateful. Over the next five years, I assumed the role of her caretaker, a role that was difficult for both of us.

Just weeks before she passed away, I got up to leave her apartment and to head home. As I reached for the doorknob, I heard her behind me utter the words, "Lisa, I love you." I was stunned, my body stiffened. The air between us immediately felt awkward. I turned toward her but couldn't look into her eyes. I answered with a nervous whisper, "I love you, too, Mommy," then hurried out the door, feeling a pit in my stomach. I'd not stopped and hugged her. Saying those words had been hard for her, and I did little to acknowledge them. Hearing the words I'd spent a lifetime trying to earn were just as hard for me to hear.

In her last few days, I sensed a tad of vulnerability seep into both of us. I felt the wall between us come down. My one hope had been to make peace with her before she died, to understand the sacrifices she made on my behalf, and to feel gratitude for the gifts she had given me. That I have done by writing my story.

My kids, my heart? Emma married a wonderful young man in the infamous year of COVID. I watch with such admiration as she and her partner build their own marketing firm. Witt has been sober now for four years and is back in school to become an architectural engineer. Trey dropped out of school after his first semester, but is back now, soaring through classes like Physics II and Calc III. He's working toward his mechanical engineering degree.

And Jim, well ...

Three years after my trip in 2011, I returned to my same apartment in Manhattan for two weeks. I invited Jim to join me for one of the weekends and I took him to the Little League fields built over the Hudson. Yes, he loved it, just as I'd imagined. That evening we joined a huge group of Auburn alums at an Irish pub in Midtown. We drank beer together and cheered our football team to victory, and after it was over, we dashed through the same streets we'd run through thirty years earlier, this time in the rain, laughing like the two happy 20-year-old kids we once were. Even though we'd been separated for over three years, it was great fun to return to the way we once were, albeit for only a snippet of time.

He and I continued to live different lives, in separate homes and cities, but our lives will be forever intertwined. I lost him to cancer just three months before publishing this book.

And me?

"If you could do anything you want to do, what would it be?" the marriage counselor asked me four years into our separation, in my very last session before I filed for divorce. "I want to write my story," I blurted out, almost puzzled from whence it came. I knew in my heart the only way I'd survive the grief I faced, the only way I would come to understand myself and my part in all this, and the only way to make peace with my mother and with Jim was to plod through the sludge of my own life, word by word, chapter by chapter, deep underneath the frenetic streets on which I traveled, down deep in that rat-infested cavern, deep in my heart and soul. And that I did.

I thank God again and again for those 30 days.

~ THE END ~

acknowledgments

I close this chapter of my life with immense gratitude to the following friends, family and colleagues who've helped me through this process.

A huge thank you …

… to literary agent Stephany Evans who looked me squarely in the eyes, in 2012, and told me I needed to write this book. I brushed her off, telling her I wasn't a writer. "I don't even read!" I continued. "Then get a ghost writer," she insisted.

… to my writing tutor Jane Gassner, my Annie Sullivan. She held my hand patiently yet was tough with me through some of the roughest years of my life. I hated her on some days, and on others, I couldn't live without her.

… to my writing and walking partner Maureen Goldman. Line by line, and step by step she helped me improve my writing.

… to the Hambidge Center of the Creative Arts for providing me the most beautiful and nurturing sanctuary in which to create.

… to Laura Munson, founder of Haven Writing Programs, who invited me into the warmest and most supportive community of writers, including my Haven I group (Emily Amedée, Leah Campbell Badertscher, Anne Burks, Kelly Glenn, Katie Keridan, Chris Levenier, Barb Parker, and Rachael Spavins) and my Haven II group (Inga Canfield, Laura DiFranco, Nancy Gentry Glenn, Teri Goldner, and Lisa Orlick).

… to Trudy Wilson, who's always been my cheerleader. A huge hug to all the members of "Chat 'n Chew," her book club of Columbia, South Carolina who served as beta readers: Angel Allen, Nell Brennan, Anne Bristow, Jean Bunch, Sharmin Hill, Gloria Lattimore, Lynn Lemon, Teresa Mathis, Erin McKinney, Doris Taylor, Nancy Theus, Mary Tribble, and Susan White. You all gave so much of yourselves.

… to Debbie Hartwell DeLacey, Annie Gillespie, plus Pam and Ray Thompson. It still amazes me how each of your visits came with a purpose.

… to Bren McClain, the writer I aspire to be.

… to my spirit partners Katy Barksdale and Angie Fife. They've given so much of their time and energy and heart to get me across the finish line.

… to author Joanna Webster (pen name Lee St. John). She calls me every Thursday evening to check on my progress. Bless her!

… to Ally Kirkpatrick, owner of Old Town Books in Alexandria, VA. Ally made me feel vital–maybe even cool–even though I was 30 years her senior.

… Rachel Lankester of Magnificent Midlife who reached across the pond to interview me on her podcast. What an honor!

… to Susie Stangland. I'll never ever forget your phone call, way back in 2012.

… to editor Nancy LaFever who yes, edited my work, but more importantly has become my long-lost friend.

… to Victoria Cumbow who edited my very first attempt at writing. And to Girl Friday Productions' Christina Henry de Tessan and Shannon O'Neill who edited my still-shitty second and third drafts. And to Laura Gallagher, Barbara Tapp and Heather Karellas, all who saved me from misspellings, too many commas, and Lord help me, those damn ellipses!

… to my incredible village, those who continue to encourage me with their calls, cards, photos, Zooms, and Facebook messages: Joe Benton, Kim Bolton, Margot Dawkins, Jodianne Dybowski, Claire Everts, Irene Grubbs, Jane Kelley, Penny Randolph Kelsch, Judi Lee, Chris Levenier, Glenda Moreland, Janis Miller, Melodie Randolph, and Georganne Young. To my Davidson High School girlfriends who gave me a kick in the butt when I needed it, and to my Alpha Gam sisters who are right there with me, even after fifty years! I am surely blessed.

... to my church friends including those who said, "HELL YEAH, you're going!" that day in the class and who gave me a going-away party or who wrote me notes of encouragement: Megan Ball, Laura Boyd, Cathy Goulding Brashear, Patti Brennan, Stacey Dougan, Porter Draughton, Janice Gallagher, Elizabeth Johnson, Susan Lowery, Joan Millett, Glenda Moreland, Tavye Morgan, Allison O'Sullivan, Alicia Ottley, Kelli Spencer, Maxine Watkins, and Candace Zahner.

... to author Frances Mayes who so generously gave of her time to help me with my book. Her memoir *Under Magnolia* remains one of my very favorites. I love hearing it read in her own Southern voice.

... to my cousin Renee Stapleton who asked, "What's Plan B?" I wonder if she even realizes how instrumental she was in getting me there.

... to my cousin Sandy Thomas who has welcomed me to New York with open arms. She and her sister Jennie Stultz have both opened their homes and their hearts throughout this entire journey.

... to Constance Trover who liked and commented on every single Facebook and blog post when first got started. I WILL meet her in person one day.

... to my idol Martha Cooper who invited me into the inner sanctum of street art. No, she admitted, not even she had seen the Underbelly Project.

... to George Weinstein and for all you do for us, the members of the Atlanta Writers Club. You have no idea how much you've taught me.

... to Mary Gresham, Mindy Strich, and Rebecca Parker who've helped me spiritually, emotionally, and energetically navigate through this crazy journey.

... to my social media friends who continue to support me and follow along on this never-ending journey.

... to Mommy. I love you.

... and finally to my family: Jim, Emma and John, Witt, Trey, and Michele.

Scan this code to see photos from my journey.

CPSIA information can be obtained
at www.ICGtesting.com
Printed in the USA
LVHW051410090622
720874LV00009B/587